Sai

CATECHISM FOR YOUNG CATHOLICS

Found to be in conformity with the *Catechism of the Catholic Church* by the Subcommittee on the Catechism, United States Conference of Catholic Bishops

No. 4

High School

CATECHISM OF THE CATHOLIC CHURCH

VATICAN II DOCUMENTS

and

NEW CATHOLIC BIBLE

CATHOLIC BOOK PUBLISHING, CORP.
New Jersey

Dedicated to
SAINT JOSEPH
Patron of the Universal Church

NIHIL OBSTAT: Rev. Pawel Tomczyk, Ph.D.
Censor Librorum

IMPRIMATUR: ✠ Kevin J. Sweeney, D.D.
Bishop of Paterson

May 20, 2022

(T-233)

ISBN ISBN: 978-1-953152-95-4

Printed in the U.S.A. 22 BI 1

catholicbookpublishing.com

FOREWORD

As the Catholic Church revitalizes the mission of teaching the Faith, the 2020 edition of the *Directory for Catechesis* provides clear guidance for catechesis and presents universal norms to assist both pastors and catechists in their evangelization efforts. The *Directory* underscores the close link between evangelization and catechesis.

In concert with the *Directory*, the Saint Joseph Catechism for Young Catholics series adheres to the presentation of the Catholic Faith—as expressed in the *Catechism of the Catholic Church*—as a touchpoint for teaching while emphasizing Scripture and being mindful of papal writings, such as Pope Francis' Apostolic Exhortation *Evangelii Gaudium* (EG).

Evangelii Gaudium expresses the importance of family in forming the faith of children. "The family is experiencing a profound cultural crisis, as are all communities and social bonds. In the case of the family, the weakening of these bonds is particularly serious because the family is the fundamental cell of society, where we learn to live with others despite our differences and to belong to one another; it is also the place where parents pass on the faith to their children" (EG 66).

Pope Francis continues: "Growing numbers of parents do not bring their children for baptism or teach them how to pray.... The causes of this breakdown include: a lack of opportunity for dialogue in families, the influence of the communications media, a relativistic subjectivism, unbridled consumerism which feeds the market, lack of pastoral care among the poor, the failure of our institutions to be welcoming, and our difficulty in restoring a mystical adherence to the faith in a pluralistic religious landscape" (EG 70).

The four volumes in the Saint Joseph Catechism for Young Catholics series endeavor to assist parents in the spiritual formation of their children. Using an effective Question-and-Answer format, the essential elements of Catholic doctrine are presented in an orderly way in all four books, so children can easily retain them with greater understanding. It may even be possible that parents will reacquaint themselves with certain fundamentals of the Faith as they work with their children. What a wonderful opportunity to share God's truths within the closeness, caring, and love of family.

Catholic Book Publishing Corp.

To help the reader identify the source, the following code marks precede each text:

✠ Indicates a text from the *St. Joseph New Catholic Bible.*

▲ Indicates a quotation taken from DOCUMENTS OF VATICAN II.

● Indicates the author's explanation of the teachings of the Church.

CONTENTS

Summary of Basic Truths 7

Part One
GOD

Chapter — Page

1. The Mystery of the One God—Father, Son, Holy Spirit 11
2. True Worship of God 21
3. Knowledge of God and the Witness of Christian Love 28

Part Two
JESUS CHRIST

4. Jesus Christ, Son of God, the Firstborn of All Creation, and Savior 33
5. Creation, the Beginning of the History of Man's Salvation 39
6. Jesus Christ, the Center of All God's Saving Works.... 46
7. Jesus Christ, True Man and True God in the Unity of the Divine Person 50
8. Jesus Christ, Savior and Redeemer of the World 55
9. The Holy Spirit in the Church and in the Life of the Christian 62

Part Three
THE SACRAMENTS

10. The Sacraments, Actions of Christ in the Church 68
11. Religious Instruction on the Sacraments 78
12. The Eucharist, Center of All Sacramental Life 98
13. The Sacrament of Matrimony 111
14. We are Made New in the Spirit 122

Part Four
FREEDOM

15. Human and Christian Freedom 129

Part Five

SIN

16. The Sins of Man 133

Part Six

MORAL LIFE

17. The Moral Life of Christians 140
18. The Perfection of Christian Love 151
19. Duties Flowing from Love of God and Others 159

Part Seven

THE CHURCH

20. The Church, the People of God 177
21. The Church as a Community 193
22. The Quest for Unity 200
23. The Church as the Institution for Salvation 208
24. Mary, Mother of God, Mother and Model of the Church 212

Part Eight

FINAL REUNION WITH GOD

25. Final Reunion with God 219

APPENDICES

Appendix A—The Ten Commandments of God; The Beatitudes 232
Appendix B—Duties of Catholics 233
Appendix C—Essential Prayers 234
Index 238

SUMMARY OF BASIC DOCTRINES

I. GOD

CHAPTER 1 — Meeting with the Triune God occurs especially when we acknowledge the Father, Son, and Holy Spirit as the authors of the plan of salvation, which is completed in the death and resurrection of Christ.

The life of believers consists in developing a familiarity with the Three Divine Persons through faith, hope and love.

CHAPTER 2 — Many people today consider God as remote or even absent. True worship of God requires that we carry out his will.

CHAPTER 3 — The faithful can help an atheistic world by the witness of a life which reflects Christ's love.

II. JESUS CHRIST

CHAPTER 4 — The incarnation is the greatest of God's works. Having become obedient to death, Christ is exalted as Lord of all. Through his resurrection he is manifested to us as God's Son in power.

CHAPTER 5 — Creation is not a truth set apart, but ordered to the salvation accomplished by Christ.

CHAPTER 6 — Each Christian has a role in Christ's saving work so that creation will give glory to God.

CHAPTER 7 — Jesus was a true man and lived among men with a human mind, will, and heart. We shall be able to acknowledge his divinity if we become aware of his marvelous humanity.

CHAPTER 8 — The mystery of Christ is also the mystery of salvation. By his holy death and resurrection he redeemed humankind from the slavery of sin.

CHAPTER 9 —The Holy Spirit carries out Christ's work in the world. He is present in a special way in the community of those who acknowledge Christ as Lord.

III. THE SACRAMENTS

CHAPTER 10—The mystery of Christ is contained in the Church through the sacraments—the signs he instituted. The Church herself is in some way the universal sacrament.

CHAPTER 11—While the sacraments express the efficacious will of Christ, they demand that people be properly disposed. The life of grace of the faithful should in some way be related to the sacraments.

Baptism cleanses us from original and personal sin and incorporates us into the Church. Confirmation binds us more perfectly to the Church and gives us the strength of the Spirit to witness to Christ. Through Penance, pardon and reconciliation to the Church are obtained. Orders conform certain members to Christ the Mediator, conferring on them sacred powers. In the Anointing of the Sick, the Church commends the sick to Christ to lighten their sufferings and to save them.

CHAPTER 12 — The Eucharist is the center of the entire sacramental life. When the words of consecration are spoken, the reality of the bread and wine Is changed into the Body and Blood of Christ. The Eucharist is not only a memorial of the sacrifice of the cross, but a perpetuation of It in an unbloody manner. In the Eucharist Christ nourishes the faithful with himself so that, filled with love of God and neighbor, they may be a people more acceptable to God. Of its nature, the Eucharistic banquet Is meant to help the faithful love others.

CHAPTER 13 — Matrimony is the foundation of family life with divine laws of unity, Indissolubility, and love ordered to the procreation and education of children. Conjugal chastity must be preserved according to the teaching of the Church. When the spouses give irrevocable consent they imitate and represent the love of Christ for his Church.

CHAPTER 14 — When one accepts the Spirit of Christ and is justified, they begin a new life which is entirely unmerited.

IV. FREEDOM

CHAPTER 15 — The divine call requires a free response by us. As free beings, we have the duty to keep the moral law.

The Church has the obligation to defend human freedom against unjust force. Because freedom can be impaired or even destroyed, Christians must work for the best conditions for the exercise of freedom in the world.

V. SIN

CHAPTER 16 — The greatest obstacle to freedom is sin. At the dawn of history, man abused his liberty. Human nature stripped of grace is transmitted to all people. The multitude of sins has become the cause of many sorrows. Personal sin violates the moral law and, in a serious matter, seriously offends God.

VI. MORAL LIFE

CHAPTER 17 — The moral life of the Christian is a response to the duty of growing in the new life communicated through Christ. Docility to the Holy Spirit entails faithful observance of the commandments of

God, laws of the Church and just civil laws. Christian freedom must be regulated and be subject to the Magisterium of the Church whose duty is to explain the whole moral law with authority given by Christ himself. There are absolute moral norms which must be followed.

CHAPTER 18 — All precepts and counsels are summed up in faith working through charity.

CHAPTER 19 — God is love, and doing his will means a life in which love reigns in keeping the commandments. Holiness is the perfection of love.

VII. THE CHURCH

CHAPTER 20 — The Church, instituted by Christ, is the new people of God. She has all the means necessary for guiding herself to maturity as the communion of persons in Christ. The Church is essentially a hierarchical society guided by its Shepherds who are in union with the Supreme Pontiff.

CHAPTER 21 — The Church is also a communion, a people whom God unites by close spiritual bonds. Her structure requires a variety of gifts and offices. But these do not detract from the basic equality of persons in the Church.

CHAPTER 22 — Though Catholics should show a deep interest in separated brethren, their first obligation is to renew the Catholic Church so that it may present itself as the clear witness of Christ.

CHAPTER 23 — The Church is not only a communion of persons, but an institution to which the universal saving mission has been entrusted. She accepts all cultures and dialogues with the world to be aware of the signs of the times. Inspired by no earthly ambition, she is deeply solicitous for the needs of all.

CHAPTER 24 — Mary, ever-Virgin Mother of the Lord, occupies the highest place in the Church next to Christ himself. The Church, who honors the faithful and saints who are already with the Lord, venerates in a most special way Christ's Mother who is also our Mother.

VIII. FINAL REUNION WITH GOD

CHAPTER 25—The faithful already in this life await the coming of the Lord. The very last realities, however, will become manifest only when Christ comes in power as judge of the living and the dead. He will hand over his people to the Father. They will be judged after death; there are expiatory punishments for sin in purgatory; there is eternal death in hell; there will be a last judgment. Above all, there will be an eternal reward for those who have done right during their lifetime. We should work out our salvation with hope and salutary fear.

Part One – GOD

Chapter 1

THE MYSTERY OF THE ONE GOD —FATHER, SON, HOLY SPIRIT—

1. What is the history of salvation?

The history of salvation is the story of God's dealing with humankind. Through it, the one true God in three Persons—the Father, the Son, the Holy Spirit—(1) reveals himself to them and (2) saves them from sin.

VATICAN COUNCIL II . . .

▲ Through divine revelation God chose to show forth and communicate himself and the eternal decisions of his will regarding the salvation of men. That is to say, he chose "to share those divine treasures which totally transcend the understanding of the human mind" (Vatican I). *(Divine Revelation, 6)*

The plan of revelation is realized by deeds and words having an inner unity: the deeds wrought by God in the history of salvation manifest and confirm the teaching and realities signified by the words, while the words proclaim the deeds and clarify the mystery contained in them. *(Divine Revelation, 2)*

EXPLANATION . . .

● **(1) The history of salvation is identical with the history of the way and the plan by which God, true and one, the Father, the Son, the Holy Spirit, reveals himself to people, and reconciles and unites with himself those turned away from sin.**

(2) Out of his merciful kindness God has made us and has called us to share in his own life and glory. But sin caused us to lose God's life. God sent his Son to save us from sin and death, and to give us the divine life of grace again. God has poured out his divine goodness upon us, and continues to do so. The history of salvation tells us how God went about carrying out this plan to save us.

2. How did God reveal himself in the Old Testament?

In the Old Testament God revealed himself as the one true personal God, transcendent, beyond the limits of this world.

VATICAN COUNCIL II . . .

▲ Planning to make known the way of heavenly salvation, God from the start manifested himself to our first parents. Then after their fall his promise of redemption aroused in them the hope of being saved (cf. Gen 3:15), and from that time on he ceaselessly kept the human race in his care, in order to give eternal life to those who perseveringly do good in search of salvation (cf. Rom 2:6-7). Then, at the time he had appointed, he called Abraham in order to make him a great nation (cf. Gen 12:2). *(Divine Revelation*, 3)

EXPLANATION . . .

● God is an all-powerful being existing above and beyond humankind and his world. The true God is real. He becomes real for us when we come to know him. To know God personally, we have to be very attentive to whatever he shows us of himself. This is called revelation. By making himself known to us through divine revelation, God gave himself to us and showed us his will for the salvation of all.

God shows himself in all of creation and history. But the Catholic Church is especially interested in a personal way in which God showed and continues to show himself to us. This revelation is described in the Bible, and from it we learn what our life really is and how we must live it.

The Bible is a collection of books written under the inspiration of God who is the author of all Sacred Scripture (CCC 81, see 105).

The forty-six books of the Old Testament contain a history of the Jewish people and their faith from earliest times down to the first century. They also include books of poems and prayers, laws and stories, books of wisdom and practical advice in the art of living.

This material came from the life and experience of the Jewish people. Much of the material was passed along by word of mouth for generations before it was written the way we now have it.

The Bible is true because essentially it is the testimony of what God has done in the life of a people and what they have come to believe about him through this experience. That testimony is true.

"The inspired books teach the truth. 'Since therefore all that the inspired authors or sacred writers affirm should be regarded as affirmed by the Holy Spirit, we must acknowledge that the books of Scripture firmly, faithfully, and without error teach that truth which God, for the sake of our salvation, wished to see confided to the Sacred Scriptures'" (CCC 107).

The Bible is important because it is the written record of God's actions in the world. These make known to us the meaning of life and point the way to the future. This knowledge and hope is most important to humankind.

3. How did God prepare for a later revelation of the Trinity?

By his Old Testament words and actions, God prepared for the later revelation of the Trinity.

VATICAN COUNCIL II . . .

▲ Through the patriarchs, and after them through Moses and the prophets, he taught this nation to acknowledge him as the one living and true God, provident Father and just Judge, and to wait for the Savior promised by him. In this manner he prepared the way for the gospel down through the centuries. *(Divine Revelation, 3)*

EXPLANATION . . .

● God's revelation was carried out by his words and deeds in the Old and New Testaments. First, God revealed himself to our first parents. After their fall into sin his promise of redemption gave them the hope of being saved. He said to the serpent, "I will establish hostility between you and the woman, between your line and her line. Her offspring will crush your head and you will bruise his heel" (Gen 3:15).

After the fall of our first parents, God introduced himself to man and urged him to be open to God and to the future. God's action began in the Old Testament, about 4,000 years ago, with Abraham. Abraham answered God's invitation and followed him all of his life. Because of Abraham's faithfulness, God chose his descendants to be his own special people. The Lord said to Abraham: "Leave your country, your people and the house of your father, and go the the land to which I will lead you. I will make of you a great people, and I will bless you" (Gen 12:1-2).

Abraham welcomes three strangers into his home, who are really God and two angels, symbolic of the Holy Trinity.

The Jewish people, known in the Old Testament as "Israel," were God's people. They came out of Egypt. Originally their ancestors had come there as refugees from famine and stayed on. After several generations the Egyptians made slaves of them. God inspired Moses to convince these people that if they put their trust in the God of their fathers he would lead them out of slavery and into a land of their own.

After their escape they wandered through the Sinai desert. God had called them out of Egypt to become his own people. With the help of Moses they declared their acceptance of God and their willingness to be his people. They sealed their commitment to God in the blood of animals, which had been killed and offered to God as gifts. This commitment is called the "Covenant."

A covenant was an ancient legal form by which a king's sovereignty over a people was recognized and accepted by them. Israel's covenant was with God. The conditions of the Covenant were expressed in the ten commandments which Moses presented to the people. Later other laws were added, so that the whole life of the people was organized around their promise to God.

Over and over again Israel broke the Covenant by ignoring God's commandments. This led them into war, suffering, and defeat. But God never abandoned his people and always forgave them when they turned back to him in repentance.

Israel expected to receive special benefits as God's people because of their covenant with him. They expected to be the nation through which God would extend his kingdom over the whole world. They also expected to be the first among the nations.

During the period of the Old Testament people learned that God was real and the guiding force in their lives. They found that he was faithful to his promises and that they could live as his friends if they put their trust in him.

4. How was the mystery of the Trinity expressed?

The mystery of the Trinity was expressed in the person, words, and works of Jesus Christ.

THE BIBLE . . .

✠ *In previous times God spoke to our ancestors in many and various ways through the Prophets, but in these last days he has spoken to us through his Son, whom he appointed heir of all things and through whom he created the universe.* (Heb 1:1-2)

VATICAN COUNCIL II . . .

▲ Jesus Christ, therefore, the Word made flesh, sent as "a man to men, speaks the words of God" (Jn 3:34), and completes the work of salvation which his Father gave him to do (cf. Jn 5:36; 17:4). To see Jesus is to see his Father (Jn 14:9). For this reason Jesus perfected revelation by fulfilling it through his whole work of making himself present and manifesting himself: through his words and deeds, his signs and wonders, but especially through his death and glorious resurrection from the dead and final sending of the Spirit of truth. *(Divine Revelation, 4)*

EXPLANATION . . .

● The foreshadowings of the mystery of the Trinity are completely explained in the person, the works, and the words of Jesus Christ. God gave himself. He came among people in the person of his Son and announced that the kingdom of God had arrived to stay. This message of the "Good News" of salvation is found in the New Testament.

The New Testament is the record of what the early followers of Jesus had to say about him and his teaching. It includes four gospels or basic teachings of the followers of Jesus, a history of the early Church (Acts of the Apostles), twenty-one letters of the apostles (epistles), and a book of prophecy (Apocalypse or Book of Revelation). This material came from the earliest communities of our Lord's followers.

After speaking through the prophets, God sent his Son, the Divine Word, to dwell among men and tell them the deepest truths about God. By his words and actions, and especially in his holy person, Jesus made known how each person of the Trinity would help humankind to be saved from sin and to be brought to eternal life. Jesus gave us the names of these persons. We associate the names of each person with God giving us all we have—the Father; God showing himself to us—the Son; God living within us—the Holy Spirit.

5. What did Jesus reveal about the Trinity?

Jesus (1) revealed himself as the eternal and divine Son of God; (2) more fully revealed the Father; (3) made known a third divine Person, the Holy Spirit, whom the Father and he, as risen Lord, sent to his Church.

VATICAN COUNCIL II . . .

▲ Christ established the kingdom of God on earth, manifested his Father and himself by deeds and words, and completed his work by his death, resurrection, and glorious ascension and by the sending of the Holy Spirit. *(Divine Revelation, 17)*

EXPLANATION . . .

● (1) God chose to reveal himself through Christ that humankind might have access to the Father in the Holy Spirit and come to share in the divine nature. Jesus made himself known as God's Son through his words and deeds, but especially through his death and glorious resurrection and the sending of the Holy Spirit. He said to the Jews, "The One whom God has sent speaks the words of God, for God gives him the Spirit without measure" (Jn 3:34). "But I have testimony that is greater than John's. The works that my Father has given me to accomplish, the very works that I am doing, testify about me that the Father has sent me" (Jn 5:36).

In his talk with his disciples shortly before his death Jesus said, "Believe me when I say that I am in the Father and the Father is in me. But if you do not, then believe because of the works themselves" (Jn 14:11). "Everything that the Father has is mine. That is why I said that he will take what is mine and communicate it to you" (Jn 16:15). Thus Jesus Christ is only one Person—the second Person of the Blessed Trinity. He has two natures: the nature of God and the nature of man.

(2) Christ, the final Adam, by the revelation of the mystery of the Father and his love, fully reveals man to man himself and makes his supreme calling clear. Jesus teaches us God's love by telling us about his Father. But his very life is a lesson in which we can see God's love at work. In his person, life, and teaching Jesus shows us God giving himself to us.

Jesus said to Philip, "Have I been with you all this time, Philip, and you still do not know me? Whoever has seen me has seen the Father. How can you say, 'Show us the Father'?" (Jn 14:9).

Jesus said to his disciples, "I have used figures of speech to explain these things to you. The hour is coming when I will no longer use figures, but I will tell you about the Father in plain words. When that day comes, you will ask in my name. I do not say that I will entreat the Father on your behalf. For the Father himself loves you because you have loved me and have come to believe that I came from God. I came from the Father and have come into the world. Now I am leaving the world and returning to the Father" (Jn 16:25-28).

Jesus taught us to love our heavenly Father because he loves us and wants to help us in all the needs of our body and soul. But we must speak to him through prayer. The Father wants to bring his children to his heavenly home, and he will do so through Jesus, his Son. Jesus said to his disciples, "Your Father knows what you need before you ask him. This is how you should pray: 'Our Father in heaven, hallowed be your name. Your kingdom come, your will be done on earth as it is in heaven' " (Mt 6:8-10). It is important to have God as a Father because God gives us life and love and, in so doing, makes us realize the dignity of our person.

(3) At the Last Supper Jesus promised to send the Holy Spirit. "I have told you these things while I am still with you. However, the Advocate, the Holy Spirit, whom the Father will send in my name, will teach you everything and remind you of all that I have said to you" (Jn 14:25-26). "If I do not go away, the Advocate will not come to you, whereas if I go, I will send him to you" (Jn 16:7).

6. What did the divine Teacher give his disciples?

The Divine Teacher (1) gave his disciples knowledge of the true God by his own authority; (2) he called them to become sons and daughters of God through the gift of the Spirit which he bestows on them.

THE BIBLE . . .

✠ *To those who did accept him and who believed in his name he granted the power to become children of God. (Jn 1:12)*

You did not receive a spirit of slavery leading to fear; rather, you received the Spirit of adoption, enabling us to cry out, "Abba! Father!" (Rom 8:15)

VATICAN COUNCIL II . . .

▲ Jesus confirmed with divine testimony what revelation proclaimed, that God is with us to free us from the darkness of sin and death, and to raise us up to life eternal. *(Divine Rev., 4)*

When the work which the Father gave the Son to do on earth was accomplished (cf. Jn 17:4), the Holy Spirit was sent on the day of Pentecost in order that he might continually sanctify the Church, and thus, all those who believe would have access through Christ in one Spirit to the Father (cf. Eph 2:18). He is the Spirit of Life, a fountain of water springing up to life eternal (cf. Jn 4:14; 7:38-39). *(The Church, 4)*

EXPLANATION . . .

● (1) Jesus is the way to God. By getting to know him, we meet God in a human being and really see his love for us in action. Finding Jesus, we reach the very presence of our Father. Jesus said, "I am the gate. Anyone who enters through me will be saved. He will go in and out and will find pasture. A thief comes only to steal and kill and destroy" (Jn 10:9-10).

(2) Jesus brought a whole new life to us. He said, "I have come that they may have life, and have it in abundance" (Jn 10:10). This new life—God's own life—communicated to us by the Holy Spirit, who comes to live within us, is sometimes called "grace." Jesus said, "Whoever loves me will keep my word, and my Father will love him, and we will come to him and make our abode with him" (Jn 14:23).

This is a new life because before Jesus came no one loved God enough to be able to live his kind of life. Because he was the Son of God Jesus was able to give us a share of God's life and make us children of God through the gift of the Spirit which he gives us. St. John says, "To those who did accept him and believed in his name he granted the power to become children of God" (Jn 1:12). And St. Paul says, "You did not receive a spirit of slavery leading to fear; rather, you received the Spirit of adoption, enabling us to cry out, 'Abba! Father!' " (Rom 8:15).

God entered man's life and invited us to share his life when he personally became a man in Jesus Christ. Jesus then called us to the kingdom of his Father. He communicates his life to others through the Holy Spirit whom he sends to live within his friends. He said, "If you love me, you will keep my commandments. And I will ask the Father, and he will give you another Advocate to be with you forever, the Spirit of Truth whom the world cannot accept because it neither sees him nor knows him. But you know him because he dwells with you and will be in you" (Jn 14:15-17).

7. How do we express our devotion to the Trinity?

We should (1) become ever more aware of the Triune God dwelling in our soul; (2) try to grasp, through faith, the great truth that, beginning at baptism, we are called to a lifelong union of love with the three divine Persons.

VATICAN COUNCIL II . . .

▲ By baptism men are plunged into the paschal mystery of Christ: they die with him, are buried with him, and rise with him (cf. Rom 6:4; Eph 2:6; Col 3:1; 2 Tim 2:11); they receive the spirit of adoption as sons "in which we cry: Abba, Father" (Rom 8:15), and thus become true adorers whom the Father seeks (cf. Jn 4:23). *(Sacred Liturgy, 6)*

EXPLANATION . . .

● (1) The night before he died Jesus said to his disciples, "Anyone who has received my commandments and observes them is the one who loves me. And whoever loves me will be loved by my Father, and I will love him and reveal myself to him" (Jn 14:21). "I will ask the Father, and he will give you another Advocate to be with you forever" (Jn 14:16). The Holy Spirit lives in our soul by grace. We first received this grace through baptism.

We ought to speak to God in our soul frequently. This is a beautiful way of honoring the Father and the Son and the Holy Spirit, for Jesus said, "Whoever loves me will keep my word, and my Father will love him, and we will come to him and make our abode with him" (Jn 14:23).

(2) We belong to God who is closest to us. God is our Father; Jesus Christ is our Lord and Savior; the Holy Spirit is our teacher and guide. Because of Jesus Christ the Father shares his unending life with us, and the Holy Spirit will make us so like Jesus that, even though we die, our Father will again raise us to life as he did his Son.

DISCUSSION QUESTIONS

1. What does the history of salvation tell us? (1)
2. What is the Bible? What does it contain? Why is it true? Why is it important? (2)
3. How did God give himself to us? (2)
4. How did God reveal himself to our first parents? (3)
5. How did God reveal himself to Abraham? (3)
6. How did God reveal himself through Moses? (3)
7. What is the New Testament? (4)
8. What does the New Testament include? (4)
9. How did Jesus reveal himself? (5)
10. How did Jesus reveal the Father? (5)
11. How did Jesus reveal the Holy Spirit? (5)
12. How do we know the true God through Jesus? (6)
13. What does it mean to be children of God? (6)
14. How do we show our devotion to the three Divine Persons? (7)

Chapter 2

TRUE WORSHIP OF GOD

8. What are some of the perfections of God?

God is all-good, holy, just, merciful, wise and perfect.

VATICAN COUNCIL II . . .

▲ Freely creating us out of his surpassing and merciful kindness, and graciously calling us moreover to communicate in life and glory with himself, God has generously poured out his divine goodness and does not cease to do so. *(Church in the Modern World, 2)*

EXPLANATION . . .

● God is *all-good.* He is goodness itself. God made the earth for us: the heat of the sun to give us warmth and make things grow for our benefit and pleasure; the grains, the animals that they might give food and help us in our work. God permits some evil like illness, poverty, only to bring good out of evil.

God has given us all the good things we have because he loves us. He created us and then by Baptism made us his children. He gave us the benefits of the Catholic Church: truth, the sacraments, the promise of eternal life.

God is *all-holy* because he is God. Isaiah tells us that the angels cry out in the presence of God: "Holy, holy, holy is the Lord of hosts! The entire earth is filled with his glory!" (Isa 6:3).

God invites us and helps us to a life of holiness. Jesus tells us, "Strive to be perfect just as your heavenly Father is perfect" (Mt 5:48).

God is *all-just.* He is honest and fair with everybody. He promised to reward those who do good and punish those who do evil, and he will keep his word.

God is *all-merciful.* Jesus teaches us to have confidence in the mercy of God, as in the parable of the Prodigal Son. He taught us to pray: "Our Father in heaven . . . forgive us our debts as we forgive our debtors" (Mt 6:12). He assured us of forgiveness: "If you forgive others for the wrongs they have done, your heavenly Father will also forgive you" (Mt 6:14). On the evening of his resurrection he instituted the sacrament of penance and told his apostles, "If you forgive anyone's sins, they are forgiven. If you retain anyone's sins, they are retained" (Jn 20:23). If we are truly sorry for our sins, God will forgive us because he is all-merciful.

God is *all-knowing.* He knows all things, past, present, and future, even our most secret thoughts, words, and actions. He knows those who serve him and those who offend him. Nothing can be hidden from him. St. Paul says, "Nothing in creation is hidden from his sight. Everything is uncovered and exposed to the eyes of the one to whom we must all render an account" (Heb 4:13).

9. How has God shown his goodness to us?

God (1) has made firm commitments to us and bound us to himself by solemn covenants. (2) He has each of us always in view. (3) He loves us with the love of a father, the love of a spouse.

VATICAN COUNCIL II . . .

▲ In his goodness and wisdom God chose to reveal himself and to make known to us the hidden purpose of his will (cf. Eph 1:9) by which through Christ, the Word made flesh, man might in the Holy Spirit have access to the Father and come to share in the divine nature (cf. Eph 2:18; 2 Pet 1:4). Through this revelation, therefore, the invisible God (cf. Col 1:15; 1 Tim 1:17) out of the abundance of his love speaks to men as friends (cf. Ex 33:11; Jn 15: 14-15) and lives among them (cf. Bar 3:38), so that he may invite and take them into fellowship with himself. *(Divine Revelation, 2)*

EXPLANATION . . .

● (1) After our first parents sinned, God made a promise to save humankind. He kept his promise. God chose Abraham's descendants to be his own special people. With the help of Moses the Jewish people made their commitment to God which was called the "Covenant." Its conditions were expressed in the ten commandments. Israel often broke the Covenant, but God never abandoned his people. Finally, God came among his people in the person of his Son, who established the New Covenant in his blood by his death on the cross.

(2) It is through Jesus Christ that God most perfectly shows his love for us. God spoke to us in revelation. Through Jesus he revealed to us his loving plan of salvation. He wished to share his life with us. He now does so through Jesus. Through the passion, death, and resurrection of Jesus we have received grace and God's life. Through Jesus we have hope of eternal life with God in heaven.

(3) God truly loves us and takes care of us as a loving Father. He has made us his children through Baptism and has prepared his heavenly kingdom to be our eternal home. His love is expressed in the love of Jesus, who loved the Church as his bride, and gave his life for her.

10. What should the thought of God's goodness prompt us to do?

The thought of God's goodness (1) should awaken joy in the God who is the cause of our eternal hope and (2) should prompt us to worship him.

THE BIBLE . . .

✠ *Blessed be the God and Father of our Lord Jesus Christ. In his great mercy he has given us a new birth to a living hope through the resurrection of Jesus Christ from the dead, and to an inheritance that is imperishable, undefiled and unfading. It is reserved in heaven for you. (1 Pet 1:3-4)*

VATICAN COUNCIL II . . .

▲ The spiritual life, however, is not limited solely to participation in the liturgy. The Christian is indeed called to pray with his brethren, but he must also enter into his chamber to pray to the Father, in secret (cf. Mt 6:6); yet more, according to the teaching of the Apostle, he should pray without ceasing (cf. 1 Thes 5:17). *(Sacred Liturgy, 12)*

EXPLANATION . . .

● **(1) As Christians we must be convinced that God is real. The final explanation of who we are and what our life means is to be found in him, though he is only partly known. Our faith teaches us that God is our Father, and that fact makes us very important. Our life really means something because God has given it to us. We belong to him. He loves us and asks that we love him. Thus we have something to live for that deserves the best we have. God wanted us in this world and made us his children in baptism so that someday we might be with him forever in heaven. God's love for us should make us find our joy in him and trust him.**

(2) We owe God loving service and worship. St. Peter wrote: "Blessed be the God and Father of our Lord Jesus Christ. In his great mercy he has given us a new birth to a living hope through the resurrection of Jesus Christ from the dead and to an inheritance that is imperishable, undefiled, and unfading. It is reserved in heaven for you" (1 Pet 1:3-4).

11. How do we worship God?

We worship God (1) especially in the sacred liturgy, offering ourselves to him through our Lord Jesus Christ. (2) We commit ourselves to carrying out his will in our every activity, and to use and increase the talents he has given us.

THE BIBLE . . .

✠ *"The kingdom of heaven will be like a man going on a journey who summoned his servants and entrusted his property to them. To one he gave five talents, to another two talents, to a third one talent—to each according to his ability. Then he set forth on his journey." (Mt 25:14f)*

VATICAN COUNCIL II . . .

▲ Through the ministry of the priests, the spiritual sacrifice of the faithful is made perfect in union with the sacrifice of Christ. He is the only mediator who in the name of the whole Church is offered sacramentally in the Eucharist and in an unbloody manner until the Lord himself comes (cf. 1 Cor 11:26). *(Ministry and Life of Priests, 2)*

EXPLANATION . . .

● **(1) We worship God especially by adoring him in the Holy Sacrifice of the Mass, uniting ourselves to him through Jesus Christ. We worship God also when we pray.**

(2) We worship God by keeping his commandments as obedient children. The purpose of our life is to answer our Father's invitation to know him and to love him and to give ourselves to him and also to serve others. We fulfill the purpose of our life when we do God's will. It will be finally fulfilled when we give ourselves completely over to God at our death.

We worship God especially in the Eucharistic Sacrifice.

12. What graces can we expect from God's goodness?

From God's goodness we receive the graces needed (1) to profess the truth in love and, (2) to bring forth the fruits of love, justice and peace, all to his glory.

THE BIBLE . . .

✠ *Rather, professing truth and love, we will in all things grow into him who is the head, Christ.* (Eph 4:15)

VATICAN COUNCIL II . . .

▲ Man would not exist were he not created by God's love and constantly preserved by it; and he cannot live fully according to truth unless he freely acknowledges that love and devotes himself to his Creator. (*Church in the Modern World*, 19)

EXPLANATION . . .

● (1) St. Paul says, "Rather, professing truth and love, we will in all things grow into him who is the head, Christ" (Eph 4:15). We cannot live according to the truth unless we freely acknowledge God's love and devote ourselves to our Creator.

(2) Since God loves us, he also wants to help us to love him in return. We are in this world to know, love, and serve God. He offers us his help to do so through his grace, which he offers us when we pray and receive the sacraments, especially the Holy Eucharist. Our life can be a joyous life with God if only we open our heart to him and try to use the graces he offers us each day. We should be grateful to God for his love.

13. Why do many people today pay little attention to God?

Many people pay little attention to God because (1) modern life is self-centered, not God-centered; (2) its climate is unfavorable to faith.

VATICAN COUNCIL II . . .

▲ Man is split within himself. As a result, all of human life, whether individual or collective, shows itself to be a dramatic struggle between good and evil, between light and darkness. Indeed, man finds that by himself he is incapable of battling the assaults of evil successfully, so that everyone feels as though he is bound by chains. *(Church in the Modern World, 13)*

EXPLANATION . . .

● (1) Freely creating us out of his merciful kindness, and graciously calling us to share in life and glory with himself, God has poured out his divine goodness upon us, and continues to do so. And yet there are very many people in the world who hardly ever think of him; many even break his commandments. They are too interested in their own pleasures and in the things the world offers them. They are self-centered, not God-centered.

(2) To live a God-centered life one must have faith, because we know God through what he has revealed to us about himself. We must accept his word with deep faith, relying only on his love for us and his faithfulness to his promises. We can make up for the care-

lessness and lack of faith in the world by trying to serve God even more earnestly. He will surely reward us for our devotion to him.

14. Does everyone have some desire for God?

God has placed in every one some desire for him, no matter how hidden.

VATICAN COUNCIL II . . .

▲ The root reason for human dignity lies in man's call to communion with God. From the very circumstance of his origin man is already invited to converse with God. *(Church in the Modern World, 19)*

EXPLANATION . . .

● **An outstanding cause of human dignity lies in one's call to converse with God. God has made us for himself and we cannot find true happiness unless we look for it in him. The Psalmist prayed: "My heart and my flesh cry out for the living God" (Ps 84:3). Even when we do not want to think so, there is a secret desire in our hearts for God. Since God has helped us to know him more than many other people do, he expects us to love him more and serve him better. Our life will be blessed if we do so. We can look forward to being with God forever in heaven.**

DISCUSSION QUESTIONS

1. Why is God all-good? all-holy? all-just? all-merciful? all-knowing? (8)
2. How did God show his love through Abraham? Moses? Jesus? (9)
3. How does God show us his goodness? (9)
4. Why should we find joy in God and put our trust in him? (10)
5. How do we worship God in Holy Mass? In prayer? In keeping his commandments? (11)
6. How do we profess the truth in love? (12)
7. How can we live a God-centered life? (13)
8. What should the secret desire in our hearts for God prompt us to do? (14)

Chapter 3

KNOWLEDGE OF GOD AND THE WITNESS OF CHRISTIAN LOVE

15. Can one come to know God through created things?

(1) Sacred Scripture shows that one can come to know God through the things God has made. (2) The Church teaches that from reflection on created things human reason can come to a knowledge of God as the beginning and end of all that is.

THE BIBLE . . .

✠ *Ever since the creation of the world the invisible attributes of God's eternal power and divine nature have been clearly understood and perceived through the things he has made. Therefore, the conduct of these people is inexcusable.* (Rom 1:20)

"After this I will return and rebuild the fallen tent of David. From its ruins I will rebuild it and raise it up again, so that the rest of mankind may seek out the Lord, as well as all the Gentiles whom I have claimed as my own." (Acts 15:16-17)

The heavens proclaim the glory of God; the firmament shows forth the work of his hands. (Ps 19:2)

For all people were inherently foolish who remained in ignorance of God and did not come to know him who is, even while observing the good things around them, nor recognize the artisan while studying his works. To their way of thinking, either fire or wind or the swift air, or the periphery of the stars, or tempestuous water, or the luminaries of heaven were the gods that govern the world. If they have been deluded by the beauty of these things into believing that these were gods, let them come to understand how far superior to these things is their Lord, since he was the source of beauty that fashioned them. And if they were astonished at their power and energy, let them realize from observing these things how much more powerful is he who made them. For from the grandeur and the beauty of created things is derived a corresponding perception of the creator. Yet these people incur minimal blame, for they may have gone astray while seeking God and eagerly desiring to find him. For while diligently searching among his works, they are distracted by the beauty of these things. But even so, they cannot be completely absolved of guilt. For if they achieved a sufficient degree of knowledge to investigate the world, how did they fail to find its Lord more quickly? (Wis 13:1-9)

VATICAN COUNCIL II . . .

▲ As a sacred synod has affirmed, God, the beginning and end of all things, can be known with certainty from created reality by the light of human reason (cf. Rom 1:20); but the Synod teaches that it is through his revelation that those religious truths which are by their nature accessible to human reason can be known by all men with ease, with solid certitude and with no trace of error, even in this present state of the human race. *(Divine Revelation, 6)*

EXPLANATION . . .

● (1) The faithful must learn the deepest meaning and value of creation, and how to relate it to the praise of God. They must assist one another to live holier lives. The God who loves us makes himself known to us in various ways. He wants to gain our love and to unite us to himself now and forever. God teaches us through the things he has made. He also teaches us through the revelation he has made of himself.

(2) The Catholic Church teaches us to know God better. This is the reason why the study of our religion is so important. We cannot love what we do not know. If we really want to love God more, we will try to learn as much as we can about him. St. Paul tells us, "God's eternal power and divine nature have been clearly understood and perceived through the things he has made" (Rom 1:20).

When the early astronauts caught sight of the earth from outer space, they paid tribute to the fact that God can be known through the magnificent works he has made.

16. How can we help unbelievers to find God?

Like the first Christians we can help unbelievers to find God by the compelling witness of a life (1) which shows a firm and mature faith in God, (2) which is lived in personal love of Christ, and (3) which carries out works of justice and charity.

THE BIBLE . . .

✠ *They devoted themselves to the teaching of the apostles and to the communal fellowship, to the breaking of bread and to prayers. A sense of awe was felt by all for many wonders and signs were performed by the apostles. All the believers were together and owned everything in common. They would sell their property and possessions and distribute the proceeds to all according to what each one needed. Every day, united in spirit, they would assemble together in the temple. They would break bread in their homes and share their food with joyful and generous hearts as they praised God, and they were regarded with favor by all the people. And day by day the Lord added to those who were being saved.* (Acts 2:42-47)

VATICAN COUNCIL II . . .

▲ There are innumerable opportunities open to the laity for the exercise of their apostolate of evangelization and sanctification. The very testimony of their Christian life and good works done in a supernatural spirit has the power to draw men to belief and to God; for the Lord says, "Your light must shine so that it can be seen by others; this will enable them to observe your good works and give praise to your Father in heaven" (Mt 5:16).

However, an apostolate of this kind does not consist only in the witness of one's way of life; a true apostle looks for opportunities to announce Christ by words addressed either to non-believers with a view to leading them to faith, or to the faithful with a view to instructing, strengthening, and encouraging them to a more fervent life. (*Apostolate of the Laity*, 6)

EXPLANATION . . .

● (1) We can help people to turn to God if we give them a good example of our own deep faith in God, (2) and our love for Jesus Christ. We can be like missionaries in the world by letting them see the goodness of our life.

(2) God has willed that all people should make up one family and treat one another in a spirit of charity, for all are called to the same goal, God himself. God our Father made this world and the whole universe. He put us in it and we take much of our life from it. As we grow to love our Father, we will find that we shall be putting more of ourselves into his world and helping it to grow; most of all, we shall help others to grow in their love for our heavenly Father and Creator.

17. Does faith in God and union with Christ free us of concern for the world's troubles?

Christians must show by their actions that faith in God and union with Christ entail an obligation to work at solving the world's problems.

THE BIBLE . . .

✠ *"Our ancestors worshiped on this mountain, but you say that the place where people must worship is in Jerusalem." Jesus told her, "Believe me, woman, the hour is coming when you will worship the Father neither on this mountain nor in Jerusalem." (Jn 4:20-21)*

VATICAN COUNCIL II . . .

▲ Such a life requires a continual exercise of faith, hope, and charity. Only by the light of faith and by meditation on the word of God can one always and everywhere recognize God in whom "we live, and move, and have our being" (Acts 17:28), seek his will in every event, see Christ in everyone whether he be a relative or a stranger, and make correct judgments about the true meaning and value of temporal things both in themselves and in their relation to man's final goal. *(Apostolate of the Laity, 4)*

EXPLANATION . . .

● **We can help people to love God by loving God ourselves. We owe God this love and service. We also owe this to our neighbor—the people around us—because we are to love them for the love of God. In this way we can help them in what they need most—to find their peace and joy in God. Love for our neighbor obliges us to work earnestly for the betterment of the world—to improve conditions in the world and to help to solve its problems.**

DISCUSSION QUESTIONS

1. Why does God make himself known through creation? (15)
2. Why is the study of religion important? (15)
3. How do we lead unbelievers to God: By our faith? By our love for Christ? By love of neighbor? (16)
4. How can we improve conditions in the world? (17)

Part Two – JESUS CHRIST

Chapter 4

JESUS CHRIST, SON OF GOD, THE FIRSTBORN OF ALL CREATION, AND SAVIOR

— Son of God —

18. What is the greatest of God's works?

The greatest of God's works is the taking on of human flesh by his Son, Jesus Christ, which is called the incarnation.

VATICAN COUNCIL II . . .

▲ This decree, however, flows from the "fount-like love" or charity of God the Father who is the "principle without principle" from whom the Son is begotten and the Holy Spirit proceeds through the Son. *(Mission Activity of the Church, 2)*

For when the fullness of time arrived (cf. Gal 4:4), the Word was made flesh and dwelt among us in his fullness of grace and truth (cf. Jn 1:14). *(Divine Revelation, 17)*

EXPLANATION . . .

● In the plan of our heavenly Father, his Son was to come to this world born of a woman. He sent the angel Gabriel to a town of Galilee named Nazareth, to a virgin promised to a man named Joseph. Her name was Mary. The angel said to her: "Hail, full of grace! The Lord is with you. Blessed are you among women." When Mary wondered

what his greeting meant, the angel went on to say to her: "Do not be afraid, Mary, you have found favor with God. Behold, you will conceive in your womb and bear a son, and you will name him Jesus. He will be great and will be called Son of the Most High."

Mary said to the angel, "How will this be?" The angel answered her: "The Holy Spirit will come upon you, and the power of the Most High will overshadow you. Therefore, the child to be born will be holy, and he will be called the Son of God." Mary said: "Behold, I am the servant of the Lord. Let it be done to me according to your word" (cf. Lk 1:26-38). At that moment Jesus Christ, God's own Son, became man in the Blessed Virgin Mary.

The greatest of God's works is the incarnation of his Son, Jesus Christ. The Son is begotten from the Father, and the Holy Spirit proceeds from the Father through the Son. The incarnation means that the Word, the Son of God, became man and dwelt among us in the fullness of grace and truth.

St. Luke made known to us the birth of God made man in Bethlehem nine months after the message of the angel in these simple words: "She gave birth to her firstborn son. She wrapped him in swaddling clothes and laid him in a manger, because there was no room for them in the inn" (Lk 2:7).

19. Why did the Son of God come on earth?

The Son of God came on earth and entered human history (1) so as to renew the world from within and, (2) be for it an abiding source of supernatural life and salvation from sin.

VATICAN COUNCIL II . . .

▲ Jesus Christ was sent into the world as a real mediator between God and men. Since he is God, all divine fullness dwells bodily in him (Col 2:9). *(Mission Activity of the Church,* 3)

The Son of God walked the ways of a true Incarnation that he might make men sharers in the nature of God: made poor for our sakes, though he had been rich, in order that his poverty might enrich us (2 Cor 8:9). The Son of man came not that he might be served, but that he might be a servant, and give his life as a ransom for the many—that is, for all (cf. Mk 10:45). *(Mission Activity of the Church,* 3)

EXPLANATION . . .

● (1) The Word was made flesh that he might make men sharers in the divine nature, and give his life as a ransom for all. The supreme purpose of the incarnation of the Word and of the whole economy of salvation consists in this: that all people be led to the Father. By his incarnation the Son of God has united himself with every one. Born of the Virgin Mary, he has truly been made one of us, like us in all things except sin.

The human race lost God's life of grace through original sin. The Bible tells us about the temptation and fall of our first parents. Because of his love for us Jesus regained grace for all by his life and death and resurrection. He showed us what it means to be a child of God. In this way he renews the world from within.

(2) Jesus Christ, God's Son, came into human life as our brother to teach us and to show us what it means to love God and to belong to God. Jesus showed in his life and teaching that the Son of God—and he is God-Man—is powerful and good like his Father. Jesus showed us how we must belong to God. His whole life was devoted to doing the work and will of his Father. His life teaches us that to belong to God means to be like Jesus.

To receive God's life we must accept Jesus and his way of life. We do this through Baptism. Through the Catholic Church and its sacraments we are able to keep this life in our soul. With this grace we can be united with God in this world and forever in heaven. Thus through the sacraments and his grace Jesus is for us an abiding source of supernatural life and salvation from sin.

— Firstborn —

20. Why is Jesus Christ called the firstborn of all creation?

St. Paul teaches that Jesus Christ is the firstborn of all creation. (1) He is before all; all things hold together in him; all have been created in him, through him, and for him. (2) Obedient unto death, he was exalted as Lord of all. (3) Through his resurrection he was made known to us as God's Son in power. (4) Being the firstborn of the dead, he gives eternal life to all. (5) In him we are created anew.

THE BIBLE . . .

✠ *He is the image of the invisible God, the firstborn of all creation. For in him were created all things in heaven and on earth, whether visible and invisible, whether thrones or dominions, or rulers or powers—all things were created through him and for him. He exists before all things, and in him all things hold together.* (Col 1:15-17)

The gospel concerning his Son who according to the flesh was descended from David, and who according to the Spirit of holiness was proclaimed to be the Son of God in power by his resurrection from the dead: Jesus Christ our Lord. (Rom 1:3-4)

Just as in Adam all die, so all will be brought to life in Christ. (1 Cor 15:22)

We are God's handiwork, created in Christ Jesus for a life of good works that God had prepared for us to do. (Eph 2:10)

VATICAN COUNCIL II . . .

▲ The eternal Father, by a free and hidden plan of his own wisdom and goodness, created the whole world. His plan was to raise men to a participation of the divine life. After they had fallen in Adam, God did not leave men to themselves, but ceaselessly offered helps to salvation, in view of Christ, the Redeemer "who is the image of the invisible God, the firstborn of all creation" (Col 1:15).

All the elect, before time began, the Father "foreknew and predestined to become conformed to the image of his Son, that he should be the firstborn among many brethren" (Rom 8:29). He planned to assemble in the holy Church all those who would believe in Christ. *(The Church,* 2)

EXPLANATION . . .

● (1) All things were created in and through and for Jesus Christ, because he is God's own Son. St. John says of him: "In the beginning was the Word, and the Word was with God, and the Word was God. . . . Through him all things came into existence, and without him there was nothing that came into being. In him was life, and the life was the light of the human race" (Jn 1:1-4). He is the "firstborn of all creation" because he is before all that was created. All things find life in him.

(2) Jesus in his great love for us died on the cross to make up for our personal sins and to regain for us the life of grace. He also atoned for the sin of Adam. Sin is an offense against God. Only God can forgive our sins. God chose his Son to be the one to suffer and to die for our sins. Jesus is called our Savior because he saved us from sin.

(3) By conquering death through his own power in his resurrection, Jesus has shown himself Master of life and death; therefore, Jesus the Son of God, the Second Person of the Blessed Trinity, is true God as well as true man. He showed himself as the King of Kings and Lord of Lords, our own Savior.

(4) Christ's passage from death to life brought about our passage from the death of sin to life in Christ. Being the firstborn of the dead, he gives eternal life to all.

(5) God made all through Christ, and appointed him heir of all things so that he might restore them all. According to his human nature, Christ is the new Adam because he was made head of a renewed humanity, and is full of grace and truth.

We receive the new life of grace in Baptism because in Christ we are created new. We are now God's children. United to Christ, we should try to avoid sin because of Christ's resurrection and our Baptism. St. Peter says: "Blessed be the God and Father of our Lord Jesus Christ. In his great mercy he has given us a new birth to a living hope through the resurrection of Jesus Christ from the dead and to an inheritance that is imperishable . . . It is reserved in heaven for you" (1 Pet 1:3-4).

— Savior —

21. Why is Jesus Christ called the Savior?

Jesus Christ is called the Savior because (1) through him all creatures will be saved from the slavery of corruption. (2) Scripture says: "There is no salvation in anyone else" (Acts 4:12), nor has there ever been, from the very beginning.

THE BIBLE . . .

✠ *Indeed, creation itself eagerly awaits the revelation of the children of God. For creation was subjected to frustration, not of its own choice but by the will of the one who subjected it in the hope that creation itself will be freed from its slavery to corruption and share in the glorious freedom of the children of God. (Rom 8:19-21)*

"There is no salvation in anyone else, nor is there any other name under heaven given to men by which we can be saved." (Acts 4:12)

VATICAN COUNCIL II . . .

▲ In order to establish peace or the communion of sinful human beings with himself, as well as to fashion them into a fraternal community, God determined to intervene in human history in a way both new and final. For he sent his Son, clothed in our flesh, in order that through him he might snatch men from the power of darkness and Satan (cf. Col 1:13; Acts 10:38) and reconcile the world to himself in him (cf. 2 Cor 5:19). *(Mission Activity of the Church*, 3)

By the preaching of the word and by the celebration of the sacraments, the center and summit of which is the most holy Eucharist, missionary activity brings about the presence of Christ, the author of salvation. *(Mission Activity of the Church*, 9)

EXPLANATION . . .

● (1) St. Paul speaks of sin as a slavery. Jesus is our Savior because he saved us from sin. "He has rescued us from the power of darkness and transferred us into the kingdom of his beloved Son, in whom we have redemption, the forgiveness of sins" (Col 1:13-14). "We know that our old self was crucified with him, so that our sinful body might be destroyed and we might no longer be enslaved to sin" (Rom 6:6).

(2) All stand in need of Christ, their Model, their Savior, their source of life. By his own power no one is freed from sin and slavery. To prepare us for our resurrection and ascension, he asks us to make him King of our minds by accepting him as the Truth, King of our wills by our obedience to his laws, and King of our hearts by accepting the love he offers us.

DISCUSSION QUESTIONS

1. What does the incarnation mean? (18)
2. What took place during the visit of the angel to Mary? (18)
3. What is the purpose of the incarnation? (19)
4. Why is Christ the firstborn of all creation? (20)
5. How are we created new in Christ? (20)
6. Why is Jesus our Savior? (21)
7. How do we accept Jesus as our Savior? (21)

Chapter 5

CREATION, THE BEGINNING OF THE HISTORY OF MAN'S SALVATION

22. What is creation?

Creation means that the entire universe was made out of nothing. This includes our world in which salvation and redemption are accomplished through Jesus Christ.

VATICAN COUNCIL II . . .

▲ The eternal Father, by a free and hidden plan of his own wisdom and goodness, created the whole world. His plan was to raise men to a participation of the divine life. *(The Church,* 2)

EXPLANATION . . .

● The entire world created out of nothing is the world in which salvation and redemption are in fact accomplished through Jesus Christ.

"Creation" is the way God gave life and the world to us. It seems that creation was a gradual evolutionary development that took place a very long time ago. We do not know how it happened. The important thing for faith is that we owe all that we have to God.

The Bible does not try to explain creation. God's people knew that he was Lord of life and the universe. Millions of years after the events they could only imagine how creation took place.

23. What did God's creative action show in the Old Testament?

In the Old Testament, God's creative action (1) showed his power (2) and proved that he is always with his people.

THE BIBLE . . .

✠ *Why do you say, O Jacob, and complain, O Israel: "My way is hidden from the Lord, and my cause is disregarded by my God"? Do you not know? Have you not heard? The Lord is the eternal God, the creator of the earth's farthest boundaries. He does not faint or grow weary; his understanding cannot be scrutinized. (Isa 40:27-28)*

I, I alone, am the one who comforts you. Why then do you fear mortal men who must die, human beings who must perish like grass? You have forgotten the Lord, your maker, who stretched out the heavens and laid the foundations of the earth. (Isa 51:12-13)

VATICAN COUNCIL II . . .

▲ God, who has fatherly concern for everyone, has willed that all men should constitute one family and treat one another in a spirit of brotherhood. For having been created in the image of God, who "from one man has created the whole human race and made them live all over the face of the earth" (Acts 17:26), all men are called to one and the same goal, namely, God himself. *(Church in the Modern World, 24)*

EXPLANATION . . .

● **(1) In the Old Testament the truth of God's creative action enters the minds of the Israelites, with the help of a notion of the oneness of God, as a message declaring the power and victory of God.**

(2) God's creative action also serves as the basis for showing that the Lord remains always with his people. God did wonderful things to protect and help them. All these deeds of power and victory show that he kept his promises and that he loved his people, and that he remains always with them.

24. What is the beginning of the mystery of salvation?

(1) The creation of the angels and the world is the beginning of the mystery of salvation; (2) the creation of humankind is the first gift leading to Christ.

VATICAN COUNCIL II . . .

▲ Sacred Scripture teaches that man was created "to the image of God," is capable of knowing and loving his Creator, and was appointed by him as master of all earthly creatures (cf. Gen 1:26; Wis 2:23) that he might subdue them and use them to God's glory (cf. Sir 17:3-10). "What is man that you should care for him? You have made him little less than the angels, and crowned him with glory and honor. You have given him rule over the works of your hands, putting all things under his feet" (Ps 8:5-7).

But God did not create man as a solitary, for from the beginning "male and female he created them" (Gen 1:27). Their companionship produces the primary form of interpersonal communion. *(Church in the Modern World, 12)*

EXPLANATION . . .

● (1) Long before God created humankind, he made the angels. They were spirits, meaning that they had no body. They had a brilliant mind to understand God's goodness and beauty; they had a free will to love and praise him. God did not need anyone else to make him happy and yet he wanted to make the angels and people to share his happiness with them. But some of the angels sinned and became evil spirits.

(2) Sacred Scripture teaches that man was created to the image of God, is able to know and love his Creator, and was appointed by him as master of all earthly creatures that he might use them to God's glory. God created them male and female for companionship.

Man has a mind to know the Creator and a will to love him. We were created by God for an eternity of happiness. Our greatest dignity is to be able to know and love God and to be able to talk to him. To reach eternal happiness with God one must freely accept God's love and be devoted to his service. But Jesus is the one whom God sent to lead people to God. It is only through him that we can be saved. That is why we can say that the creation of man is the first gift of God leading to Christ.

25. Where do we especially see the all-powerful action of God in the mystery of salvation?

In Christ's resurrection from the dead the same all-powerful action of God stands out splendidly.

THE BIBLE . . .

✠ *Such was the power he exhibited in Christ when he raised him from the dead and enthroned him at his right hand in heaven. (Eph 1:20)*

VATICAN COUNCIL II . . .

▲ The wonderful works of God among the people of the Old Testament were but a prelude to the work of Christ the Lord in redeeming humankind and giving perfect glory to God. He achieved his task principally by the paschal mystery of his blessed passion, resurrection from the dead, and glorious ascension, whereby "dying, he destroyed our death and, rising, he restored our life" (Easter Preface). *(Sacred Liturgy, 5)*

EXPLANATION . . .

● **Though he was made by God in a state of holiness, man turned against God of his own free will, being led to do so by the evil spirit. His mind was darkened and he turned from his last goal. But God sent his Son to free us from the slavery of sin and to make us holy again. He did this through the sufferings and death of Jesus and through his glorious resurrection. God's power as the Creator is manifested in a splendid way in Christ's resurrection, in which is revealed the immeasurable extent of his omnipotence.**

God's action as Creator is seen especially in Christ's resurrection from the dead.

26. How is the doctrine of creation to be considered?

The doctrine of creation is to be considered as directly relating to the salvation accomplished by Jesus Christ, that is, as God's continuing activity as he works out our salvation.

VATICAN COUNCIL II . . .

▲ The Church has been taught by divine revelation and firmly teaches that man has been created by God for a blissful purpose beyond the reach of earthly misery. *(Church in the Modern World, 18)*

God, who through the Word creates all things (cf. Jn 1:3) and keeps them in existence, gives men an enduring witness to himself in created realities (cf. Rom 1:19-20). *(Divine Revelation, 3)*

EXPLANATION . . .

● **When we think of the creation of the angels, the creation of the world, and the creation of humankind, we should see how God's all-powerful action saved all people. It was his great love for us that led him to do so.**

The entire economy of salvation receives its meaning from the incarnate Word. It prepared his coming; it manifests and extends his kingdom on earth from the time of his death and resurrection up to his second glorious coming, which will complete the work of God. So it is that the mystery of Christ illumines the whole content of our holy Faith.

27. How is God present in human history?

God is actively and lovingly present in human history from start to finish, using his limitless power in our behalf.

VATICAN COUNCIL II . . .

▲ God's Word, through whom all things were made, was himself made flesh and dwelt on the earth of men (cf. Jn 1:3 and 14). Thus he entered the world's history as a perfect man, taking that history up into himself and summarizing it (cf. Eph 1:10). He himself revealed to us that "God is love" (1 Jn 4:8) and at the same time taught us that the new command of love was the basic law of human perfection and hence of the world's transformation. *(Church in the Modern World, 38)*

EXPLANATION . . .

● **When we hear about the creation, we should not only think of God's act of making the world but also turn our mind to all that he did to save the people in this world. His deeds of salvation can be seen in the history of man and of the world, especially in the history of Israel. They lead to the most important events in our Lord's life, his death and resurrection.**

28. Is God present among us today?

Just as his presence shines forth in the history of Israel, just as he was powerfully at work in the life, death, and resurrection of his Incarnate Son, so God is present among us today and will be for all generations.

VATICAN COUNCIL II . . .

▲ The council focuses its attention on the world of men . . . that world which the Christian sees as created and sustained by its Maker's love, fallen indeed into the bondage of sin, yet emancipated now by Christ. He was crucified and rose again to break the stranglehold of personified evil, so that the world might be fashioned anew according to God's design and reach its fulfillment. *(Church in the Modern World, 2)*

The Church holds that the recognition of God is in no way hostile to man's dignity, since this dignity is rooted and perfected in God. For man was made an intelligent and free member of society by God who created him. Even more important, he is called to commune with God and share in his happiness. *(Church in the Modern World, 21)*

EXPLANATION . . .

● **The life, death, and resurrection of Jesus is the decisive event of all time through which God shows himself and his love for people. However, he also shows himself in other events. Over the centuries certain special events have been recognized as signs of God by people of faith. These events are found in the Bible and in the life of the Church. The Bible and the Church are witnesses to these events and they explain their meaning. Hence Bible and Church are both essential for the Christian. God will continue to be present among us, showing his power and his love.**

29. When will God finally complete his saving work?

God will finally complete his saving work only at the end of the world, when there will be "new heavens and a new earth."

THE BIBLE . . .

✠ *We eagerly await the promised new heavens and a new earth in which righteousness dwells.* (2 Pet 3:13)

VATICAN COUNCIL II . . .

▲ The Church, to which we are all called in Christ Jesus, and in which we acquire sanctity through the grace of God, will attain her full perfection only in the glory of heaven, when there will come the time of the restoration of all things (Acts 3:21). At that time the human race as well as the entire world, which is intimately related to man and attains to its end through him, will be perfectly reestablished in Christ (cf. Eph 1:10; Col 1:20; 2 Pet 3:10-13). *(The Church, 48)*

EXPLANATION . . .

● God will finish his saving work at the end of the world, when there will be new heavens and a new earth. Heaven and earth are new because of the new moral relationship between God and us. This was predicted by Isaiah: "For behold, I am about to create new heavens and a new earth. The past will not be remembered or ever again called to mind. Rather, rejoice and be filled with delight forever" (Isa 65:17).

Everything of evil and of punishment—the things that had been associated with the "former heavens and the former earth"—is past. Nothing remains but to wonder at the magnificence of the eternal Kingdom of God. The new Jerusalem is the Church. God is the cause of the new order.

DISCUSSION QUESTIONS

1. What does creation mean? (22)
2. How did God show his creative action in the Old Testament? (23)
3. Who are the angels? (24)
4. Why was man created? (24)
5. How is God's power as the Creator shown in the resurrection of Jesus? (25)
6. Why is the doctrine of creation related to the work of salvation? (26)
7. Where can God's deeds of salvation be seen? (27)
8. What are other witnesses of the event of salvation? (28)
9. What do we mean by "new heavens and a new earth"? (29)

Chapter 6

JESUS CHRIST, THE CENTER OF ALL GOD'S SAVING WORKS

30. Why is Jesus Christ the center of all God's saving works?

Jesus Christ is the center of all God's saving works because in him we are joined to all history and to all people.

VATICAN COUNCIL II . . .

▲ God's Word, by whom all things were made, was himself made flesh so that as perfect man he might save all men and sum up all things in himself. The Lord is the goal of human history, the focal point of the longings of history and of civilization, the center of the human race, the joy of every heart and the answer to all its yearning. (*Church in the Modern World*, 45)

EXPLANATION . . .

● Jesus Christ is the center of the work of salvation because he, the Son of God, became man so that as perfect man he might save all people and sum up all things in himself. He summed up in himself the mysteries of our salvation by his death and his resurrection; he had received all power in heaven and on earth; he founded his Church as a means for our salvation. So in Christ, our Redeemer, we are joined to all people.

Christ Jesus, the incarnate Word of God, since he is the supreme reason why God intervenes in the world and manifests himself to men, is the center of the gospel message within salvation history.

31. What is the aim of God's plan for our salvation?

The aim of God's plan for us is to form his people into "the unity of faith and knowledge of the Son of God . . . as measured by the full stature of Christ" (Eph 4:13).

THE BIBLE . . .

✠ *It was he who established some as apostles, some as prophets, some as evangelists, and some as pastors and teachers, to equip the saints for the work of ministry in building up the body of Christ, until all of us attain the unity of faith and knowledge of the Son of God, to full maturity, as measured by the full stature of Christ. (Eph 4:11-13)*

VATICAN COUNCIL II . . .

▲ That messianic people has Christ for its head, "who was delivered up for our sins. and rose again for our justification" (Rom 4:25), and now, having won a name which is above all names, reigns in glory in heaven.

The state of this people is that of the dignity and freedom of the sons of God, in whose hearts the Holy Spirit dwells as in his temple. Its law is the new commandment to love as Christ loved us (cf. Jn 13:34). Its end is the kingdom of God, which has been begun by God himself on earth, and which is to be further extended until it is brought to perfection by him at the end of time, when Christ, our life (cf. Col 3:4), shall appear, and "creation itself will be delivered from its slavery to corruption into the freedom of the glory of the sons of God" (Rom 8:21).

So it is that this messianic people, although it does not actually include all men, and at times may look like a small flock, is nonetheless a lasting and sure seed of unity, hope, and salvation for the whole human race. Established by Christ as a communion of life, charity, and truth, it is also used by him as an instrument for the redemption of all, and is sent forth into the whole world as the light of the world and the salt of the earth (cf. Mt 5:13-16). *(The Church*, 9)

EXPLANATION . . .

● **A Christian recognizes that in Jesus Christ he is linked with all of history and is in communion with all people. The history of salvation is being accomplished in the midst of the history of the world. By this**

history of salvation God fulfills his plan, and thus the People of God, that is, "the whole Christ," is being perfected in time.

Jesus Christ gave himself for us in his passion that he might redeem us from sin and cleanse for himself a people pleasing to God. He then poured out on his people the spirit of adoption by making them children of God. In this way he made in himself a new people, filled with the grace of God. United with Jesus, the new People of God are "the whole Christ." He offers them to his Father and gives him glory. This is the aim of his Father's plan for the salvation of all.

Jesus appears to the apostles after his resurrection. United with Jesus, the new People of God are "the whole Christ."

32. What is the appointed task of the Christian in regard to God's plan of salvation?

Christians are dedicated to the appointed task of making creation give glory to God to the full extent of their abilities and opportunities through the power of Jesus the Savior.

THE BIBLE . . .

✠ *When all things are subjected to him, then the Son himself will also be subjected to the one who made all things subject to him, so that God may be all in all.* (1 Cor 15:28)

VATICAN COUNCIL II . . .

▲ The faithful, therefore, must learn the deepest meaning and the value of all creation, as well as its role in the harmonious praise of God. They must assist each other to live holier lives even in their daily occupations. In this way the world may be permeated by the spirit of Christ and it may more effectively fulfill its purpose in justice, charity, and peace. *(The Church, 36)*

EXPLANATION . . .

● Since Christ is the center of all God's works of salvation, through him we can make all creation give glory to God. All this was made possible through his love and power.

We must be convinced that God is the full meaning of life and that Jesus Christ is the way to God. Jesus asks that we accept him as the keystone of our lives for the future. This turning to Jesus is called "conversion." Jesus said, "The Father loves the Son and he has entrusted everything into his hand. Whoever believes in the Son has eternal life" (Jn 3:35-36).

How thankful we should be to God for having sent his Son to save us! How thankful we should be to Jesus Christ for having given his life for our salvation, for having given us his grace to be children of God, God's own people, and for having made it possible for us to be one with God in eternal happiness!

DISCUSSION QUESTIONS

1. Why is Jesus the center of the work of salvation? (30)
2. What do we mean by "the whole Christ"? (31)
3. How can we make creation give glory to God? (32)

Chapter 7

JESUS CHRIST, TRUE MAN AND TRUE GOD IN THE UNITY OF THE DIVINE PERSON

33. Why is Jesus Christ true man?

Jesus Christ, the Son of God, is true man because he was "made visible in the flesh" (1 Tim 3:16).

(1) He lived among men. (2) As man he thought with a human mind, acted with a human will, loved with a human heart. (3) By becoming man, he joined himself in a real way with every human being except in sin. (4) He showed the human person such respect and concern as no one before had done. (5) He reached out to all—the virtuous and sinners, the poor and the rich, especially the suffering and rejected. In him God's love for humankind is seen.

THE BIBLE . . .

✠ *In the beginning was the Word, and the Word was with God, and the Word was God. He was with God in the very beginning. Through him all things came into existence, and without him there was nothing. That which came to be found life in him, and the life was the light of the human race. The light shines in the darkness, and the darkness has been unable to overcome it.*

A man appeared, sent by God, whose name was John. He came as a witness to give testimony to the light, so that through him all might come to believe. He himself was not the light; his role was to bear witness to the light. The true light that enlightens everyone was coming into the world. He was in the world, which had come into existence through him, yet the world did not recognize him. He came to his own, but his own did not accept him.

However, to those who did accept him and who believed in his name he granted the power to become children of God, who were born not from blood or human desire or human will, but from God.

And the Word became flesh and dwelt among us. And we saw his glory, the glory of the Father's only Son, full of grace and truth.

John testified to him, proclaiming, "This is the one of whom I said, 'The one who comes after me ranks ahead of me because he existed before me.' "

From his fullness we have all received grace upon grace. The law was given through Moses, but grace and truth came through Jesus Christ. No one has ever seen God. It is the only Son, God, who is at the Father's side, who has made him known. (Jn 1:1-18)

VATICAN COUNCIL II . . .

▲ By his incarnation the Son of God has united himself in some fashion with every man. He worked with human hands. He thought with a human mind, acted by human choice and loved with a human heart. Born of the Virgin Mary, he has truly been made one of us, like us in all things except sin (cf. Heb 4:15). *(Church in the Modern World, 22)*

EXPLANATION . . .

● **(1) St. John says, "The Word became flesh and dwelt among us" (Jn 1:14). The incarnation means that the Word, the Son of God, became man and dwelt among us.**

(2) As man Jesus thought with a human mind, acted with a human will, loved with a human heart.

The Son of God became a real man, having real flesh, a human body and soul. He is a man as we are; he felt the joys and sorrows, pleasures and pains that we feel as human beings. This means that he

was born into this world, and lived a real human life. He died like the rest of us.

(3) The Fathers of the Church proclaim that what Christ took up was our entire human nature though without our sin. "The deepening of faith in the virginal motherhood led the Church to confess Mary's real and perpetual virginity even in the act of giving birth to the Son of God made man. In fact, Christ's birth 'did not diminish his mother's virginal integrity but sanctified it'" (CCC 499). Because of this extraordinary action of God, Mary is called the "Blessed Virgin." Joseph was Mary's husband and acted as foster father to Jesus during his childhood.

(4) Jesus had the greatest respect for the human person because as God he alone knew the full value of a human soul—he was ready to die for its salvation. He showed his concern for all people, and in his concern we see the very love of God for us.

(5) In the four gospels of the New Testament we find very little about Christ's childhood and early life. We know about his public life, for he spent several years traveling all over Israel, teaching the people about his Father and his love for them, and performing miraculous cures and wonders. He loved especially the poor, the sick, and the sinners. We read of his tender acts of compassion for people. He loved sinners and forgave their sins, even those who put him to death. That is why he could say, "Come to me, all you who are weary and overburdened, and I will give you rest. Take my yoke upon you and learn from me, for I am meek and humble of heart, and you will find rest for your souls. For my yoke is easy and my burden is light" (Mt 11:28-30).

We cannot see God. But when God sent his Son to live among us and to save us by his death on the cross, we can see how much God really loves us. Our Lord's whole teaching is about loving God with our whole heart.

34. Why is Jesus also true God?

Jesus is not only the perfect man, but God's only-begotten Son: in him there is all fullness of divinity.

VATICAN COUNCIL II . . .

▲ Jesus Christ was sent into the world as a real mediator between God and men. Since he is God, all divine fullness dwells bodily in him (Col 2:9). *(Mission Activity of the Church, 3)*

Jesus says, "Receive your sight." He showed his concern for all people.

EXPLANATION . . .

• Jesus Christ is true God, the Son of the Father, the Divine Word of God incarnate. He has two natures: the nature of God and the nature of man. But he is only one Person; and that Person is the Second Person of the Blessed Trinity, the Divine Word. St. John wrote: "In the beginning was the Word, and the Word was with God, and the Word was God" (Jn 1:1).

Jesus said he was God. He said to the Jews, "The very works that I am doing, testify about me that the Father has sent me" (Jn 5:36). "I declare what I have seen in my Father's presence. . . . If God were your father, you would love me, for I came from God, and now I am present among you. . . . I do know him , and I keep his word. . . . Amen, amen, I say to you, before Abraham was, I AM" (Jn 8:38, 42, 55, 58).

The night before Jesus died he prayed, "Father, the hour has come. Glorify your Son, so that your Son may glorify you, since you have given him authority over all people, so that he may give eternal life to all those you have given him. . . . So now, Father, glorify me in your presence with the glory I had with you before the world began" (Jn 17:1-5).

35. How does the Church express her faith in Christ's divinity?

The Church prays in her Creed: "God from God, Light from Light, true God from true God, begotten not made, consubstantial with the Father" (Nicene Creed).

THE BIBLE . . .

✠ *No one has ever seen God. It is the only Son, God, who is at the Father's side, who has made him known. (Jn 1:18)*

VATICAN COUNCIL II . . .

▲ From God the Father, who is "the origin without origin," the Son is begotten and the Holy Spirit proceeds through the Son. *(Church in the Modern World,* 2)

EXPLANATION . . .

● People come to believe in God because he shows something of himself to them. All real faith is the result of such a personal meeting between God and us. Christians believe because they are sure that God shows himself in a fully personal way in Jesus Christ. In Jesus God shows himself in what he says and does, how he lives with others, by what he reveals of his thoughts and feelings. In the person of Jesus Christ, God reveals as much of himself as we can understand.

For this reason Jesus is the center of Christian faith. Everything that he said and did is important because in him we find God our Father and come to believe in him. Jesus Christ is our way, our truth, and our life.

The chief teaching of the Catholic Church about Jesus Christ is that he is God made man. She expresses this in her Creed. It is Jesus Christ the God-Man whom we see and hear in the gospels, the God-Man whom we receive in the Eucharist. It is to him with the Father and the Holy Spirit that we pray: Glory be to the Father, and to the Son, and to the Holy Spirit. With St. Peter we profess our faith in the God-Man: "You are the Christ, the Son of the living God." (Mt 16:16).

DISCUSSION QUESTIONS

1. How does the Son of God show that he is a real man? (33)
2. How many natures does Jesus Christ have? (34)
3. In what words did Jesus state that he was true God? (34)
4. What is the chief teaching of the Church about Jesus Christ? (35)

Chapter 8

JESUS CHRIST, SAVIOR AND REDEEMER OF THE WORLD

36. Why is Jesus Christ the Savior and Redeemer of the world?

(1) Jesus Christ came into the world as God made man, to be its Savior and Redeemer. (2) God so loved sinners that he gave his Son, reconciling the world to himself.

THE BIBLE . . .

✠ *In other words, God was in Christ, reconciling the world to himself, not holding people's transgressions against them, and he committed to us the message of reconciliation.* (2 Cor 5:19)

VATICAN COUNCIL II . . .

▲ Christ, whom the Father sanctified, consecrated and sent into the world (cf. Jn 10:36), "gave himself for us that he might redeem us from all iniquity and cleanse for himself an acceptable people, pursuing good works" (Tit 2:14), and thus through suffering entered into his glory (cf. Lk 24:26). *(Ministry and Life of Priests, 12)*

EXPLANATION . . .

● **(1) God sent his Son, clothed in our human nature, that he might snatch us from the power of Satan and make peace between God and us. To do this Jesus had to become man, to preach his truth about the**

kingdom of his Father, to give his life for us on the cross. He is our Savior. He restored to humankind the divine likeness which had been disfigured from the first sin, and raised up human nature to a divine dignity.

Jesus is also our Redeemer because he paid our debt for sin and bought heaven back for us.

(2) God gave his Son as a sacrifice for sin to reconcile the world to himself. Christ's humanity, united with the person of the Word, was the instrument of our salvation. In him come perfect satisfaction for our reconciliation and the means for giving worthy worship to God.

37. How were all people saved?

All people were saved by the obedience of the Son to the will and command of his Father.

THE BIBLE . . .

✠ *Just as through the disobedience of one man the many were made sinners, so by the obedience of one man the many will be made righteous. (Rom 5:19)*

VATICAN COUNCIL II . . .

▲ The Son came, sent by the Father. It was in him, before the foundation of the world, that the Father chose us and predestined us to become adopted sons, for in him it pleased the Father to reestablish all things (cf. Eph 1:4-5, 10).

To carry out the will of the Father, Christ inaugurated the kingdom of heaven on earth and revealed to us the mystery of that kingdom. By his obedience he brought about redemption. The Church, or, in other words, the kingdom of Christ now present in mystery, grows visibly through the power of God in the world. *(The Church, 3)*

EXPLANATION . . .

● **Having become obedient unto death, Jesus Christ was exalted as Lord of all things, and was manifested to us through his resurrection as God's Son in power. Being the firstborn of the dead, he gives life to all; through him all creatures will be liberated from the slavery of corruption. He gave himself for us in his passion that he might redeem us from sin and cleanse for himself an acceptable people.**

38. How did Jesus carry out his earthly mission?

As the Messiah fulfilling Old Testament prophecy and history, (1) Jesus carried out his earthly mission. (2) He preached the gospel of the kingdom of God and summoned us to interior conversion and faith. (3) He persisted in his ministry despite the resistance of religious leaders of his day and their threats to his life.

THE BIBLE . . .

✠ *"The time of fulfillment has arrived, and the kingdom of God is close at hand. Repent and believe in the gospel!"* (Mk 1:15)

VATICAN COUNCIL II . . .

▲ After speaking in many and varied ways through the prophets, "now at last in these days God has spoken to us in his Son" (Heb 1:1-2). For he sent his Son, the eternal Word, who enlightens all men, so that he might dwell among men and tell them of the innermost being of God (cf. Jn 1:1-18). *(Divine Revelation, 4)*

EXPLANATION . . .

● (1) Jesus is the Messiah, God's own Son, who fulfilled Old Testament prophecy, as he carried out his mission on earth. He often stated that what he was doing was done that the Scriptures might be fulfilled, because in them he recognized the will of his Father.

(2) The main point of Jesus' teaching was that with him the kingdom of God had come into the world. This means that God's way of life has been begun among people and they are called to enter it. They are called also to live and work together with God for the growth and completion of the kingdom. St. Mark writes that Jesus appeared in Galilee proclaiming the Good News of God: "The time of fulfillment has arrived, and the kingdom of God is close at hand. Repent and believe in the gospel!" (Mk 1:15).

(3) In order to do his Father's will Jesus was willing to face the persecution and resistance of the Jewish leaders. For the truth of his word he even offered his life, for the religious leaders of the Jewish people finally arranged for his execution by the Roman authorities because he claimed to be the Son of God.

39. Why did Jesus give himself up to death?

Out of filial love for his Father and redemptive love for us, Jesus gave himself up to death and passed through it to the glory of the Father.

THE BIBLE . . .

✠ *"The world must come to understand that I love the Father and I do just as the Father has commanded me."* (Jn 14:31)

And now it is no longer I who live, but it is Christ who lives in me. The life I live now in the flesh I live by faith in the Son of God who loved me and gave himself up for me. (Gal 2:20)

This is how we know what love is: Jesus laid down his life for us, and we in turn must be prepared to lay down our lives for our brethren. (1 Jn 3:16)

Because of this, God greatly exalted him and bestowed on him the name that is above all other names, so that at the name of Jesus every knee should bend of those in heaven and on earth and under the earth, and every tongue should proclaim to the glory of God the Father: Jesus Christ is Lord. (Phil 2:9-11)

Such was his mighty power that he exhibited in Christ when he raised him from the dead and enthroned him at his right hand in heaven. (Eph 1:20)

VATICAN COUNCIL II . . .

▲ As the Church has always held and holds now, Christ underwent his passion and death freely, because of the sins of men and out of infinite love, in order that all may reach salvation. It is, therefore, the burden of the Church's preaching to proclaim the cross of Christ as the sign of God's all-embracing love and as the fountain from which every grace flows. *(Non-Christian Religions, 4)*

EXPLANATION . . .

● **The mystery of Christ appears in the history of men and of the world—a history subject to sin—not only as the mystery of the incarnation but also as the mystery of salvation and redemption. God so loved sinners that he gave his Son, reconciling the world to himself. Christ in his boundless love freely underwent his passion and death because of the sins of all, so that all might attain salvation.**

Our Lord's life shows God's own love for us because all that he said and did, his whole life and death, was for the sake of others.

He spent his life teaching people the truth about his Father and about themselves; he shared their life and suffering and their illness. He did all this out of love for them and for his Father who called him to this service. The life of Jesus shows us in a human way that God's life is a life of love. Father, Son, and Holy Spirit are forever giving themselves to each other. Having received from Jesus a perfect human life of love, the Father now gives his own life to people who turn to him in faith.

40. From what did Jesus redeem humankind?

By his death and resurrection Jesus redeemed humankind from slavery to sin and to the devil.

VATICAN COUNCIL II . . .

▲ The Lord himself came to free and strengthen man, renewing him inwardly and casting out that prince of this world (cf. Jn 12:31) who held him in the bondage of sin (cf. Jn 8:34). For sin has diminished man, blocking his path to fulfillment. The call to grandeur and the depths of misery, both of which are a part of human experience, find their ultimate and simultaneous explanation in the light of this revelation. *(Church in the Modern World, 13)*

EXPLANATION . . .

● By his most holy death Christ redeemed humankind from the slavery of sin and of the devil, and he poured out on it the spirit of adoption, thus creating in himself a new humanity. Christ has risen, destroying death by his death, and gave us life so as to become children of God.

We were slaves of the devil because of original sin and because of our personal sins. But Jesus made us free with the freedom of the children of God. St. Paul tells us: "Let your attitude be identical to that of Christ Jesus. Though he was in the form of God, he did not regard equality with God as something to be grasped. Rather, he emptied himself, taking the form of a slave, being born in human likeness. Being found in appearance as a man, he humbled himself, and became obedient to death, death even death on a cross. Because of this, God greatly exalted him and bestowed on him the name that is above all other names, so that at the name of Jesus every knee should bend of those in heaven and on earth and under the earth, and every tongue should proclaim to the glory of God the Father: Jesus Christ is Lord!" (Phil 2:5-11).

41. How did the Risen Lord benefit the human race?

Risen truly and literally, (1) the Lord became the unfailing source of life and of the outpouring of the Holy Spirit upon the human race. (2) He is the firstborn among many brethren. (3) He created in himself a new humanity.

THE BIBLE . . .

✠ *Now he was referring here to the Spirit whom those who believed in him were to receive. As yet the Spirit had not been bestowed because Jesus had not yet been glorified.* (Jn 7:39)

"Exalted at God's right hand, he received from the Father the promise of the Holy Spirit and has poured out what you now see and hear." (Acts 2:33)

This was also meant for us as well, to whom God will credit righteousness—for us who believe in him who raised from the dead Jesus our Lord who was handed over to death for our sins and who was raised to life for our justification. (Rom 4:24-25)

If the Spirit of him who raised Jesus from the dead dwells in you, then the one who raised Christ from the dead will also give life to your mortal bodies through his Spirit that dwells in you. (Rom 8:11)

As it is written, the first man, Adam, became a living being; the last Adam has become a life-giving spirit. (I Cor 15:45)

Although he was a Son, he learned obedience through his sufferings, and when he had been made perfect, he became the source of eternal salvation for all who obey him. (Heb 5:8-9)

Those whom he foreknew he also predestined to be conformed to the image of his Son so that he might be the firstborn among many brethren. (Rom 8:29)

VATICAN COUNCIL II . . .

▲ In the human nature united to himself the Son of God, by overcoming death through his own death and resurrection, redeemed man and remolded him into a new creation (cf. Gal 6:15; 2 Cor 5:17). *(The Church, 7)*

EXPLANATION . . .

● **(1) Jesus, glorious and immortal, rose from the dead. Scripture states it as a fact through the words of the angel to the women, "Why do you look among the dead for one who is alive? He is not here. He has been** raised. Remember what he told you while he was still in Galilee: that the Son of Man must be handed over to sinners and be crucified and rise again on the third day" (Lk 24:5-7).

The Father raised Jesus up to life within a few days after his crucifixion and Jesus showed himself to many of his followers for forty days after that. He assured them that he was really alive and he stressed even more the things he had already taught them. He ended his appearances, and returned to the Father where he lives in glory.

Christ established the kingdom of God on earth, manifested his Father and himself by deeds and words, and completed his work by his death, resurrection, and ascension, and by the sending of the Holy Spirit.

(2) Christ is the firstborn among many brethren because dying he destroyed our death and, rising, he restored our life. As the Risen Lord, he now shares with us his divine life of grace, especially through the sacraments, and gives us his Holy Spirit to make us holy and pleasing to God.

(3) Having received from Jesus a perfect human life of love, the Father now gives his own life to people who turn to him in faith. We receive this new life by putting our faith, hope, and love in Jesus Christ whose life, death, and resurrection has opened up the life of God to us. The Father, Son, and Holy Spirit come and share their love with those who give themselves to Jesus.

We must live the life of God as Jesus did. United to him, we must die to self and rise to a new life for God and in the service of others. We see this gift of new life in the resurrection of Jesus, who was beaten and crucified and buried, but the Father raised him up to a new life and together they give this new life to his followers.

DISCUSSION QUESTIONS

1. Why is Jesus Christ the Savior of the world? (36)
2. Why is Jesus Christ the Redeemer of the world? (36)
3. Why was the humanity of Christ the instrument of our salvation? (36)
4. Why were all saved by the obedience of Jesus? (37)
5. What was the main point of the teaching of Jesus? (38)
6. How did Jesus show his love for his Father? (39)
7. How did Jesus show his love for us? (39)
8. From what did Jesus redeem us? (40)
9. How did Jesus establish the Kingdom of God on earth? (41)
10. Why is Jesus the firstborn among many brethren? (41)
11. How does the Father give his own life to people? (41)

Chapter 9

THE HOLY SPIRIT IN THE CHURCH AND IN THE LIFE OF THE CHRISTIAN

42. What is the role of the Holy Spirit in the world?

The Holy Spirit carries out Christ's work in the world when persons answer God's invitation to love him and one another.

VATICAN COUNCIL II . . .

▲ United in Christ, they [the followers of Christ] are led by the Holy Spirit in their journey to the kingdom of their Father and they have welcomed the news of salvation which is meant for every man. (*Church in the Modern World*, 1)

EXPLANATION . . .

● The Holy Spirit is the Third Person of the Blessed Trinity, truly God just as the Father and the Son are truly God. He is the Love of the Father and the Son.

As Jesus Christ is the center of the history of salvation, so the mystery of God is the center from which this history takes its origin and to which it is ordered as to its last end. The crucified and risen Christ leads us to the Father by sending the Holy Spirit upon the People of God.

The Holy Spirit was already at work in the world before Christ was glorified. But to complete the work of the salvation of humankind, Jesus sent the Holy Spirit from the Father. The Spirit was to carry out his saving work in our souls and to spread the Church throughout the world.

43. What has Christ said concerning the Holy Spirit?

(1) Christ promised the coming of the consoling Paraclete.

(2) He pledged that the Spirit of Truth would be with us and remain with us.

THE BIBLE . . .

✠ *"I will ask the Father, and he will give you another Advocate to be with you forever." (Jn 14:16)*

"When the Advocate comes whom I will send you from the Father, the Spirit of Truth who comes from the Father, he will testify on my behalf." (Jn 15:26)

"The Spirit of Truth whom the world cannot accept because it neither sees him nor knows him. But you know him, because he dwells with you and will be in you." (Jn 14:17)

VATICAN COUNCIL II . . .

▲ The Lord Jesus, before freely giving his life for the world, did so arrange the apostles' ministry and promise to send the Holy Spirit that both they and the Spirit might be associated in effecting the work of salvation always and everywhere. *(Mission Activity of the Church, 4)*

EXPLANATION . . .

● **(1) Jesus so arranged the ministry of the apostles and so promised to send the Holy Spirit, that both they and the Spirit were associated in effecting the work of salvation.**

(2) Jesus said to his disciples, "I will ask the Father, and he will give you another Advocate to be with you forever, the Spirit of Truth whom the world cannot accept because it neither sees him nor knows him. But you know him, because he dwells with you and will be in you" (Jn 14:16-17).

44. When did the Holy Spirit come to humankind?

The Holy Spirit came at Pentecost, never to depart.

THE BIBLE . . .

✠ *When the day of Pentecost arrived, they were all assembled together in one place. Suddenly, there came from heaven a sound similar to that of a violent wind, and it filled the entire house in which they were sitting. Then there appeared to them tongues as of fire, which separated and came to rest on each one of them. All of them were filled with the Holy Spirit and began to speak in different languages, as the Spirit enabled them to do so.* (Acts 2:1-4)

VATICAN COUNCIL II . . .

▲ When the work which the Father gave the Son to do on earth (cf. Jn 17:4) was accomplished, the Holy Spirit was sent on the day of Pentecost in order that he might continually sanctify the Church, and thus, all those who believe would have access through Christ in one Spirit to the Father (cf. Eph 2:18). He is the Spirit of Life, a fountain of water springing up to life eternal (cf. Jn 4:14; 7:38-39). To men, dead in sin, the Father gives life through him, until in Christ he brings to life their mortal bodies (cf. Rom 8:10-11). *(The Church, 4)*

EXPLANATION . . .

● **Fifty days after Easter, on Pentecost Sunday, the Holy Spirit came to the early Church and changed the apostles from weak, fearful men to brave men of faith that Christ needed to spread his gospel to the nations. The Holy Spirit came to remain with them forever, the Church was publicly revealed to the people, the gospel began to spread among the nations, and there occurred a foreshadowing of the union of all peoples in a universal faith.**

45. Where is the Holy Spirit present in a special way?

The Spirit is present in a special way in the community of those who acknowledge Christ as Lord, the Church.

VATICAN COUNCIL II . . .

▲ On the day of Pentecost, the Holy Spirit came down upon the disciples to remain with them forever (cf. Jn 14:16). The Church was publicly displayed to the multitude, the Gospel began to spread among the nations by means of preaching, and there was presaged that union of all peoples in the catholicity of the faith by means of the

Church of the New Covenant, a Church which speaks all tongues, understands and accepts all tongues in her love. *(Mission Activity of the Church, 4)*

EXPLANATION . . .

● **The Holy Spirit remains in the Catholic Church to help it to continue the work of Christ in the world. The knowledge of the mystery of Christ and the way to the Father are realized in the Holy Spirit. By his presence people are continually moved to have communion with God and others and to fulfill their duties.**

46. How does the Holy Spirit help the Church?

(1) The Church is enlivened by the abiding Spirit of Truth. (2) Our lives also are to be guided by that same Holy Spirit, the Third Person of the Trinity.

VATICAN COUNCIL II . . .

▲ The Spirit dwells in the Church and in the hearts of the faithful, as in a temple (cf. 1 Cor 3:16; 6:19). In them he prays on their behalf and bears witness to the fact that they are adopted sons (cf. Gal 4:6; Rom 8:15-16, 26). *(The Church, 4)*

The Bishops of the United States quote the statement of Vatican Council II: " 'Christ so arranged the ministry of the apostles and so promised to send the Holy Spirit that both they and the Spirit were to be associated in effecting the work of salvation always and everywhere.' It is the Holy Spirit who 'instills into the hearts of the faithful the same mission spirit which motivated Christ himself.' " *(Mission Activity of the Church, 4)*

EXPLANATION . . .

● **(1) Christ sent the Holy Spirit from the Father to accomplish the salvation of humankind. The Spirit was to carry out his saving work inwardly and to impel the Church toward her expansion. He was sent in order that he might forever sanctify the Church; through him the Father gives life to those who are dead from sin, because he is the Spirit of life.**

The Holy Spirit guides the Pope, the bishops and the priests of the Church in their holy work of Christ—teaching his doctrine, guiding souls and giving grace to the people through the sacraments. He directs all the work of Christ in the Church—the care of the sick, the teaching of children, the guidance of youth, the comforting of the sorrowful, the support of the needy. The Holy Spirit is the life and the very soul of the Catholic Church. This is what Jesus promised.

The Holy Spirit comes down upon Mary and the disciples. The Church is enlivened by the Spirit of Truth.

(2) In the faithful the Spirit prays and bears witness to the fact that they are adopted sons and daughters, guides the Church into the fullness of truth and gives her a unity of fellowship and service, furnishes and directs her with various gifts, and adorns her with the fruits of his grace. By the power of the gospel he makes the Church grow, always renews her, and leads her to perfect union with her Spouse.

47. What is our duty toward the Holy Spirit?

We should (1) recognize the importance of the Holy Spirit and his work in the Church and in our lives; (2) honor him as our God with a personal love as we honor the Father and the Son; (3) frequently call upon him for strength and guidance.

VATICAN COUNCIL II . . .

▲ This cult [of the Mother of God], as it always existed, although it is altogether singular, differs essentially from the cult of adoration which is offered to the Incarnate Word, as well as to the Father and the Holy Spirit, and it is most favorable to it. *(The Church, 66)*

Let Christians pray also that the strength and the consolation of the Holy Spirit may descend copiously upon all those many Christians of whatsoever church they be who endure suffering and deprivations for their unwavering avowal of the name of Christ. *(The Eastern Rite, 30)*

EXPLANATION . . .

● (1) Every Christian receives the Holy Spirit in the sacrament of Baptism and in the sacrament of Confirmation. Through the Holy Spirit we share in the life of grace, God's life in our soul. We are always reminded that we are holy because the Holy Spirit dwells in us, as St. Paul asks, "Do you not realize that you are God's temple, and that the Spirit of God dwells in you?" (1 Cor 3:16). By his presence we are continually moved to have communion with God and others and to fulfill their duties.

(2) United in Christ, the followers of Jesus are led by the Holy Spirit in their journey to the kingdom of their Father. We should love the indwelling Spirit as we honor the Father and the Son.

(3) We should often ask the Spirit for the light and strength we need to live a holy life and to save our soul.

DISCUSSION QUESTIONS

1. Who is the Holy Spirit? (42)
2. How does Jesus lead us to the Father? (42)
3. What did Jesus promise concerning the Holy Spirit? (43)
4. What happened at Pentecost? (44)
5. Why does the Holy Spirit remain in the Church? (45)
6. What does the Holy Spirit do in the Church? (45)
7. What does the Holy Spirit do in the lives of the faithful? (46)
8. How do we show our devotion to the Holy Spirit? (47)

Part Three –THE SACRAMENTS

Chapter 10

THE SACRAMENTS, ACTIONS OF CHRIST IN THE CHURCH

48. How is the saving work of Christ continued in the Church?

Through the gift of the Holy Spirit the Church enjoys the presence of Christ and carries on his ministry and saving mission.

VATICAN COUNCIL II . . .

▲ To accomplish this [the salvation of mankind], Christ sent from the Father his Holy Spirit, who was to carry on inwardly his saving work and prompt the Church to spread out. *(Mission Activity of the Church, 4)*

EXPLANATION . . .

● Before ascending into heaven, Jesus gave his apostles a command to teach all nations and to baptize them. He said, "[Teach] them to observe all that I have commanded you. And behold, I am with you always, to the end of the world" (Mt 28:20). Christ is with his Church also through the gift of the Holy Spirit. He promised this the night before he died. "It is much better for you that I depart. For if I do not go away, the Advocate will not come to you, whereas if I go, I will send him to you. And when he comes, he will prove the world wrong about sin and righteousness and judgment. . . . When the Spirit of Truth comes, he will guide you into all the truth. . . . He will glorify me, for he will take what is mine and communicate it to you" (Jn 16:7-14).

49. What means does the Church have for carrying on Christ's works?

The Church has been entrusted with special means for carrying on Christ's works: namely, the sacraments which he instituted.

VATICAN COUNCIL II . . .

▲ Just as Christ was sent by the Father, so also he sent the apostles, filled with the Holy Spirit. This he did that, by preaching the Gospel to every creature (cf. Mk 16:15), they might proclaim that the Son of God, by his death and resurrection, had freed us from the power of Satan (cf. Acts 26:18) and from death, and brought us into the kingdom of his Father. His purpose also was that they might accomplish the work of salvation which they had proclaimed, by means of sacrifice and sacraments, around which the entire liturgical life revolves. *(Sacred Liturgy, 6)*

EXPLANATION . . .

● Christ's work of salvation is continued in the Church, which always enjoys his presence and serves him. This is done in a special way through the signs that Christ instituted to bring grace to the soul. They are called sacraments. The sacraments are special actions in the Church through which the life of God is communicated to his people.

50. What are the sacraments?

The sacraments are outward signs both of God's grace and man's faith.

VATICAN COUNCIL II . . .

▲ The purpose of the sacraments is to sanctify men, to build up the body of Christ, and, finally, to give worship to God. Because they are signs they also instruct. They not only presuppose faith, but by words and objects they also nourish, strengthen, and express it; that is why they are called "sacraments of faith." They do indeed impart grace, but, in addition, the very act of celebrating them most effectively disposes the faithful to receive this grace in a fruitful manner, to worship God duly, and to practice charity. *(Sacred Liturgy, 59)*

EXPLANATION . . .

● The sacraments are signs because they also instruct; by words and objects they nourish, strengthen, and express faith; they impart grace to worship God and to practice charity.

The sacraments are signs we can see which let us know that God's grace is being given to the soul of the person who receives the sacrament. We can see the signs with our bodily eyes, but it is only through faith that we know God's grace is given to us. We believe this on the word of Christ himself who gave us the sacraments to make it possible for us to share God's own life through grace.

Jesus tells the Samaritan woman about the living water he will give to us through the sacraments.

51. What do the sacraments show?

The sacraments effectively show (1) God's intention to sanctify us, and (2) our willingness to receive this sanctification. In this way they bring us God's grace.

VATICAN COUNCIL II . . .

▲ By the sacraments, especially the Eucharist, that charity toward God and man which is the soul of the apostolate is communicated and nourished. *(The Church, 33)*

EXPLANATION . . .

● (1) The sacraments are the signs that Christ instituted, which signify the gift of grace and produce it. Their very institution shows

God's intention to make people holy by giving them his grace. By grace we share in the very life of God himself, for through Baptism we are born again. We are God's temple and God lives in us. We are truly children of God through grace, as St. John says, "See what great love the Father has bestowed on us, enabling us to be called the children of God, and that is what we are" (1 Jn 3:1). All this happens when Jesus comes to us in the sacraments.

(2) We show our willingness to receive Christ's grace if we frequently and earnestly receive the sacraments for our sanctification. We cannot afford to neglect the means God has given us to grow holy and pleasing to him by sharing his divine life.

52. Why is the Church the universal sacrament?

The Church is not only the People of God, but by her relationship with Christ, the Church is, as it were, a sacrament (or sign and instrument) of intimate union with God and of the unity of all humankind.

VATICAN COUNCIL II . . .

▲ The Lord Jesus had by his death and his resurrection completed once for all in himself the mysteries of our salvation and the renewal of all things; he had also received all power in heaven and on earth (cf. Mt 28:18). Now, before he was taken up into heaven (cf. Acts 1:11), he founded his Church as the sacrament of salvation and sent his apostles into all the world just as he himself had been sent by his Father (cf. Jn 20:21). *(Mission Activity of the Church, 5)*

EXPLANATION . . .

● **The Church is the worldwide community of those whom God has called to give witness to his Son Jesus and to the new life he has brought to us. This assembly is called "the People of God" and "the body of Christ." The Church ministers to our spiritual needs by providing a community of faith, where people can find support and guidance in their response to God. Within this community the Holy Spirit communicates and strengthens the life of God through the sacraments, prayers, and works of service. Because the Church is the means of uniting us with God and forming God's People, she is called the universal sacrament.**

53. Why are sacraments the actions of Christ?

(1) The sacraments are the principal actions through which Christ gives his Spirit to Christians and makes them a holy people. (2) The sacraments get their power from Christ.

VATICAN COUNCIL II . . .

▲ By his power Christ is present in the sacraments, so that when a man baptizes it is really Christ himself who baptizes. *(Sacred Liturgy*, 7)

EXPLANATION . . .

● (1) Sacraments are the principal and fundamental actions whereby Jesus Christ unceasingly bestows his Spirit on the faithful, thus making them the holy people which offers itself, in him and with him, as an oblation acceptable to the Father. In the sacraments Christ gives us his grace, bought for us on the cross, to help us to become more like him. In every sacrament it is Christ our high priest bringing his grace to us. The priests who administer the sacrament are only his ordained representatives.

(2) To the Church belongs the power of administering the sacraments; and yet they are always to be referred to Christ, from whom they receive their power. "In case of necessity, any person can baptize provided that he have the intention of doing that which the Church does and provided that he pours water on the candidate's head while saying: I baptize you in the name of the Father, and of the Son, and of the Holy Spirit." (CCC 1284).

54. What is the purpose of the sacraments?

The purpose of the sacraments is (1) to sanctify us, (2) to build up the body of Christ, (3) to give worship to God, and (4) because they are signs they also instruct.

VATICAN COUNCIL II . . .

▲ The purpose of the sacraments is to sanctify men, to build up the body of Christ, and, finally, to give worship to God; because they are signs they also instruct. *(Sacred Liturgy*, 59)

EXPLANATION . . .

● (1) The sacraments are the ordinary channels of God's grace and are necessary to keep the life of grace in our soul. St. John reminds us that

Jesus gives us his grace for our sanctification. "From his fullness we have all received, grace upon grace. The law was given through Moses, but grace and truth came through Jesus Christ" (Jn 1:16-17).

(2) Each of the sacraments plays an indispensable part in the life of the Church. Baptism, Confirmation, Marriage and Holy Orders confer an office in the Mystical Body. Baptism makes us members of the Body and gives us a share in the priesthood of Christ. Confirmation makes us mature and responsible Christians and increases our participation in Christ's priesthood. Holy Orders confers the actual powers of the priesthood and provides for the continuation of the Church. Marriage makes a man and a woman one and provides for the growth of the Body of Christ by conferring the vocation of parenthood and guaranteeing the graces which enable parents to guide the new members of Christ. The anointing of the sick prepares us for entrance into the ranks of the Church Triumphant in heaven. The sacrament of Penance gives us pardon for sin and strength to resist temptation, and the sacrament of the Eucharist nourishes our souls and gives us an increase of the power to love God and our neighbor.

(3) By means of the Eucharist Christ continually reoffers himself to the Father through the ministry of his priests in the Sacrifice of the Mass. This is the greatest act of worship that can be given to God, because it is offered by the God-Man in the spirit in which he offered himself on the cross for our redemption. All of us, members of Christ's body, can participate in this oblation and thereby give worthy adoration, thanksgiving, and atonement to God through Christ.

(4) Signs are actions which convey an idea. Words are signs which convey an idea. In the sacraments the words together with the action make up the sacred sign. Water, since it is so necessary for life, can be used as a sign of life; hence water is an appropriate sign of the divine life. Oil is used to strengthen and heal the body. In Confirmation it is used to signify the strength we receive from this sacrament and to give us that strength. In the sacrament of the Anointing of the Sick it is used both to signify and to impart health of soul and body. But the sacraments are signs which not only communicate an idea but also produce what they signify. Baptism not only signifies life, it actually produces it. Confirmation not only signifies strength but gives us that strength. Anointing of the Sick not only signifies health but imparts it to soul and body.

55. What is the effect of the act of celebrating the sacraments?

The very act of celebrating the sacraments disposes the faithful more effectively (1) to receive grace in a fruitful manner, (2) to worship God duly, and (3) to practice charity.

VATICAN COUNCIL II . . .

▲ The sacraments do indeed impart grace, but, in addition, the very act of celebrating them most effectively disposes the faithful to receive this grace in a fruitful manner, to worship God duly, and to practice charity. *(Sacred Liturgy,* 59)

EXPLANATION . . .

● (1) Jesus Christ is the source of divine life. He speaks of it as living water in his conversation with the Samaritan woman. "Whoever drinks the water that I will give him will never be thirsty. The water that I will give him will become a spring of water within him, welling up to eternal life" (Jn 4:14). He gives us this life and increases it within us by means of the seven channels of grace which are called the sacraments.

Through the sacraments Jesus unites us to himself, ever deepening our union with him, ever increasing our holiness. Through the sacraments Christ is with us throughout our lives to provide us with all the help and strength we need to grow in the divine life. He is always there to strengthen us, to forgive us, to nourish us, and to fit us for the vocation in which we serve him in the Church.

(2) Though Jesus now reigns in glory, he continues his saving work on earth. At Mass he has the assembly of believers daily adore the Father. With Christ they give glory to God; they praise him for his mercy and generosity toward humankind. Their first work as God's holy people is to thank and honor God joyfully, and this; they do in the Mass in a manner worthy of God, because they are united with Christ in his offering of himself.

(3) When we eat the flesh of Christ in Holy Communion, Christ keeps making us one body with himself. The gift of sanctifying grace, through which the Spirit of Christ carries on his work of sanctification, makes steady progress in our hearts if we cooperate with it. Christ said that he would share everlasting life with those who ate his flesh and drank his blood.

As Christ grafts us onto himself, he brings us closer to one another. Israel's sacrificial meals united them as a nation. So the Eucharist unites us as God's family: it makes the Church one. since the Eucharist makes us one in Christ, it strengthens our charitable respect for one another. This food enables us who eat it to sacrifice ourselves for our neighbor's good. For the Eucharist inspires us with the memory of Christ's holy death, when he offered his body and blood for our salvation. If we partake of the Bread of Life in faith, we too will be enabled to sacrifice ourselves for our neighbor's sake.

56. What is the wish of the Church concerning the sacraments?

It is of capital importance (1) that the faithful easily understand the sacramental signs, and (2) with great eagerness have frequent recourse to the sacraments, instituted to nourish Christian life.

VATICAN COUNCIL II . . .

▲ It is of the highest importance that the faithful should easily understand the sacramental signs, and should frequent with great eagerness those sacraments which were instituted to nourish the Christian life. *(Sacred Liturgy*, 59)

EXPLANATION . . .

● (1) Christ himself determined the signs to be used in the sacraments. He made them the instruments he uses at the present time to produce grace in us. This is what we mean when we say that Christ instituted the sacraments. There are references in the Bible that Christ instituted Baptism, Penance, the Eucharist and Holy Orders. The Church infallibly teaches that he also instituted the others.

(2) That the faithful may nourish their Christian life, the Church considers it very important not only that Catholics understand the meaning of all the sacraments but that they receive them eagerly and frequently.

Three of the sacraments, Baptism, Confirmation and Holy Orders, produce in the soul a mark which can never be lost. This mark or character is a kind of badge of our membership in Christ, a participation in his eternal priesthood, by which we are dedicated to sacred worship. These sacraments may be received only once.

57. How must we regard the sacraments?

The Christian's union with God in grace is an important measure connected with the sacraments. Therefore the sacraments must be seen (1) as sources of grace for individuals and communities, (2) as well as remedies for sin and the effects of sin.

VATICAN COUNCIL II . . . *(The Church, 12)*

▲ It is not only through the sacraments and the ministries of the Church that the Holy Spirit sanctifies and leads the People of God and enriches it with virtues, but "allotting his gifts to everyone according as he wills" (1 Cor 12:11), he distributes special graces among the faithful of every rank. By these gifts he makes them fit and ready to undertake the various tasks and offices which contribute toward the renewal and building up of the Church, according to the words of the Apostle: "The manifestation of the Spirit is given to everyone for profit" (1 Cor 12:7).

EXPLANATION . . .

● **(1) The sacraments are sources of grace for individuals and communities. All the sacraments produce the divine life. In addition, each sacrament gives its own particular actual graces and a right to future actual graces. A sacrament is a sacred sign instituted by Christ to give grace. This grace is given for the benefit of the person who receives the sacrament, and also for the benefit of the entire community of faith. The sacraments are instruments of divine life for the family of God.**

(2) Mortal sin is the greatest evil in the world because it drives out of our soul the divine life of sanctifying grace and turns us away from God, the source of all life, peace, and joy. But our Lord protects our soul from serious sin by giving us more sanctifying grace in the sacraments, especially in Holy Communion.

Through the sacraments we also receive actual or sacramental grace, which gives us the light to see what is evil and the strength we need to fight against it. In this way our soul is strengthened against temptation.

This is especially true of Holy Communion. "This is the bread that comes down from heaven, so that one may eat it and not die" (Jn 6:50). Just as bodily food repairs what we lose by daily wear and tear so likewise this divine food is a remedy for the spiritual infirmities of each

day. The sacramental grace we receive in the sacrament of Penance is a remedy for our spiritual sickness and all the effects of sin.

58. What attitude should we have toward the sacraments?

Since they are sacraments of faith, (1) the right attitude of faith must be encouraged (2) as well as the sincerity and generosity required for celebrating and receiving them worthily.

VATICAN COUNCIL II . . . *(Ministry and Life of Priests, 4)*

▲ In the Christian community, especially among those who seem to understand and believe little of what they practice, the preaching of the word is needed for the very ministering of the sacraments. They are precisely sacraments of faith, a faith which is born of and nourished by the word.

EXPLANATION . . .

● **(1) The more faith and love we have when we receive the sacraments the more grace they will confer on us. It is true that the sacraments worthily received always give grace, even if they are received without due preparation. But it is also true that the better prepared we are to receive them the more fruitful will be our reception.**

(2) If the sacrament is properly received it will always produce grace, provided we do not place an obstacle in the way. An example of such an obstacle would be mortal sin in one who receives Confirmation, Holy Orders or Marriage. In such a case the grace which should have been given, but was impeded by the obstacle of mortal sin, will be given when the sinner repents.

DISCUSSION QUESTIONS

1. How did Jesus assure us that his work of salvation would be continued through the Holy Spirit? (48)
2. How is the life of God communicated to his people? (49)
3. Why are sacraments signs of God's grace and our faith? (50)
4. How do we show our willingness to receive God's grace? (51)
5. Why is the Church a means of uniting us with God? (52)
6. Why are sacraments actions of Christ? (53)
7. What is the purpose of the sacraments? (54)
8. What are the effects of the sacraments? (55)
9. Why does the Church encourage us to receive the sacraments frequently? (56)
10. Why are the sacraments sources of grace and remedies for sin? (57)
11. What is required for the reception of the sacraments? (58)

Chapter 11

RELIGIOUS INSTRUCTION ON THE SACRAMENTS

— Baptism —

59. What is Baptism?

Baptism is (1) the sacrament of rebirth as a child of God sanctified by the Spirit, (2) of unity with Jesus in his death and resurrection, (3) of cleansing from original sin and personal sins, and (4) of welcome into the community of the Church.

VATICAN COUNCIL II . . .

▲ From the wedlock of Christians there comes the family, in which new citizens of human society are born, who by the grace of the Holy Spirit received in baptism are made children of God, thus perpetuating the People of God through the centuries. *(The Church, 11)*

Whenever the sacrament of baptism is duly administered as our Lord instituted it, and is received with the right dispositions, a person is truly incorporated into the crucified and glorified Christ, and reborn to a sharing of the divine life, as the Apostle says: "You were buried together with him in baptism, and in him also rose again—through faith in the working of God, who raised him from the dead" (Col 2:12; cf. Rom 6:4). *(Ecumenism, 22)*

By baptism men are truly brought into the People of God. *(Ministry and Life of Priests, 5)*

EXPLANATION . . .

(1) Baptism is directed toward the acquiring of the fullness of Christ's divine life. By this sacrament a person becomes truly incorporated into Christ and is reborn to a sharing of the divine life. Baptism is a new birth as a child of God, a beginning of a new life in us, which is God's own life of grace brought to us by Jesus Christ.

St. John says, "To those who did accept him . . . he granted power to become children of God" (Jn 1:12). Jesus said to Nicodemus, "Amen, amen, I say to you, no one can enter the kingdom of God unless he is born of water and the Spirit" (Jn 3:5). It is Christ himself who baptizes and makes us holy with the gifts of the Holy Spirit and impresses on the soul a character or mark that cannot be taken away.

(2) Baptism unites the new Christian so closely to Jesus that he shares in his death and resurrection. Through this sacrament he dies to his old self and rises to new life. St. Paul says, "Do you not know that all of us who have been baptized into Christ Jesus were baptized into his death? Through that baptism into his death we were buried with him, so that, just as Christ was raised from the dead by the glory of the Father, so we too might begin to live a new life. For if we have been united with Christ Jesus in a death like his, we shall also be united with him in his resurrection" (Rom 6:3-4).

(3) Baptism cleanses the soul from original sin and from all personal sins. The result of Baptism is that a person is reconciled with God: their sins are forgiven, they receive the life of God, and become part of God's people.

Water is a sign of life-giving and of cleansing. The words signify that the life the person enters is that of God—the Father, Son, and Holy Spirit. The Holy Spirit unites us to Jesus so that we may share with him the life of God he brought into the world.

(4) For believing Christians the Church is the only place where they can live out their faith to the fullest. They need to hear the gospel again and again and to be a part of the continuing work of Jesus in the world. They need the company of other Christians as they grow in faith.

(5) "Those who die for the faith, those who are catechumens, and all those who, without knowing of the Church but acting under the inspiration of grace, seek God sincerely and strive to fulfill his will, are saved even if they have not been baptized (cf. LG 16)." (CCC 1281) "With respect to children who have died without Baptism, the liturgy of the Church invites us to trust in God's mercy and to pray for their salvation." (CCC 1283).

60. What relationship with God and Christ is begun at Baptism?

Baptism (1) permanently relates one to God with a relationship that can never be erased, and (2) joins them to the priestly, prophetic, and kingly works of Christ.

VATICAN COUNCIL II . . .

▲ Of itself baptism is only a beginning, an inauguration wholly directed toward the fullness of life in Christ. Baptism, therefore, envisages a complete profession of faith, complete incorporation into the system of salvation such as Christ willed it to be, and finally complete ingrafting in Eucharistic Communion *(Ecumenism*, 22)

EXPLANATION . . .

● (1) Baptism is directed toward the acquiring of the fullness of life in Christ, that is, toward a complete profession of faith, a complete incorporation into the system of salvation, and participation in Eucharistic Communion. Faith in Jesus Christ and the desire to follow him with his Church is necessary for Baptism. Thus Baptism permanently relates one to God.

(2) The People of God share in the *kingly* and *priestly* offices of Christ because by regeneration in Baptism and the anointing of the Holy Spirit they are consecrated into a spiritual house and a holy priesthood. Through their works befitting a Christian they can offer spiritual sacrifices.

The People of God share in Christ's *prophetic* office by being a living witness to him by means of a life of faith and charity and by offering to God a sacrifice of praise. As Christians we should now show forth, by the example of our life, the new person which we became at Baptism. We are children of God and followers of Jesus Christ.

— Confirmation —

61. What is Confirmation?

Confirmation is the sacrament by which those born anew in Baptism now receive the seal of the Holy Spirit.

VATICAN COUNCIL II . . .

▲ The faithful are more perfectly bound to the Church by the sacrament of confirmation, and the Holy Spirit endows them with special strength so that they are more strictly obliged to spread and defend the faith, both by word and by deed, as true witnesses of Christ. *(The Church, 11)*

EXPLANATION . . .

● **Confirmation is a sacrament that confirms or strengthens the life of the Spirit received at Baptism.**

"In the Latin rite, 'the sacrament of Confirmation is conferred through the anointing with chrism on the forehead, which is done by the laying on of the hand, and through the words: 'Accipe signaculum doni Spiritus Sancti' [Be sealed with the Gift of the Holy Spirit.]'" (CCC 1300).

62. What are the sacraments of Christian initiation?

Confirmation, as the sealing of the candidate with the Spirit, is linked with the other sacraments of Christian initiation, Baptism and the Eucharist.

"In the East this sacrament is administered immediately after Baptism and is followed by participation in the Eucharist; this tradition highlights the unity of the three sacraments." (CCC 1318)

VATICAN COUNCIL II . . .

▲ The faithful, already marked with the seal of baptism and confirmation' are through the reception of the Eucharist fully joined to the Body of Christ. *(Ministry and Life of Priests, 5)*

EXPLANATION . . .

● **After Baptism, through the sacrament of Confirmation Jesus sends the Holy Spirit once more to the Christian souls with new grace and new strength to lead the Christian life. In the third century, St. Cyprian wrote: "They who are baptized . . . are presented to the bishops . . . and by our prayers and the imposition of hands they receive the Holy Spirit and are perfected with the seal of the Lord."**

Candidates renew their baptismal promises before Confirmation because of the intimate connection of Confirmation with the Christian initiation. In the Eucharist we can receive even daily the nourishment we need to live the Christian life that we might bear witness to Jesus Christ and serve others.

63. What is the purpose of the sealing of the Spirit?

The sealing of the Spirit is a preparation (1) for the witness of a mature, Christian life, and (2) for the apostolate of living in the world and extending and defending the faith.

VATICAN COUNCIL II . . .

▲ The laity derive the right and duty to the apostolate from their union with Christ the head; incorporated into Christ's Mystical Body through baptism and strengthened by the power of the Holy Spirit through confirmation, they are assigned to the apostolate by the Lord himself. *(Apostolate of the Laity*, 3)

There are many forms of the apostolate whereby the laity build up the Church, sanctify the world, and give it life in Christ. A particular form of the individual apostolate as well as a sign specially suited to our times is the testimony of the whole lay life arising from faith, hope, and charity. It manifests Christ living in those who believe in him. Then by the apostolate of the spoken and written word, which is utterly necessary under certain circumstances, lay people announce Christ, explain and spread his teaching in accordance with their status and ability, and faithfully profess it. *(Apostolate of the Laity*, 16)

EXPLANATION . . .

● **(1) Confirmation binds the Christian more perfectly to the Church and enriches them with a special strength of the Holy Spirit, that they may live in the world as a witness of Christ and serve others.**

(2) Incorporated into Christ's Mystical Body through Baptism and strengthened by the Holy Spirit through Confirmation, the laity are assigned to the apostolate by the Lord himself.

We should remember the duty placed upon us when we were confirmed: we have the task of bringing Jesus Christ, his example, his way of life and his Church to others. The strength of the grace of the Holy Spirit will help us each day to fulfill our apostolate when we are generous enough to show some effort and to ask for his help in prayer.

— Penance —

64. What is Penance?

The sacrament of Reconciliation, or Penance, brings to the Christian God's merciful forgiveness for sins committed after Baptism.

VATICAN COUNCIL II . . .

▲ In the bosom of the Church not only does the Christian receive through baptism the fundamental gift of "metanoia" ("change of heart"), but this gift is restored and reinvigorated through the sacrament of penance in those members of the Body of Christ who have fallen into sin. *(Apostolic Constitution on Fast and Abstinence: The Sacred Congregation of Rites, May 25, 1967)*

EXPLANATION . . .

● **In the sacrament of Penance Jesus comes to forgive the sins of a baptized Christian, bringing the sinner consolation and peace. St. John writes: "However, if we confess our sins, he who is faithful and just will forgive our sins and cleanse us from all wrongdoing" (1 Jn 1:9).**

65. What is sacramental absolution?

Sacramental absolution, which follows upon sincere confession of sin, true sorrow, and resolution not to sin again, is (1) a means of obtaining pardon from God. (2) It also brings about a reconciliation with the faith community, the Church, which is wounded by our sins.

VATICAN COUNCIL II . . .

▲ Those who approach the sacrament of penance obtain pardon from the mercy of God for the offense committed against him and are at the same time reconciled with the Church, which they have wounded by their sins, and which by charity, example, and prayer seeks their conversion. *(The Church, 11)*

EXPLANATION . . .

● (1) As God's Son, Jesus had the power of forgiving sins. One day he said to a paralyzed man who was brought to him, "Friend, your sins are forgiven you." Then the scribes and the Pharisees began to ask each other, " . . . Who can forgive sins but God alone?" . . . [Jesus] said in reply, ". . . that you may come to realize that the Son of Man has authority on earth to forgive sins"—he said to the paralyzed man—"I say to you, stand up, and take your bed, and go to your home." Immediately, the man stood up before them (Lk 5:20-25).

Jesus gave the power of forgiving sins to his apostles when he appeared to them on the evening of the day of his resurrection. "Peace be with you," he said to them again. "As the Father has sent me, so I send you." After saying this, he breathed on them and said, "Receive the Holy Spirit. If you forgive anyone's sins, they are forgiven. If you retain anyone's sins, they are retained" (Jn 20:21-23). This power has been handed down through the years to the priests of the Church today.

In the sacrament of Penance a person repents of his sins, confesses to a priest, receives absolution from the priest and does penance. Absolution means the words of forgiveness spoken by the priest in confession. These words are a sign of assurance of God's forgiveness. To do penance means to say the prayers or to do the acts of charity assigned by the priest in confession or freely done by the penitent.

(2) When we approach the sacrament of Penance we not only obtain pardon from God for sins we have committed against him, but we are also reconciled to the Church, which we have wounded by our sins. By

doing penance we show repentance in action and make our relationship with God and others more firm. We have damaged this union by sin.

66. How does Penance aid our spiritual growth?

The sacrament of Penance brings to each individual (1) special direction toward growth, (2) eliminating habits of sin, and (3) working for perfection.

VATICAN COUNCIL II . . .

▲ Pastors should also be mindful of how much the sacrament of penance contributes to developing the Christian life and, therefore, should always make themselves available to hear the confessions of the faithful. *(Office of Bishops, 30)*

EXPLANATION . . .

● **(1) Through each sacrament the Holy Spirit makes our soul more pleasing to God because of the graces he gives us. Through the sacrament of Penance Jesus, the Good Shepherd, forgives our sins and sends his Holy Spirit once more to our soul with new grace and new strength to lead the Christian life and to grow spiritually.**

(2) The purpose of the sacrament of Penance is to make visible and present God's mercy and forgiveness. In this sacrament we can join ourselves to Jesus, dying to sin and selfishness and rising with him to new life with God. Only with God's help can we overcome temptation and avoid sin. Since the human will is unsteady and wounded by sin, peace can be reached only by mastering one's passions and respecting lawful authority. Only by the help of God's grace can we be brought to relationship with God.

(3) The sacrament of Penance not only forgives sin; it also develops virtues which make us more Christ-like. Penance reminds us of the great *love* God has for us. His love must inspire us to greater *love* for him. We should grow in the love of God each time we receive this sacrament. This sacrament also increases our *hope.* We realize that even though we are sinners we can obtain from God the help we need to reach heaven. *Faith* is strengthened in the sacrament of Penance because like any other sacrament Penance demands the exercise of faith. We believe that Christ instituted this sacrament for the forgiveness of our sins and for our reconciliation with God and his people.

67. What is confession?

Confession is for the Catholic the sacramental way of obtaining pardon for sins, of submitting our offenses to the mercy and forgiving grace of God.

VATICAN COUNCIL II . . .

▲ The same Lord, however, has established ministers among his faithful to unite them together in one body in which "not all the members have the same function" (Rom 12:4). These ministers in the society of the faithful are able by the sacred power of orders to offer sacrifice and to forgive sins, and they perform their priestly office publicly for men in the name of Christ. *(Ministry and Life of Priests,* 2)

EXPLANATION . . .

● The sinner's manifestation of sorrow by word or gesture, the sins confessed, the sinner's willingness to make satisfaction and the words of the priest, "I absolve you from your sins in the name of the Father, and of the Son, and of the Holy Spirit," constitute the sign of the sacrament of Penance. Thus confession is the sacramental way of obtaining pardon for sin.

In this sacrament Jesus forgives our sins, no matter how terrible they are, as long as we are sorry for them and resolve, even though we are weak, not to commit the sins again. We trust in the help of God's grace to do so.

According to the Rite of confession, the priest greets the penitent. The penitent makes the sign of the cross. The priest invites the penitent to have trust in God, to which the penitent answers: Amen. The priest may read a text of Scripture on God's mercy. The penitent then confesses their sins, after which the priest gives suitable counsel and proposes an act of penance. The penitent expresses their sorrow by making an act of contrition. The priest then extends his right hand and imparts absolution ending with the words: "I absolve you from your sins in the name of the Father, and of the Son, and of the Holy Spirit." The penitent answers: Amen. The priest continues: "Give thanks to the Lord, for he is good," to which the penitent answers: "His mercy endures for ever." The priest dismisses the penitent with the words: "Go in peace."

68. When is confession the ordinary way of reconciliation?

If one has fallen into serious sin, sacramental confession is the ordinary way established in the Church to reconcile the the sinner with Christ and with his Church.

VATICAN COUNCIL II . . .

▲ By baptism men are truly brought into the People of God; by the sacrament of penance sinners are reconciled to God and his Church. *(Ministry and Life of Priests, 5)*

EXPLANATION . . .

● Since the life of Christians, which on earth is a warfare, is subject to temptations and sins, the sacrament of Penance is open for them, so that they may obtain pardon from the merciful God and reconcile themselves with the Church.

Repentance is a change of heart which leads a sinner to turn back to God and accept his loving forgiveness. God never refuses forgiveness if the sinner is sincerely sorry and willing to give up their evil ways. The sinner can repent through the grace of God. God continues to speak to sinners even though they keep on refusing God.

Repentance and forgiveness of sins committed after Baptism are expressed in the Church through the sacrament of Penance. It is the ordinary way offered by the Church to reconcile the sinner with Christ and with his Church.

69. In what other way can a sinner be restored to grace?

It is also true that a sinner can be restored to grace by perfect sorrow or perfect contrition in the sense of the Church's Tradition.

VATICAN COUNCIL II . . .

▲ As regards instruction it is important to impress on the minds of the faithful not only the social consequences of sin but also that essence of the virtue of penance which leads to the detestation of sin as an offense against God. *(Sacred Liturgy, 109)*

It is therefore necessary for the full remission and—as it is called—reparation of sins not only that friendship with God be reestablished by a sincere conversion of the mind and amends made for the offense against his wisdom and goodness. In addition, all the personal as well as social values and those of the universal order itself, which have been diminished or destroyed by sin, must also be fully reintegrated.

This can be done either through voluntary reparation which will involve punishment or through acceptance of the punishments established by the just and most holy wisdom of God, from which there will shine forth throughout the world the sanctity and the splendor of his glory. The very existence and the gravity of the punishment enable us to understand the foolishness and malice of sin and its harmful consequences. *(Apostolic Constitution on Indulgences, Pope Paul VI, January 1, 1967, 3)*

EXPLANATION . . .

● **We have sorrow or contrition for our sins when we are sorry for them because they have offended the good God, our Father, and when we do not want to commit them again. Our sorrow is sincere when it comes from the heart. The real meaning of the virtue of penance is hatred for sin as an offense against God. The virtue of penance is based on a sense of the holiness of God. The realization of the goodness of God must be the basis of all our sorrow. This realization should grow each time we say the act of contrition or go to confession.**

We should have contrition for mortal sin because it is the greatest of all evils: it offends God seriously, keeps us out of heaven, and condemns us forever to hell. By perfect contrition we can be restored to grace.

The remedy for sin is Jesus Christ who came into the world to save his people from their sins. By sharing in his death and resurrection, one can triumph over sin and death. St. Paul says, "Now that we have been justified by Christ's blood, how much more certainly will we be saved through him from divine retribution. For if, while we were enemies, we were reconciled to God through the death of his Son, how much more certain it is that, having been reconciled, we shall be saved by his life. And not only that, but we now even trust exultantly in God through our Lord Jesus Christ, through whom we have already been granted reconciliation" (Rom 5:9-11).

70. Does the Church urge the use of Penance?

Every Catholic, from his early years, should be instructed how to receive and best profit from the regular reception of this sacrament.

VATICAN COUNCIL II . . .

▲ In the spirit of Christ the Shepherd, priests must prompt their people to confess their sins with a contrite heart in the sacrament of penance, so that, mindful of his words: "Repent for the kingdom of God is at hand" (Mt 4:17), they are drawn closer to the Lord more and more each day. *(Ministry and Life of Priests, 5)*

EXPLANATION . . .

● **The Church urges the faithful to confess their sins to the Church with a contrite heart in the sacrament of Penance. She makes it very clear that she wishes the faithful to use frequently those sacraments which foster the Christian life, and the sacrament of Penance is one of them. After the Eucharist, it can be received most frequently.**

71. Why is confession useful even when venial sins are in question?

We should keep in mind the usefulness of confession, (1) which retains its efficacy even when only venial sins are in question, (2) and which gives an increase of grace and of charity, (3) increases our good dispositions for receiving the Eucharist, and (4) also helps to perfect the Christian life.

VATICAN COUNCIL II . . .

▲ Since man's freedom has been damaged by sin, only by the aid of God's grace can he bring such a relationship with God into full flower. Before the judgment seat of God each man must render an account of his own life, whether he has done good or evil (cf. 2 Cor 5:10). *(Church in the Modern World, 17)*

EXPLANATION . . .

● **(1) In the sacrament of Penance Christ forgives mortal sin, restores the divine life in even greater abundance, and removes the sentence of hell for those who had been guilty of serious sin. "The contrition called 'imperfect' (or 'attrition') is also a gift of God, a prompting of the Holy Spirit. It is born of the consideration of sin's ugliness or the fear of eternal damnation and the other penalties threatening the sinner (contrition of fear). Such a stirring of conscience can initiate an interior process which, under the prompting of grace, will be brought to completion by sacramental absolution. By itself however, imperfect contrition cannot obtain the forgiveness of grave sins, but it disposes one to obtain forgiveness in the sacrament of Penance" (CCC 1453).**

(2) Christ gives us a pledge of the actual graces we need to atone for past sins and to avoid sin in the future.

(3) The abundance of the fruit of Holy Communion is measured by the degree of our love, since the special fruit of Holy Communion is an increase of sanctifying grace and the virtue of charity.

Christ does not find in all souls the willingness to permit him to act freely in them. Their vanity, self-love, sensuality, and lack of charity prevent the union between them and Christ from being made perfect. The secret of spiritual success through Holy Communion lies in the absence of obstacles to God's grace. The grace of the sacrament of Penance helps us to overcome such obstacles.

(4) Though we are a community of believers, we are also a sinful people. God has called us to greatness, but conscious of the forces of sin within us, we look to Christ for understanding and mercy. We make our humble appeal for mercy in the sacrament of Penance, and for the grace we need to live the Christian life according to God's will. Christ gives us whatever we need to love sincerely and to promote peace and common respect among God's people.

— Holy Orders —

72. What is Holy Orders?

Holy Orders (1) in a special way conforms certain members of the People of God to Christ the Mediator, (2) puts them in positions of special service for building up the Body of Christ, and (3) gives them a sacred power to fulfill that ministry of service.

THE BIBLE . . .

✠ *It was he who established some as apostles, some as prophets, some as evangelists, and some as pastors and teachers, to equip the saints for the work of ministry in building up the body of Christ. (Eph 4:11-12)*

VATICAN COUNCIL II . . .

▲ Christ, "whom the Father has sanctified and sent into the world" (Jn 10:36), has, through his apostles, made their successors, the bishops, partakers of his consecration and his mission. They have legitimately handed on to different individuals in the Church various degrees of participation in this ministry. Thus the divinely established ecclesiastical ministry is exercised on different levels by those who from antiquity have been called bishops, priests, and deacons. *(The Church, 28)*

EXPLANATION . . .

● (1) Holy Orders is the act by which the Church chooses and gives power to certain individuals to carry out special functions for the building up of the Church of Jesus by the power of the Holy Spirit. The major orders of the Church are deacon, priest, and bishop.

Jesus Christ extends his priestly work in the world through this sacrament. St. Paul says, "Therefore, he had to be made like his brethren in every way in order that he might become a compassionate and faithful high priest before God and expiate the sins of the people" (Heb 2:17). Christ is the mediator between us and the Father. "There is one God, and there is one mediator between God and man, Christ Jesus himself a man, who gave himself as a ransom for all" (1 Tim 2:5-6).

Through his priesthood Jesus, the mediator between God and man, preached his gospel to the people, established his Church to carry on his work among men in all ages and gave his life, a sacrifice for our sins. Jesus offered to the Father the sacrifice of his life on the cross. He continues this sacrifice in the Church in the Sacrifice of the Mass through the ministry of his priests.

(2) Through the sacrament of Holy Orders Jesus Christ shares the work of his priesthood with other men—the bishops and priests of the Catholic Church. Through them he makes himself present to offer sacrifice, to baptize, to give the sacrament of Confirmation, to give his Body and Blood in Holy Communion, to forgive sins in the sacrament of Penance, to Anoint the Sick and to bless and sanctify marriages.

(3) By his own authority Jesus appointed the apostles to be his priests to carry on his work in the world. At the Last Supper he gave the apostles the power to change bread and wine into his Body and Blood: "Do this in memory of me" (Lk 22:19). After his resurrection he gave

them the power to forgive men's sins: "If you forgive anyone's sins, they are forgiven. If you retain anyone's sins, they are retained" (Jn 20:23).

Before ascending into heaven Jesus said to his apostles: "All authority in heaven and on earth has been given to me. Go, therefore, and make disciples of all nations, baptizing them in the name of the Father, and of the Son, and of the Holy Spirit, and teaching them to observe all that I have commanded you. And behold, I am with you always, to the end of the world" (Mt 28:18-20).

73. What special graces does Christ give in the sacrament of Holy Orders?

Through this sacrament Christ bestows a permanent charism or grace of the Holy Spirit enabling the recipients to (1) guide and shepherd the faith community, (2) proclaim and explain the Gospel, (3) and guide and sanctify God's people.

VATICAN COUNCIL II . . .

▲ Priests do not possess the highest degree of the priesthood and are dependent on the bishops in the exercise of their power. Nevertheless, they are united with the bishops in sacerdotal dignity. By the power of the sacrament of orders, in the image of Christ the eternal high Priest (Heb 5:1-10; 7:24; 9:11-28), they are consecrated to preach the gospel and shepherd the faithful and to celebrate divine worship, so that they are true priests of the New Testament. *(The Church,* 28)

EXPLANATION . . .

● (1) Before Jesus ascended into heaven, he gave special instructions to his apostles. He wanted to be certain that there would be helpers to carry on the work of shepherding his flock.

(2) He sent his apostles to preach the gospel of the New Covenant to every nation, because he intended his kingdom, the Church, for all people.

(3) The apostles continued Christ's priestly work of being mediators between God and man. They brought God's mercy and grace to the people of the New Covenant and, in return, gave their praise to God. When they performed priestly functions, Christ the high priest was present, acting through them.

74. What can priests do as Christ's representatives?

Representing Christ, priests (1) primarily offer the Sacrifice of the Mass, (2) administer the sacrament of Penance for the forgiveness of sins, and (3) administer the sacrament of the Anointing of the Sick.

VATICAN COUNCIL II . . .

▲ The same Lord has established ministers among his faithful to unite them together in one body in which "not all the members have the same function" (Rom 12:4). These ministers in the society of the faithful are able by the sacred power of orders to offer sacrifice and to forgive sins, and they perform their priestly office publicly for men in the name of Christ. *(Ministry and Life of Priests,* 2)

EXPLANATION . . .

● (1) Knowing that Christ's priesthood and his Church were to be continued to the end of time, the apostles by consecrating bishops and ordaining priests passed on their priestly power to others. In this sacrament a man is made a priest and receives the grace necessary to make the sacrifices required of a life that is so much like that of Christ.

By the imposition of the hands of the bishop a man is made a priest and becomes a representative of Christ, having the priestly powers of Christ. The most important work of the priest is the offering of the Holy Sacrifice of the Mass. He acts in the name of Christ and in union with him as Jesus renews the sacrifice of the cross in an unbloody manner for the glory of God and the salvation of humankind.

(2) Through his priests, Christ forgives sins. He becomes for all of us a merciful and faithful high priest; as St. Paul says, "He had to be made like his brothers in every way in order that he might become a compassionate and faithful high priest before God and expiate the sins of the people" (Heb 2:17).

(3) Through his priests Christ gives comfort to the suffering members of his Mystical Body and prepares them for their eternal union with God in the sacrament of the Anointing of the Sick.

— The Anointing of the Sick —

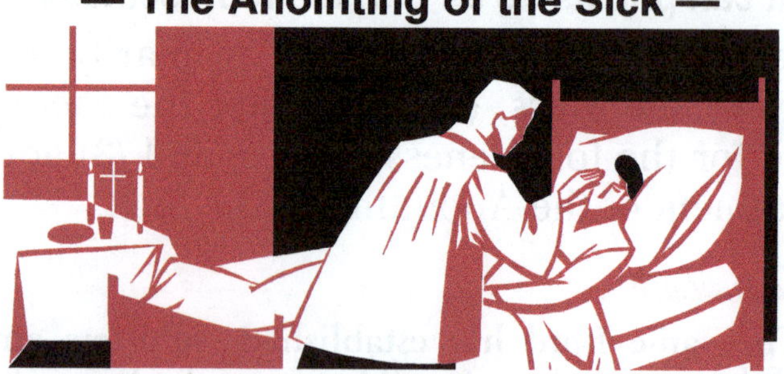

75. What is the anointing of the sick?

The Anointing of the Sick is the sacrament for the seriously ill, infirm and aged.

VATICAN COUNCIL II . . .

▲ For the sick and the sinners among the faithful, priests exercise the ministry of alleviation and reconciliation and they present the needs and the prayers of the faithful to God the Father (cf. Heb 5:1-4). *(The Church, 28)*

EXPLANATION . . .

● **Jesus showed a great love for sinners and the sick. He gave special care to the sick and cured them. "At sunset they brought to him all those who were sick with various diseases. He laid his hands on each of them and healed them" (Lk 4:40). Jesus continues to come to the sick in the sacrament of the Anointing of the Sick.**

The priest takes the oil and anoints the sick person on the forehead and the hands, saying once: "Through this holy anointing may the Lord in his love and mercy help you with the grace of the Holy Spirit. Amen. May the Lord who frees you from sin save you and raise you up. Amen."

76. When is this sacrament best received?

This sacrament is best received as soon as there is danger of death from either sickness or old age.

VATICAN COUNCIL II . . .

▲ "Extreme unction," which may also and more fittingly be called "anointing of the sick," is not a sacrament for those only who are at the point of death. Hence, as soon as any one of the faithful begins to be in danger of death from sickness or old age, the fitting time for him to receive this sacrament has certainly already arrived. *(Sacred Liturgy, 75)*

EXPLANATION . . .

● This sacrament is for those who are seriously sick, rather than for the dying. The sacrament can be repeated for persons who get well and become seriously ill again. Sorrow for sins is required to have sins forgiven in any sacrament. The priest should be called early to a sick person so that he can help the person to sincere sorrow for sins.

77. What does the Church ask for by this anointing?

By this anointing and the accompanying prayers for the restoration of health, the entire Church through the priest asks the Lord (1) for possible restored health for the sick, (2) to lighten the suffering of the sick, (3) forgive their sins, and (4) bring them to eternal salvation.

VATICAN COUNCIL . . .

▲ By the sacred anointing of the sick and the prayer of her priests the whole Church commends the sick to the suffering and glorified Lord, asking that he may lighten their suffering and save them (cf. Jas 5:14-16). *(The Church, 11)*

EXPLANATION . . .

● (1) Christ comes to the sick in the sacrament of the Anointing of the Sick. The sacrament may restore the sick person to health, as St. James says, "The prayer of faith will save the sick person, and the Lord will raise him up" (Jas 5:15).

In this sacrament Christ gives us graces which enable us to bear the pain and distress of our illness with patience. Christ comes with consolation for the soul often in pain and sometimes in fear and temptation.

(2) Christ also gives us graces which enable us to have deep sorrow for our sins. Sorrow for sins is required to have sins forgiven in this sacrament. Therefore, the parish priest should be called early to a sick person so that he can help the person to sincere sorrow for sins and a fruitful reception of the sacrament. To neglect to call the priest early is to neglect the sick person.

(3) By this sacrament we are prepared for immediate entrance into glory. Besides forgiving our sins, Jesus helps us to offer ourselves, our life, and the pains of our last illness to him with sincere Christian resignation, and with deep sorrow for our sins, so that we can hope to go immediately into heaven if we die.

Jesus heals the cripple. The pool called Bethsaida is a symbol of the healing power of the sacraments.

78. What does the Church encourage the sick to do?

The Church encourages the sick to contribute to the spiritual good of the entire People of God by associating themselves freely to the suffering and death of Christ.

VATICAN COUNCIL II . . .

▲ The Church exhorts the sick, moreover, to contribute to the welfare of the whole People of God by associating themselves freely with the passion and death of Christ (cf. Rom 8:17; Col 1:24; 2 Tim 2:11-12; 1 Pet 4:13). *(The Church, 11)*

EXPLANATION . . .

● The Anointing of the Sick prepares us for heaven if it is our time to die. It restores us to health if it is God's will that we serve him still longer here on earth. Since Christ increases the divine life in the soul in this sacrament, he enables us to offer our sufferings in union with his own on the cross that we might share in the work of redemption. Thus we can contribute to the welfare of the Church not only by atoning for sin, but also by meriting grace for the sanctification of the Church. If we share in the sufferings of Christ, we can expect to share also in his glory.

Before the sacrament of the Anointing of the Sick the priest usually gives the sick person the sacrament of Penance and after the anointing gives the Body and Blood of Christ. The Last Blessing which brings with it a plenary indulgence is given at this time too. This is what St. James had in mind when he said, "Confess your sins to one another and pray for one another, so that you may be healed" (Jas 5:16). The loving Christ pours forth his love and consolation upon a sick Christian through this sacrament.

DISCUSSION QUESTIONS

1. What are the effects of the sacrament of Baptism? (59)
2. How do the People of God share in the kingly, priestly, and prophetic office of Christ? (60)
3. What are the effects of the sacrament of Confirmation? (61)
4. Why are the sacraments of Confirmation, Baptism and the Eucharist called sacraments of initiation? (62)
5. What is the duty placed upon us when we are confirmed? (63)
6. What is the purpose of the sacrament of Penance? (64)
7. What does sacramental absolution do for us? (65)
8. How did the apostles receive the power of forgiving sins? (65)
9. How does penance help us in our spiritual growth? (66)
10. What is the sign of the sacrament of Penance? (67)
11. Why is confession the ordinary way of forgiveness of serious sins? (68)
12. When do we have perfect contrition for sin? (69)
13. Why does the Church urge us to receive the sacrament of Penance regularly? (70)
14. Why is frequent confession useful? (71)
15. What is Holy Orders? (72)
16. What graces does Holy Orders give? (73)
17. What are the principal duties of priests? (74)
18. What is the sign of the sacrament of the Anointing of the Sick? (75)
19. When should the Anointing of the Sick be received? (76)
20. What are the effects of the Anointing of the Sick? (77)
21. What are the sick encouraged to do? (78)

Chapter 12

THE EUCHARIST, CENTER OF ALL SACRAMENTAL LIFE

79. Why does the Eucharist have primacy among the sacraments?

The Eucharist has primacy among the sacraments because it is of the greatest importance for the uniting and strengthening of the Church.

VATICAN COUNCIL II . . .

▲ The other sacraments, as well as every ministry of the Church and every work of the apostolate, are tied together with the Eucharist and are directed toward it. The most blessed Eucharist contains the entire spiritual wealth of the Church, that is, Christ himself, our Passover and living bread; through his very flesh, rendered vital and vitalizing by the action of the Holy Spirit, he gives life to men who are thus invited and encouraged to offer themselves, their labors and all created things, together with him.

In this light, the Eucharist shows itself as the source and the apex of the whole work of preaching the Gospel. Those under instruction are introduced by stages to a sharing in the Eucharist, and the faithful, already marked with the seal of baptism and confirmation, are through the reception of the Eucharist fully joined to the Body of Christ. *(Ministry and Life of Priests, 5)*

EXPLANATION . . .

● Baptism begins the Christian life. It initiates one into the life of the Father, Son, and Holy Spirit. But the Christian must grow ever more alive with this divine life through prayer, the sacraments, hearing the word of God, and the Christ-like service of others.

Of all the sacraments, the most important and indeed the central act of the Christian Church is the sacrament of the Eucharist. The Body and Blood of Christ is called the Holy Eucharist. When the Eucharist is offered to God in sacrifice it is called the Sacrifice of the Mass. When the Eucharist is given to a person as food for his soul it is called Holy Communion.

Jesus Christ is present in the Holy Eucharist to be our sacrifice, our food, our life, our companion to strengthen and nourish us with his flesh and blood and to unite us with himself and with all the members of the Church. Therefore, the Eucharist is the center of all the sacramental life of the Church.

80. Why is the Eucharistic celebration carried out?

The Eucharistic celebration is carried out in obedience to the words of Jesus at the Last Supper: "Do this in memory of me."

VATICAN COUNCIL II . . .

▲ At the Last Supper, on the night when he was betrayed, our Savior instituted the Eucharistic sacrifice of his body and blood. He did this in order to perpetuate the sacrifice of the cross throughout the centuries until he should come again, and so to entrust to his beloved spouse, the Church, a memorial of his death and resurrection: a sacrament of love, a sign of unity, a bond of charity, a paschal banquet in which Christ is eaten, the mind is filled with grace, and a pledge of future glory is given to us. *(Sacred Liturgy, 47)*

EXPLANATION . . .

● The Mass is the Church's way of doing what Jesus did at the Last Supper. Taking bread and giving thanks, Jesus broke it and gave it to his disciples, saying, "This is my body, which will be given for you. Do this in memory of me." And he did the same with the cup after supper, "This cup is the new covenant in my blood, which will be poured out for you" (Lk 22:19-20).

Jesus gave the apostles the command and the power to bring the Eucharist to us when he said, "Do this in memory of me."

The Mass is the Church's way of doing what Jesus did at the Last Supper. St. Paul wrote, "The tradition I received from the Lord I handed on to you: the Lord Jesus, on the night he was betrayed, took bread, and

after giving thanks he broke it and said, 'This is my body that is for you. Do this in remembrance of me.' In the same fashion, after the supper, he also took the cup and said, 'This cup is the new covenant in my blood. Whenever you drink it, do this in remembrance of me.' And so, whenever you eat this bread and drink this cup, you proclaim the death of the Lord until he comes." (1 Cor 11:23-26).

The Church does this to remember Jesus and to be reunited with him. At the Last Supper Jesus gave bread and wine to his apostles to eat and drink, telling them that it was his own body and blood. He then asked them to remember him always by doing this same thing among themselves.

The Eucharist is the sacrificial meal which recalls the Last Supper.

81. What takes place when a priest pronounces the words of Eucharistic consecration?

When a priest pronounces the words of Eucharistic consecration, the underlying reality of bread and wine is changed into the Body and Blood of Christ, given for us in sacrifice.

VATICAN COUNCIL II . . .

▲ Christ is present in the Sacrifice of the Mass, not only in the person of his minister, "the same one now offering, through the ministry of priests, who formerly offered himself on the cross," but especially under the Eucharistic species. (*Sacred Liturgy*, 7)

EXPLANATION . . .

● His words and power made Jesus truly present in the bread and wine that he gave his apostles to eat so that they actually received Jesus in that meal and were united with him. This made the apostles one with Jesus and all that he did. They shared his gift of himself to his Father on the cross and in the Father's gift of life to Jesus in the resurrection. The apostles then gave Christ to the People of God in the Eucharist.

The Church recreates the Last Supper by bringing followers of Jesus together and recalling through readings and prayers what God has done for his people. Then the priest announces what Jesus said and did at the Last Supper and himself offers the consecrated bread and, on some occasions, consecrated wine to the people to eat and drink.

82. What does "transubstantiation" mean?

Transubstantiation means that Christ himself, true God and true Man, is really and substantially present, in a mysterious way, under the appearances of bread and wine.

VATICAN COUNCIL II . . .

▲ Even in the reserved sacrament Christ is to be adored because he is substantially present there through that conversion of bread and wine which, as the Council of Trent tells us, is most aptly named transubstantiation. *(Instruction on Worship of the Eucharistic Mystery: Sacred Congregation of Rites, May 25, 1967)*

EXPLANATION . . .

● After the priest speaks the words of consecration, the appearances of bread and wine remain, meaning something appears to be there but it is not really there. When our Lord gave the apostles his body, the body looked like bread and even tasted like bread but it was not bread; it was his body for he said so. When our Lord gave the apostles his blood, the blood appeared to be wine and even tasted like wine, but it was not wine; it was his blood for he said so.

This holy sacrament looks like bread and tastes like bread but it is not bread; it is Jesus. To come to us Jesus covers himself with the appearances of bread and wine. We cannot understand all this, but we take the word of God that it is so. We have such trust in God who

is all-truthful that we take his word that all he said about the Holy Eucharist is true. This is faith. The Eucharist is called the Mystery of Faith.

All priests in the Catholic Church have the power to change bread and wine into Christ. In the Eucharist it is Christ himself who consecrates through the priest as the words of consecration are said: "This is my Body. This is the chalice of my Blood, the Blood of the new and eternal covenant."

83. What is the Sacrifice of the Mass?

The Sacrifice of the Mass is not merely a ritual which commemorates the sacrifice of Calvary. In it, through the ministry of priests, Christ perpetuates the sacrifice of the cross in an unbloody manner.

VATICAN COUNCIL II . . .

▲ Through the ministry of the priests, the spiritual sacrifice of the faithful is made perfect in union with the sacrifice of Christ. He is the only mediator who in the name of the whole Church is offered sacramentally in the Eucharist and in an unbloody manner until the Lord himself comes (cf. 1 Cor 11:26). *(Ministry and Life of Priests, 2)*

EXPLANATION . . .

● The Mass does more than remember Jesus, for he is more than a memory. Through his resurrection he is present and active among us in his Spirit. The Mass is a sacrifice where the Church not only remembers Jesus but truly brings him and his saving death-resurrection into the present so that his followers may become part of it. The Church can do this because Jesus is united to his Church in the Holy Spirit. When the Church celebrates the Eucharist, Jesus is truly there, and it is he who does once more what he did at the Last Supper.

At the Last Supper, our Savior instituted the Eucharistic Sacrifice of his Body and Blood to continue for all time the sacrifice of the cross until he would come again. He gave his Church a remembrance of his death and resurrection. But the Mass is a true sacrifice. Through the hands of priests and in the name of the whole Church, the sacrifice of Jesus is offered in the Eucharist in an unbloody and sacramental man-

ner. The priest, by the sacred power he enjoys, acting in the person of Christ, brings about the Eucharistic Sacrifice, and offers it to God in the name of all the people.

The faithful join in the offering of the Eucharist and give themselves and all their works and sufferings to God. United with Jesus, the divine Victim of Calvary, they offer to God adoration and thanksgiving which are worthy of God. They ask pardon for their sins and beg for God's blessings in the best way they can—through Jesus Christ our Lord.

The Mass is a prayer to the Father in which his people give him thanks and praise for the wonderful future he has given us in his Son Jesus Christ. There are times in the Mass in which we ask forgiveness for our sins and beg the Father's blessing upon ourselves and others.

The Mass is a sacrifice because it brings into the present our Lord's own offering of himself to his Father on the cross. By doing this in memory of him, we enter into that offering and become a part of it.

The Mass brings us Jesus' resurrection because his sacrifice established a common life of friendship and love between the Father and his children. Just as we share in Jesus' death at Mass, so we also share in the new life of the Spirit poured out on Jesus in his resurrection.

The Mass is very important because it brings together all the gifts the Father has given us in Jesus Christ. It brings into our lives the very presence of Jesus, his sacrifice of himself on the cross, and the new life of the Spirit opened to us in his resurrection.

By remembering what Jesus did at the Last Supper and doing it with him, the Church thanks the Father for opening his life to us. By entering into the self-giving life and death of Jesus, the Church joins him in giving to the Father the only perfect worship the world has seen.

84. What is the Eucharist?

The Eucharist is a meal which (1) recalls the Last Supper, (2) celebrates our unity together in Christ, and (3) anticipates the messianic banquet of the kingdom.

VATICAN COUNCIL II . . .

▲ Really partaking of the body of the Lord in the breaking of the Eucharistic bread, we are taken up into communion with him and with one another. "Because the bread is one, we, though many, are one body, all of us who partake of the one bread" (1 Cor 10:17). In this way all of us are made members of his body (cf. 1 Cor 12:27), "but severally members of one another" (Rom 12:5). *(The Church, 7)*

EXPLANATION . . .

● **(1) In the Sacrifice of the Mass Jesus Christ not only offers himself to his Father as he did on the cross, though in a sacramental way, together with us, but he nourishes our soul with himself, the Bread of Life. We are nourished with the Victim of the sacrifice of the cross, because at this sacrificial meal we recall what happened at the Last Supper and actually partake of the body and blood of the Victim of our Redemption. Thus St. Paul reminded the people: "The cup of blessing that we bless, is it not a sharing in the blood of Christ? The bread that we break, is it not a sharing in the body of Christ?" (1 Cor 10:16).**

(2) The whole Jesus is in Holy Communion. He has passed through death into the fullness of life with the Father. Here is Jesus who is God, who can do everything, who is all-good and all-merciful. He is the God-Man in this sacrificial meal.

The Communion of the Mass is the meal of consecrated bread that nourishes us with the life of God and unites us to Jesus and to one another. In drawing us to union with Jesus, our Father draws us closer to each other. The Holy Spirit guides our responses with God's own love. As an assembly of Jesus' followers, the Eucharist is both an expression of that unity and love which binds us to each other and to Jesus and an action through which the bonds are strengthened.

(3) Holy Communion is already giving us a part in the banquet of Christ in the kingdom of heaven because it is the same Son of God made man who will be united with us in a union of joy forever in heaven, if we are judged worthy. At the Last Supper Jesus said, "I tell you, from now on I shall not drink this fruit of the vine until the day when I shall drink it anew with you in the kingdom of my Father" (Mt 26:29).

Jesus also promised that our body would someday enjoy his presence also. "Whoever feeds upon my flesh and drinks my blood has eternal life, and I will raise him up on the last day" (Jn 6:54). In this way Jesus anticipates the messianic banquet of the kingdom. The Eucharistic meal not only reminds us of the Church's heavenly reunion with Christ, but prepares us to take part in that heavenly communion with Christ and his Father.

85. What does Jesus do for us in the Eucharist?

In the Eucharist Jesus nourishes Christians with his own self, the Bread of Life, so that they may become a people (1) more acceptable to God and (2) filled with greater love of God and neighbor.

VATICAN COUNCIL II . . .

▲ To preach this gospel the Lord sent forth his disciples into the whole world, that being reborn by the word of God (cf. 1 Pet 1:23), men might be joined to the Church through baptism— that Church which, as the body of the Word Incarnate, is nourished and lives by the word of God and by the Eucharistic bread (cf. Acts 2:43). *(Mission Activity of the Church, 6)*

The renewal in the Eucharist of the Covenant between the Lord and man draws the faithful into the compelling love of Christ and sets them on fire. From the liturgy, therefore, and especially from the Eucharist, as from a font, grace is poured forth upon us; and the sanctification of men in Christ and the glorification of God, to which all other activities of the Church are directed as toward their end, is achieved in the most efficacious possible way. *(Sacred Liturgy, 10)*

EXPLANATION . . .

● (1) Holy Communion is Jesus Christ himself under the appearances of bread and wine uniting himself to the Christian to nourish their soul. Jesus said, "I am the living bread that came down from heaven. Whoever eats this bread will live forever; and the bread that I will give is my flesh, for the life of the world" (Jn 6:51).

By uniting us to himself in Holy Communion Jesus gives himself, the Second Person of the Blessed Trinity, the Author of grace, so that we may live his divine life, for he said, "Just as the living Father sent

me and I have life because of the Father, so whoever feeds upon me will live because of me" (Jn 6:57).

In this great celebration of their common faith, the followers of Jesus relive the experience of him and thank their Father for it. We remember what our Father has given us. At the same time, we receive again the same gift of Jesus Christ and enter more deeply into union with him in the Holy Spirit. Mass is the place where the Christian community both acts out its faith and is renewed and strengthened in all its members. Especially in the Mass do we become a people acceptable to God.

(2) Holy Communion helps us to love God more because of the divine grace which is increased in our souls. This same grace helps us to love others for the love of God. Our Lord came into this world to redeem us and to keep us from sin; he comes into our soul for the same purpose. He strengthens us through actual or sacramental grace that we may overcome temptation and avoid sinning against God and our neighbor. Only by his help can we succeed in living a life of true charity and thus fulfill his greatest commandment.

86. What is necessary to receive the Eucharist worthily?

To receive the Eucharist worthily the Christian must be in the state of grace.

THE BIBLE . . .

✠ *Therefore, anyone who eats the bread and drinks the cup of the Lord in an unworthy manner is guilty of an offense against the body and blood of the Lord. Everyone should examine himself about eating the bread and drinking from the cup.* (1 Cor 11:27-28)

VATICAN COUNCIL II . . .

▲ On those who receive the Body and Blood of Christ, the gift of the Spirit is poured out abundantly like living water (cf. Jn 7:37-39), provided that this Body and Blood have been received sacramentally and spiritually, namely by that faith which operates through charity. (*Instruction on Worship of the Eucharistic Mystery*, 38)

EXPLANATION . . .

● **St. Paul reminds us that we must receive the Eucharist worthily: "Anyone who eats the bread and drinks the cup of the Lord in an unworthy manner is guilty of an offense against the body and blood of the**

Lord" (1 Cor 11:27). As long as we are in the state of grace, we are prepared to receive our Lord each time that we are present at the Holy Sacrifice of the Mass because his body is the fruit of the Sacrifice, and for us the way to eternal life.

The best way to prepare our soul for union with Jesus in Holy Communion is to offer him and to offer ourselves with him reverently to God the Father in the Sacrifice of the Mass. Confession is not necessary before Holy Communion unless we have a serious sin to confess.

87. Why is the Eucharist a sacrament of unity?

The Eucharist is a sacrament of unity because it is meant to unite the faithful more closely each day with God and with one another.

VATICAN COUNCIL II . . .

▲ In the sacrament of the Eucharistic bread, the unity of all believers who form one body in Christ (cf. 1 Cor 10:17) is both expressed and brought about. All men are called to this union with Christ, who is the light of the world, from whom we go forth, through whom we live, and toward whom our whole life strains. *(The Church, 3)*

EXPLANATION . . .

● By eating the Body of the Lord, we are taken up into a close union with him and with one another. In this sacrament the unity of all those who believe in Jesus is not only shown but also brought about. This is what St. Paul meant when he said, "Because there is one bread, we who are many are one body, for we all partake of the one bread" (1 Cor 10:17).

88. What is expected of the Christian nourished by the Eucharist?

Having been nourished by the Lord himself, the Christian should with active love eliminate all pre-judices and all barriers to cooperation with others.

VATICAN COUNCIL II . . .

▲ No Christian community, however, is built up unless it has its basis and center in the celebration of the most Holy

Eucharist; from this, therefore, all education to the spirit of community must take its origin. This celebration, if it is to be genuine and complete, should lead to various works of charity and mutual help, as well as to missionary activity and to different forms of Christian witness. *(Ministry and Life of Priests, 6)*

EXPLANATION . . .

● **In the Eucharist Jesus nourishes our soul with himself, the Bread of Life. In this way he fills us with love of God and our neighbor, and makes us a people more pleasing to God. Having been nourished with the Victim of the sacrifice of the cross, we should be willing to treat all people with love and fairness as children of God and brothers and sisters of Jesus.**

When we eat the flesh of Christ in the sacrificial meal prepared by our heavenly Father, Christ keeps making us one body with himself. The gift of sanctifying grace, through which the Spirit of Christ carries on this work of incorporation, makes steady progress in our hearts if we cooperate with it.

As Christ grafts us onto himself, he brings us closer to one another. Israel's sacrificial meals united them as a nation. So the Eucharist unites us as God's family: it makes the Church one. Thus, the Eucharist, when eaten in faith, brings about gradual changes within the hearts of Christ's faithful. It is a transforming food, which continues to make us like Christ who dwells in us.

Since the Eucharist makes us one in Christ, it strengthens our charitable respect for one another. This food enables us who eat it to sacrifice ourselves for our neighbor's good. As the Eucharist inspires us with the memory of Christ's holy passion and death, when he offered his body and blood for our salvation, so when we eat this Bread of Life we too will be enabled to sacrifice ourselves for our neighbor's sake and to practice charity.

89. What is due to the real presence of Christ in the Blessed Sacrament reserved?

Gratitude, adoration and devotion are due to the real presence of Christ in the Blessed Sacrament reserved.

VATICAN COUNCIL II . . .

▲ There should be no doubt in anyone's mind "that all the faithful ought to show to this most holy sacrament the worship which is due to the true God, as has always been the custom of the Catholic Church. Nor is it to be adored any the less because it was instituted by Christ to be eaten. . . . The mystery of the Eucharist should therefore be considered in all its fullness, not only in the celebration of Mass but also in devotion to the sacred species which remain after Mass and are reserved to extend the grace of the sacrifice."*(Instruction on Worship of the Eucharistic Mystery*, 3)

EXPLANATION . . .

● **Jesus is present at Mass in his word as the people listen to the Scripture readings. He is present in the priest and in the people through whom he acts to do again what he did at the Last Supper. He is also present in a real way in the bread and wine that symbolize his body and blood. The Church expresses this presence of Jesus in the Eucharist by preserving the consecrated bread.**

Reservation of the Blessed Sacrament means that at the end of Communion the remaining consecrated bread is placed in the tabernacle and reverently preserved. Thus, the Blessed Sacrament of the Eucharist is always available both as a continuing sign of Jesus' real presence among his people and as spiritual food for the sick and dying.

Gratitude, adoration, and devotion are due to the real presence of Christ. This devotion is expressed in our visits to the tabernacle in our churches and in Benediction. Benediction is a devotion in which the Blessed Sacrament is exposed to the people for reverence and adoration. It concludes with the priest blessing the people with consecrated bread. It is our duty to thank Jesus for all his blessings and to adore him as our God and Savior. We must offer ourselves to serve him with all the love in our hearts.

90. How does the Eucharist reserved in our churches help us?

The Eucharist, reserved in our churches, is a powerful help to prayer and service of others.

VATICAN COUNCIL II . . .

▲ The house of prayer in which the most Holy Eucharist is celebrated and reserved, where the faithful gather and where the presence of the Son of God, our Savior, offered for us on the altar of sacrifice bestows strength and blessings on the faithful, must be spotless and suitable for prayer and sacred functions. *(Ministry and Life of Priests, 5)*

EXPLANATION . . .

● **The Jewish Passover of the Old Covenant was a symbol of the Eucharist of the New Covenant. Jesus fulfilled the Jewish Passover meal when he instituted the Eucharist at the Last Supper. As the first People of God, the Jews, ate the manna in the desert, the new People of God, Christians, eat of the Eucharist. As the ark of the Covenant and the pillar of fire were a sign of God's special presence with his people during their long journey through the desert, so Jesus is present with us in the tabernacle to be our comfort in our journey through life as our Emmanuel—God with us.**

He keeps his promise made before ascending into heaven: "And behold, I am with you always, to the end of the world!" (Mt 28:20). His presence in the Blessed Sacrament reserved will enable us to grow in our prayer-life of union with God. It should be our strength and inspiration in the service of others.

The Eucharist was the center of the early Christian community and is still the center of all worship of God today and to the end of time.

DISCUSSION QUESTIONS

1. Why is the Eucharist the central act of the Christian Church? (79)
2. Why is the Mass the Church's way of doing what Jesus did at the Last Supper? (80)
3. What takes place at the Eucharistic consecration? (81)
4. What is "transubstantiation"? (82)
5. Why is the Mass a sacrifice? (83)
6. Why does the Eucharistic meal recall the Last Supper? (84)
7. Why does Holy Communion celebrate our unity together in Christ? (84)
8. Why does Holy Communion anticipate the heavenly banquet? (85)
9. Why does Jesus nourish us with himself? (85)
10. How is the Eucharist to be received? (86)
11. Why is the Eucharist a sacrament of unity? (87)
12. Why does Holy Communion increase our love for our neighbor? (88)
13. How do we express our devotion to the real presence of Christ? (89)
14. How does the Eucharist reserved help us? (90)
15. How can we compare the Eucharist with the Jewish Passover? (90)

Chapter 13

THE SACRAMENT OF MATRIMONY

91. Who instituted marriage?

Marriage was instituted by the Creator himself and given by him certain purposes, laws, and blessings.

VATICAN COUNCIL II . . .

▲ The intimate partnership of married life and love has been established by the Creator and qualified by his laws. (*Church in the Modern World, 48*)

EXPLANATION . . .

● **At the very beginning of the human race, when he created Adam and Eve, God instituted marriage. A loving Father gave marriage to us. We read in the Book of Genesis: "God created mankind in his image, in the image of God he created them, male and female he created them. God blessed them and told them, 'Be fruitful and multiply, and fill the earth and subdue it' " (Gen 1:27-28).**

God instituted marriage for the procreation and education of children and for the loving companionship of husband and wife.

92. Who raised marriage to the dignity of a sacrament?

Christ raised marriage of the baptized to the dignity of a sacrament.

VATICAN COUNCIL II . . .

▲ Christ the Lord abundantly blessed this many-faceted love, welling up as it does from the fountain of divine love and structured as it is on the model of his union with his Church. For as God of old made himself present (cf. Jer 3:6-13, etc.) to his people through a Covenant of love and fidelity, so now the Savior of men and the Spouse of the Church (cf. Mt 9:15; 2 Cor 11:2; Eph 5:27; Rev 19:7f) comes into the lives of married Christians through the sacrament of matrimony *(Church in the Modern World, 48).*

EXPLANATION . . .

● **Jesus Christ raised marriage to the dignity of a sacrament for the baptized. He made marriage a lifelong, sacred union of husband and wife by which they give themselves in complete surrender to each other and to Christ. Christ is the third partner in every marriage.**

Christian marriage is a man and woman totally sharing life, love, and Christian faith with one another and with God. It is a sacrament. The human relationship of marriage is the sign through which God shows his love and communicates his life.

93. Who are the ministers of the sacrament?

The spouses, expressing their personal and irrevocable consent, are the ministers of the sacrament.

VATICAN COUNCIL II . . .

▲ As a mutual gift of two persons, this intimate union and the good of the children impose total fidelity on the spouses and argue for an unbreakable oneness between them. *(Church in the Modern World, 48)*

EXPLANATION . . .

● **Not the priest, but the husband and wife are the ministers of the sacrament. The sacrament of marriage is given first through the mutual promises between husband and wife in the marriage ceremony. After that it continues to be given as these promises are carried out in the years of married life. As they selflessly share their life in God, the husband is the minister of God's grace to the wife and the wife to the husband. The priest officiates at the ceremony as the Church's witness to this act of grace.**

94. In what does the dignity of matrimony consist?

The dignity of the sacrament especially consists in the fact that (1) the spouses live together in Christ's grace, and (2) imitate—and in a way represent—Christ's own love for his Church.

THE BIBLE . . .

✠ *Husbands, love your wives, just as Christ loved the Church and gave himself up for her. (Eph 5:25)*

VATICAN COUNCIL II . . .

▲ Christ abides with them thereafter so that just as he loved the Church and handed himself over on her behalf (cf. Eph 5:25), the spouses may love each other with perpetual fidelity through mutual self-bestowal. Authentic married love is caught up into divine love and is governed and enriched by Christ's redeeming power and the saving activity of the Church, so that this love may lead the spouses to God with powerful effect and may aid and strengthen them in the sublime office of being a father or a mother. *(Church in the Modern World, 48)*

EXPLANATION . . .

● (1) In the sacrament of matrimony Christ comes to a husband and wife to live with them, to give them his grace, and to help them fulfill their rights and duties to God, to each other, and to their children faithfully until death. Marriage is a sacrament because the Holy Spirit breathes God's own love into the love between husband and wife so that each becomes a grace for the other. As a result their many acts of self-giving not only strengthen their life together but also cause them to grow in the life of God. He incorporates them as husband and wife in Christ and gives them the means by which they can adjust to one another.

(2) The sacrament of matrimony shows God's love for us by showing how close Jesus is to his people. St. Paul tells us that marriage is a sign of the relationship between Jesus and his Church. "Husbands, love your wives, just as Christ loved the Church and gave himself up for her in order to sanctify her. . . . This is a great mystery. Here I am applying it to Christ and the Church" (Eph 5:25, 32).

St. Paul calls the union between Christ and the Church a great foreshadowing. He describes the Church as the bride of Christ, decked out in splendor and made beautiful by her spouse. Christ has delivered himself up for his bride, that he might sanctify her and cleanse her free of sin with his precious blood. In this best human example of love we see how deeply Jesus is committed to his followers.

95. What do Christian spouses pledge themselves to do?

By this sacrament Christian spouses are as it were consecrated (1) to uphold the dignity of matrimony, and (2) to carry out its duties.

VATICAN COUNCIL II . . .

▲ Christian spouses have a special sacrament by which they are fortified and receive a kind of consecration in the duties and dignity of their state. By virtue of this sacrament, as spouses fulfill their conjugal and family obligations, they are penetrated with the spirit of Christ, which suffuses their whole lives with faith, hope, and charity. Thus they increasingly advance the perfection of their own personalities, as well as their mutual sanctification, and hence contribute jointly to the glory of God. *(Church in the Modern World, 48)*

EXPLANATION . . .

● **(1) The goal of marriage is the fulfillment and creation of human life. Through their mutual love the couple help each other and their children to become fully what God created each to be. At the same time, through the sexual expression of their love they become partners with God in the creation of new life. Christian couples pledge themselves to uphold this dignity of marriage.**

(2) In this sacrament the spouses are given special grace to enable them to carry out the duties of Matrimony toward each other and their children. The sacrament confers an increased sanctifying grace, the divine life, and all the actual graces needed throughout married life to bring about an ever deeper union of husband and wife in soul and body to live up to what they promised in their marriage vows. They also receive the actual graces needed for the fulfillment of the vocation of parenthood.

96. What does the marriage bond entail?

The marriage bond is rooted in the conjugal covenant of personal consent, whereby spouses mutually bestow and accept each other. A relationship arises which by divine will and in the eyes of society is a lasting one. This bond no longer depends on human decisions alone.

VATICAN COUNCIL II . . .

▲ The intimate partnership of married life and love has been established by the Creator and qualified by his laws, and is rooted in the conjugal covenant of irrevocable personal consent. Hence by that human act whereby spouses mutually bestow and accept each other a relationship arises which by divine will and in the eyes of society too is a lasting one. For the good of the spouses and their offspring as well as society, the existence of the sacred bond no longer depends on human decisions alone. *(Church in the Modern World, 48)*

EXPLANATION . . .

● Marriage is for life. It lasts as long as both parties live. Marriage is permanent because Jesus taught that married people should belong completely to each other just as he belongs completely to his Church. This mutual bestowal and acceptance of each other was expressed in the personal consent in which the marriage bond is rooted.

To protect the holy state of marriage, the people who enter into it, and their children, God revealed two necessary laws: A man may marry only one wife and a woman only one husband. The marriage union lasts until death.

The love of a Christian husband and wife for each other must endure. Divorce should be unthinkable for Christians, just as it is unthinkable that Christ should separate himself from his bride, the Church. In extreme cases civil divorce is permitted, but only for its legal results. Unless the marriage is annuled, there may be no remarriage.

Jesus Christ forbade divorce and remarriage. "Therefore, what God has joined together, let no man separate. . . . If a man divorces his wife and marries another, he commits adultery against her. In the same way if a wife divorces her husband and marries another, she commits adultery" (Mk 10:9, 11-12).

St. Paul says, "A woman is bound by Law to her husband as long as he lives, but if her husband dies, she is released from her husband in regard to the Law" (Rom 7:2).

Not even the Pope can dissolve a *valid* Christian marriage. After a divorce is granted by civil courts the man and wife of a *valid* Christian marriage remain man and wife before God.

97. What are the purposes of marriage?

Marriage and conjugal love are by their nature ordained toward (1) the procreation and education of children, and (2) the mutual love of the spouses.

VATICAN COUNCIL II . . .

▲ By their very nature, the institution of matrimony itself and conjugal love are ordained for the procreation and education of children, and find in them their ultimate crown. Thus a man and woman, who by their compact of conjugal love "are no longer two, but one flesh" (Mt 19:6), render mutual help and service to each other through an intimate union of their person and of their actions. Through this union they experience the meaning of their oneness and attain to it with growing perfection day by day. *(Church in the Modern World, 48)*

EXPLANATION . . .

● **(1) From married love come children. Nature and Scripture teach us that children are a purpose and a blessing of marriage. God blessed Adam and Eve and said: "Be fruitful and multiply, and fill the earth and subdue it" (Gen 1:28). In his love for us God gives us life and the care we need as children from parents. The love of husband and wife should be a source of great strength and comfort to them in their important task of taking care of their children according to God's will.**

(2) God's holy purpose in marriage is clear. The Lord God said: "It is not good for the man to be alone. I will make another creature who will be like him" (Gen 2:18). From marriage a man and his wife have a loving companionship that is stronger than any other in life. "This is why a man leaves his father and his mother and joins with a wife, and the two become one flesh" (Gen 2:24).

98. What is the aim of conjugal love and family life?

The true practice of conjugal love, and the whole meaning of the family life which results from it, have this aim: that the couple be ready with generous hearts to cooperate with the love of the Creator and the Savior, who through them will enlarge and enrich his own family day by day.

VATICAN COUNCIL II . . .

▲ Christian spouses, in virtue of the sacrament of matrimony, whereby they signify and partake of the mystery of that unity and fruitful love which exists between Christ and his Church (cf. Eph 5:32), help each other to attain to holiness in their married life and in the rearing and education of their children. By reason of their state and rank in life they have their own special gift among the People of God (cf. 1 Cor 7:7). From the wedlock of Christians there comes the family, in which new citizens of human society are born, who by the grace of the Holy Spirit received in baptism are made children of God, thus perpetuating the People of God throughout the centuries. *(The Church, 11)*

EXPLANATION . . .

● **The most complete expression of the unity of husband and wife is the sexual act, the fulfillment of the mutual love Christ so desires for them. A man and woman united in Christian marriage are a sign of the union between the Risen Christ and his Church.**

The married couple's responsibility for new life is this: Each couple must determine in the light of all the circumstances of their married life what is the unique creative partnership God invites them to share with him. They plan their family through a conscientious assessment of what they should do to further the good of their whole family and of society.

In this they are helped by the teaching of the Church, their own knowledge of themselves and their family situation, and the example of other faithful Christians. As in all of life's decisions, there, too, people finally decide according to a well-informed Christian conscience.

99. What is the vocation of every Christian family?

The vocation of every Christian family is to be and act as a community—that is, a group of persons sharing life together at a deep, personal level.

VATICAN COUNCIL II . . .

▲ The family, in which the various generations come together and help one another grow wiser and harmonize personal rights with the other requirements of social life, is the foundation of society. All those, therefore, who exercise influence over communities and social groups should work efficiently for the welfare of marriage and the family. *(Church in the Modern World, 52)*

EXPLANATION . . .

● **The family is the most sacred of all societies. In his love for us God gives us life from parents and the care we need as children. Our character, our beliefs, thoughts and virtues come from good, loving parents. The members of the family form a community and share life together at a deep, personal level. Through a truly Christian marriage the family can function perfectly as a community. It is part of the family's vocation to become a community, one which is also open to**

Jesus blesses the children. Through them he enriches and enlarges his own family, the Church.

the Church and to the world. Problems and misunderstandings should be expected in marriage, for marriage is a union of two human beings. In the sacrament of matrimony, however, Christ gives husband and wife the power to deal with these tensions, and the grace to destroy the sins which cause them.

100. How does the Christian family manifest the Savior's presence in the world?

The Christian family manifests the Savior's living presence in the world (1) by the mutual love of the spouses, (2) by their generous fruitfulness, (3) by their union and faithfulness, and (4) by the loving way the members work together.

VATICAN COUNCIL II . . .

▲ The Christian family, which springs from marriage as a reflection of the loving covenant uniting Christ with the Church (cf. Eph 5:32), and as a participation in that covenant, will manifest to all men Christ's living presence in the world, and the genuine nature of the Church. This the family will do by the mutual love of the spouses, by their generous fruitfulness, their solidarity and faithfulness, and by the loving way in which all members of the family assist one another. *(Church in the Modern World, 48)*

EXPLANATION . . .

● **(1) In the sacrament of Matrimony the Holy Spirit unites a man and woman and consecrates them so that they may bring Christ's threefold mission into family life. United in Christ, they build up the Church by teaching, guiding, and sanctifying their children and one another.**

Marriage is a lifelong partnership of love. Since Christ elevated Matrimony to the dignity of a sacrament for the baptized, the husband and wife, living in Christ's grace, imitate and in a certain way represent the love of Christ himself for his Church. By their love for each other they manifest Christ's presence in the world.

(2) Children are a great blessing in marriage. The giving of self in marriage brings children who make the love of husbands and wives richer and fulfill one of the purposes of marriage. If husbands and wives are generous to God in working with him according to his will, enlarging his own family on earth, he will bless them in this life and especially in heaven. Their fruitfulness manifests Christ's presence in the world.

(3) Christian marriage teaches people self-giving and sacrifice. It creates a climate of care for the raising of children. It educates the young to cooperation and concern for others. All this can be accomplished only with the help of Christ's grace, and thus the Christian family manifests his presence.

If they are to carry on Christ's mission, it is essential that a couple present themselves to their family and to the world as one in Christ. With the generous actual graces of the Spirit, given in the sacrament of Matrimony, they can grow ever closer together. The Spirit gives them power to dedicate themselves fully to each other and to do something about whatever divides them: indifference to each other's needs, hurt feelings, failing to understand.

(4) Anything expressive of love is already a reaching out to God. God uses our efforts at selflessness to draw us ever more deeply into his own life.

In making it a sacrament Christ gave marriage a new beauty and a new power of sanctifying. Marriage is now not merely the lawful union of man and wife; it is a source of holiness, a means of closer union of a man and woman with God as well as with each other. The union of husband and wife is a life-giving union, imparting grace to their souls. As this grace reaches also the children of a family, the Christian family manifests Christ's presence in the world.

101. What is the Church's position on mixed marriages?

"Difference of confession between the spouses does not constitute an insurmountable obstacle for marriage, when they succeed in placing in common what they have received from their respective communities, and learn from each other the way in which each lives in fidelity to Christ. But the difficulties of mixed marriages must not be underestimated. They arise from the fact that the separation of Christians has not yet been overcome" (CCC 1634).

VATICAN COUNCIL II . . .

▲ Let all the shepherds teach the faithful the religious importance and value of this sacrament [of matrimony]. Let them warn the faithful of the difficulties and dangers which are inherent in contracting a marriage with a Christian non-Catholic, and much more with a non-Christian. By all suitable means let them bring it about that young people contract marriage with a Catholic party.... it now happens that communications, acquaintances, and contacts of Catholics with non-Catholics are more frequent, and... are wont to bring on more frequent occasions of mixed marriages. *(Instructions on Mixed Marriages: Sacred Congregation for the Doctrine of the Faith, March 18, 1966.)*

EXPLANATION . . .

• The Christian family shares in the Church's work. Husband and wife involve themselves in the teaching mission of the Church by passing on to one another and to their children Christ's message of peace. Whenever they make an effort to be kind and forgiving, they are teaching one another by their example to know God and Jesus our Lord. When they encourage one another and help one another, it is Christ who encourages and helps.

Husband and wife share also in the Church's role of guiding people to God by imitating the example of Mother Church. In order that the Christian family may enjoy the fullness of the Christian life of grace, especially through the sacraments, the Church encourages her children to marry those who enjoy the same faith and appreciate and live according to the same moral principles.

DISCUSSION QUESTIONS

1. How was marriage instituted by the Creator? (91)
2. Why is marriage a sacrament? (92)
3. How is the sacrament of marriage given? (93)
4. What does the sacrament of Matrimony represent? (94)
5. What do Christian spouses pledge themselves to do? (95)
6. Why is marriage a lasting union? (96)
7. Why is procreation of children a purpose of marriage? (97)
8. Why is mutual love a purpose of marriage? (97)
9. What is the aim of conjugal love and family life? (98)
10. What is the married couple's responsibility for new life? (98)
11. What is the vocation of the Christian family? (99)
12. How does the Christian family manifest Christ's presence in the world? (100)
13. Why does the Church discourage mixed marriages? (101)

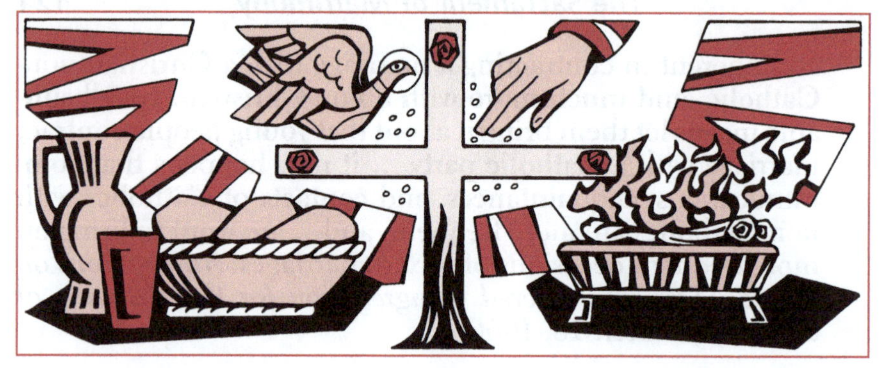

Chapter 14

WE ARE MADE NEW IN THE SPIRIT

102. What happens when a person accepts the Spirit of Christ?

When a person accepts the Spirit of Christ (1) God introduces them to a way of life completely new, which empowers them to share in God's own life. (2) The person is joined to the Father and to Christ in a vital union which not even death can break.

THE BIBLE . . .

✠ *"Whoever loves me will keep my word, and my Father will love him, and we will come to him and make our abode with him." (Jn 14:23)*

VATICAN COUNCIL II . . .

▲ All Christians, wherever they live, are bound to show forth, by the example of their lives and by the witness of their word, that new man put on at baptism and that power of the Holy Spirit by which they have been strengthened at confirmation. Thus other men, observing their good works, can glorify the Father (cf. Mt 5:16) and can perceive more fully the real meaning of human life and the universal bond of the community of mankind. *(Mission Activity of the Church, 11)*

EXPLANATION . . .

● (1) All Persons of the Blessed Trinity have a part in the holy work of getting and giving grace to people. The work of giving grace is especially attributed to the Holy Spirit because it is a work of love, and the Holy Spirit is the Spirit of Love of the Father and the Son. He sanctifies souls through the gift of grace. St. Paul says, "The love of God has been poured into our hearts through the Holy Spirit that has been given to us" (Rom 5:5).

The Spirit brings God's quality of life to us and all that we do. So deep is the effect of this that a person is said to live in the "state of grace."

St. Paul says, "God is rich in his mercy; and because he had such great love for us, he brought us to life with Christ when we were already dead through sin—it is by grace that you have been saved. . . . For it is by grace that you have been saved through faith. This has not come from you but from the gift of God. It does not come from works, so that no one can boast" (Eph 2:4-9).

(2) Grace is God's gift of himself. Jesus said, "Whoever loves me will keep my word, and my Father will love him, and we will come to him and make our abode with him" (Jn 14:23). From God's gift of himself comes our life in God which is the life of grace.

103. How does the indwelling Holy Spirit sanctify the soul?

The indwelling Holy Spirit (1) gives one hope and courage, (2) heals their weakness of soul, (3) enables them to master passion and selfishness, (4) prompts them to pursue what is good and to advance in such virtues as charity and patience, and (5) makes prayer possible and effective.

THE BIBLE . . .

✠ *The fruit of the Spirit is love, joy, peace, patience, kindness, generosity, faithfulness, gentleness, and self-control. There is no law against such things. (Gal 5:22-23)*

VATICAN COUNCIL II . . .

▲ To make this act of faith, the grace of God and the interior help of the Holy Spirit must precede and assist, moving the heart and turning it to God, opening the eyes of the mind and giving "joy and ease to everyone in assenting to the truth and believing it." To bring about an ever deeper understanding of revelation the same Holy Spirit constantly brings faith to completion by his gifts. *(Divine Revelation, 5)*

EXPLANATION . . .

● **(1) Sanctifying grace is God's gift to us; it makes our soul holy and pleasing to God. The Holy Spirit gives us the chief powers with grace: faith, hope, and love. The Spirit comes to us in many ways. He first comes from within in faith. *Faith* is what happens to us when we truly hear the word of God. It is a free gift by which the Holy Spirit enables us to accept the word completely and give our life over to the Father.**

St. Paul says, "If you confess with your lips, 'Jesus is Lord,' and believe in your heart that God raised him from the dead, you will be saved. For one believes in the heart and so is justified, and one confesses with the mouth and so is saved" (Rom 10:9-10).

Faith is possible only because God freely speaks his word to us and at the same time opens our mind and heart to his presence and love. Jesus said, "No one can come to me unless he is drawn by the Father who sent me, and I will raise up that person on the last day" (Jn 6:44).

The effect of faith is something called justification. This means that faith brings one from a stage of separation from God into communion with him and with others in God. St. Paul says, "For all have sinned and thereby are deprived of the glory of God, and all are justified by the gift of his grace that is given freely through the redemption in Christ Jesus. God designated Jesus to be a sacrifice of expiation of sin through faith by the shedding of his blood." (Rom 3:23-25).

***Hope* is the realization that God cares and that we can count on him. It is the side of faith that enables us to see good in spite of evil and to expect life forever even in the face of death. "If God is for us, who can be against us? He did not spare his own Son but gave him up for all of us. How then can he fail also to give us everything else along with him?" (Rom 8:31-32).**

We can hope because in Jesus Christ God has committed himself to us forever and will never leave us if only we remain united with him.

***Charity* is the love of God and of others because they too belong to God. St. John says, "No one has ever seen God, but if we love one another, God abides in us, and his love is made complete in us. This is**

how we know we can be certain that we abide in God and that he abides in us: he has given us a share in his Spirit" (1 Jn 4:12-13).

This kind of love is possible because God has given us his own love. The presence in us of the Holy Spirit means we are able to love with the love of God, even our enemies, if we will do so.

(2) The indwelling Holy Spirit heals the weakness of our soul. The Holy Spirit not only gives us sanctifying grace, God's life in our soul, but also *actual* grace—that supernatural help which enlightens our mind and strengthens our will to do good and to avoid evil.

(3) Evil persons, places, and things in this world can lead us into sin. The inclinations of our body also tempt us to do things unworthy of a Christian such as impurity, laziness, gluttony, anger, greed, envy, pride, and neglect of our neighbor's needs. We need the help of the Holy Spirit to lead a good Christian life. He offers us that help by giving us his grace when we really need it. It enables us to master passion and selfishness.

(4) Only by following the guidance of the Holy Spirit and using the help of his grace can we continue to share in God's divine life of sanctifying grace and live as his children; only then can we be closely united with the Most Holy Trinity by love, and persevere in the practice of virtue.

(5) Prayer is communication with the Father, Son, and Holy Spirit. In prayer, one turns to God and listens for his word. As God's word takes hold, one learns to answer with words of their own. It is the Holy Spirit who enables us to communicate with God through his grace and inspirations.

Therefore, through sanctifying grace and the gifts of faith, hope, and charity associated with it, and through actual grace, the help we need for mind and will to be good, we are sanctified by the indwelling Holy Spirit.

104. What are the effects of God's indwelling in the soul?

God's indwelling in the soul is a matchless grace and manifold gift: (1) a person dies to sin, (2) shares in the divinity of the Son through the spirit of adoption, and (3) enters into close communion with the Most Holy Trinity.

Jesus tells Thomas, "Blessed are those who have not seen and have believed." The Holy Spirit enables one to live a life of faith.

VATICAN COUNCIL II . . .

▲ The lay person should learn especially how to perform the mission of Christ and the Church by basing his life on belief in the divine mystery of creation and redemption and by being sensitive to the movement of the Holy Spirit who gives life to the People of God and who urges all to love God the Father as well as the world and men in him. This formation should be deemed the basis and condition for every successful apostolate. (*Apostolate of the Laity*, 29)

EXPLANATION . . .

● **(1) St. Paul says, "Those who belong to Christ Jesus have crucified the self with its passions and desires. If we live by the Spirit, let us also be guided by the Spirit" (Gal 5:24-25). With the help of the grace of the Holy Spirit we are able to die to sin and live to God.**

(2) By grace our soul shares in the very nature of God even while on this earth. We share in the divinity of the Son through the spirit of adop-

tion. St. Paul says, "Those whom he foreknew he also predestined to be conformed to the image of his Son so that he might be the firstborn among many brethren" (Rom 8:29).

(3) The crucified and risen Christ leads us to the Father by sending the Holy Spirit upon the People of God. St. Paul reminds Christians that they are the temple of the Holy Spirit. "Do you not realize that you are God's temple, and that the Spirit of God dwells in you?" (1 Cor 3:16).

The Holy Spirit was sent in order that he might forever sanctify the Church; through him the Father gives life to those who are dead to sin, because he is the Spirit of life. United in Christ, the followers of Christ are led by the Holy Spirit in their journey to the kingdom of their Father. He helps them to fulfill their duties. The Spirit prompts them to strive for what is good and to advance in virtue and in prayer.

105. What is one's destiny in the history of salvation?

In the history of salvation, it is divinely appointed that one is (1) to receive the sanctifying grace of adoption as God's child, and (2) to inherit eternal life.

VATICAN COUNCIL II . . .

▲ In his goodness and wisdom God chose to reveal himself and to make known to us the hidden purpose of his will (cf. Eph 1:9) by which through Christ, the Word made flesh, man might in the Holy Spirit have access to the Father and come to share in the divine nature (cf. Eph 2:18; 2 Pet 1:4). (*Divine Revelation*, 2)

EXPLANATION . . .

● (1) Grace is God's gift to us. We could never have earned it. Jesus bought grace for all by his suffering and death and resurrection. We had no right to grace. God in his goodness not only opened heaven for us by giving us divine life through his Son, but he also offers us all the help we need to reach heaven through the grace of the Holy Spirit. Our greatest honor is to be children of God. St. Paul says, "Those who are led by the Spirit of God are children of God" (Rom 8:14).

(2) Through the grace bought by Jesus we also inherit eternal life. Through his merits we hope to be united with God forever.

106. What are we given because of sanctifying grace?

Because of the grace of Christ the Savior, we are given (1) supernatural life, and (2) meaning and dignity far beyond what our own nature confers.

VATICAN COUNCIL II . . .

▲ All the Church's children should remember that their exalted status is to be attributed not to their own merits but to the special grace of Christ. If they fail moreover to respond to that grace in thought, word, and deed, not only shall they not be saved but they will be the more severely judged. *(The Church, 14)*

EXPLANATION . . .

● (1) We received two lives from God. One is the natural life we received at birth. The other is the second we received when we were baptized Christians. Jesus said to Nicodemus, "Amen, amen, I say to you, no one can see the kingdom of God without being born from above" (Jn 3:3).

We obtain natural life from our father and mother; we obtain supernatural life from God, our Father. St. John says, "See what great love the Father has bestowed on us, enabling us to be called the children of God, and that is what we are" (1 Jn 3:1).

(2) Our greatest honor is to be children of God and to have God's life in our soul because of the grace of Christ the Savior. We must strive to live a holy life and train ourselves to keep God's grace as our most precious possession. We must ask the Holy Spirit dwelling in our soul to help us to grow in our love for God and our neighbor, so that we may always live according to our great dignity as children of God and as true Christians.

DISCUSSION QUESTIONS

1. Why is the work of giving grace attributed to the Holy Spirit? (102)
2. What does the new way of life given to us by the Spirit empower us to do? (102)
3. What is sanctifying grace and its chief powers? (103)
4. What is faith? hope? charity? (103)
5. What is actual grace? (103)
6. What is prayer? (103)
7. What are the effects of God's indwelling in the soul? (104)
8. What has God in his goodness appointed for us? (105)
9. What is supernatural life? (106)
10. What is our greatest dignity? (106)

Part Four – FREEDOM

Chapter 15

HUMAN AND CHRISTIAN FREEDOM

107. What is God's plan concerning human freedom?

God's plan is that, united with Jesus Christ, we should give a free answer to God's call.

VATICAN COUNCIL II . . .

▲ It is one of the major tenets of Catholic doctrine that man's response to God in faith must be free: no one therefore is to be forced to embrace the Christian faith against his own will. This doctrine is contained in the word of God and it was constantly proclaimed by the Fathers of the Church. The act of faith is of its very nature a free act. Man, redeemed by Christ the Savior and through Christ Jesus called to be God's adopted son (cf. Eph 1:5), cannot give his adherence to God revealing himself unless, under the drawing of the Father (cf. Jn 6:44), he offers to God the reasonable and free submission of faith.

It is therefore completely in accord with the nature of faith that in matters religious every manner of coercion on the part of men should be excluded. *(Religious Freedom, 10)*

EXPLANATION . . .

● **Since we have dominion over our actions, it is very much part of our dignity and duty to be free to keep the moral law in the order of nature and in the order of grace, and in this way adhere closely to God who revealed himself in Christ.**

108. How has freedom been impaired?

At the outset, God endowed human nature with freedom. But this has been badly impaired by the sin of humanity, original sin.

VATICAN COUNCIL II . . .

▲ Peace is never attained once and for all, but must be built up ceaselessly. Moreover, since the human will is unsteady and wounded by sin, the achievement of peace requires a constant mastering of passions and the vigilance of lawful authority. *(Church in the Modern World, 78)*

EXPLANATION . . .

● God gave his grace to Adam and Eve. It was the greatest of God's gifts to them because through grace they shared in the very life of God. They were children of God; God lived in them as he lives in a temple. They were truly free with the freedom of children of God.

But through sin the human race lost God's life, grace. We place the name "original sin" on the tragedy of man losing his God. St. Paul says, "Sin entered the world as the result of one man, and death as a result of sin, and thus death has afflicted the entire human race inasmuch as everyone has sinned" (Rom 5:12).

St. Paul says, "If the transgression of one man led to the death of the many, how much greater was the overflowing effect of the grace of God and the gift of the one man Jesus Christ that has abounded for the many" (Rom 5:15).

Even our freedom was badly harmed by the sin of humanity. Our hope lies in the grace of Jesus Christ, merited for us by his redemptive death on the cross. The freedom of fallen man has been so weakened that he would be unable for long to observe even the duties of the natural law without the help of God's grace. But we have received grace. Our freedom is so elevated and strengthened that the life we live in the flesh, we are able to live in the faith of Jesus Christ. Only in this way can we truly please God.

109. How is the weakness of human nature overcome?

The weakness of human nature, impaired by original sin, is overcome by grace, so that one can live with holiness in the faith of Jesus Christ.

THE BIBLE . . .

✠ *And now it is no longer I who live, but it is Christ who lives in me. The life I live now in the flesh I live by faith in the Son of God who loved me and gave himself up for me.* (Gal 2:20)

VATICAN COUNCIL II . . .

▲ Since man's freedom has been damaged by sin, only by the aid of God's grace can he bring such a relationship with God into full flower. *(Church in the Modern World, 17)*

EXPLANATION . . .

● **Because of his love for us Jesus regained grace for all and showed us what it means to be children of God. St. John says, "For God so loved the world that he gave his only Son, so that everyone who believes in him may not perish but may attain eternal life" (Jn 3:16). Now with the help of the grace of Jesus Christ we can give a free answer to God's call to love and serve him.**

Jesus said, "Amen, Amen, I say to you, everyone who sins is a slave of sin. A slave does not remain in a household forever, but a son remains in it forever. Therefore, if the Son sets you free, you then will truly be free" (Jn 8:34-36).

110. What is the teaching of the Church concerning freedom?

Since freedom can be reduced because of psychological difficulties or external conditions, the Church states that conditions most favorable to the exercise of genuine human freedom must be promoted, not only for our temporal welfare but also for the higher good of grace and eternal salvation.

VATICAN COUNCIL II . . .

▲ The Christian faithful, in common with all other men, possess the civil right not to be hindered in leading their lives in accordance with their consciences. Therefore, a harmony exists between the freedom of the Church and the religious freedom which is to be recognized as the right of all men and communities and sanctioned by constitutional law. *(Rel. Freedom, 13)*

EXPLANATION . . .

● **The Church knows that freedom, even when assisted by divine grace, can be influenced by grave difficulties and external conditions that may diminish freedom. For this reason she is solicitous both to**

educate for and to foster genuine freedom, and also to bring about suitable conditions so that freedom will be able to be truly and justly exercised. For here it is a question not only of promoting a good that belongs to this life on earth, but also of a duty that ultimately serves the good of grace and of salvation.

111. What is the role of the Church regarding freedom?

The Church (1) will seek to communicate a true sense and appreciation of freedom, (2) will defend freedom against unjust force of every kind, (3) and will summon Christians to work together with all people of good will to safeguard freedom.

VATICAN COUNCIL II . . .

▲ This Vatican Council declares that the human person has a right to religious freedom. This freedom means that all men are to be immune from coercion on the part of individuals or of social groups and of any human power, in such wise that no one is to be forced to act in a manner contrary to his own beliefs, whether privately or publicly, whether alone or in association with others, within due limits. *(Religious Freedom, 2)*

EXPLANATION . . .

● **(1) The Church claims that our response to God in faith must be free. She always encourages an appreciation of freedom.**

(2) The Church states that no one is to be forced to embrace the Christian faith against their will. The Church claims freedom for herself as a society of people who have the right to live according to the Christian Faith, which leads to our welfare on earth and eternal salvation in eternity.

(3) The Church urges Christians to work earnestly in the temporal sphere, so that as far as possible the best conditions may be established for the right exercise of freedom. They have this duty in common with all people of good will. Yet they are to promote freedom especially for the spiritual good that will be derived from it, that is, to lead humankind to an eternal union with God.

DISCUSSION QUESTIONS

1. Why is it a part of our dignity to be free? (107)
2. How has our freedom been harmed? (108)
3. How is the weakness of human nature overcome? (109)
4. What does the Church teach concerning freedom? (110)
5. How does the Church promote religious freedom? (111)

Part Five – SIN

Chapter 16

THE SINS OF MAN

112. What is our greatest problem in working out our salvation?

In working out our salvation, we find that the greatest problem is sin.

VATICAN COUNCIL II . . .

▲ The Lord himself came to free and strengthen man, renewing him inwardly and casting out that "prince of this world" (Jn 12:31) who held him in the bondage of sin (cf. Jn 8:34). For sin has diminished man, blocking his path to fulfillment. *(Church in the Modern World, 13)*

EXPLANATION . . .

● **Sin is refusing to let God have his way in our lives. The sinner wants to live without regard for God's will and chooses whatever will make him happy even though it does not fit into God's plan. He fails to trust God completely. But working out our salvation means doing God's will.**

113. Why is original sin one's first obstacle to salvation?

Although we were made by God in a state of holiness, from the very dawn of history we abused our liberty, at the urging of the Evil One. We set ourselves against God and sought to find fulfillment apart from God.

THE BIBLE . . .

✠ *Therefore sin entered the world as the result of one man, and death as a result of sin, and thus death has afflicted the entire human race inasmuch as everyone has sinned. (Rom 5:12)*

VATICAN COUNCIL II . . .

▲ Although he was made by God in a state of holiness, from the very onset of his history man abused his liberty, at the urging of the Evil One. Man set himself against God and sought to attain his goal apart from God. Although men knew God, they did not glorify him as God, but their senseless minds were darkened and they served the creature rather than the Creator (cf. Rom 1:21-25). *(Church in the Modern World, 13)*

EXPLANATION . . .

● God wanted us to cooperate with him in making the earth a well-ordered home for the human race. We were to enjoy its fruits and use it well. Humankind was the crown of God's creation; of all on earth they alone could give back to God the love which God first gave to the world. God wanted us to live as his family, united to each other and to himself in love. Neither sickness, death, ignorance, weakness, nor any other evil thing was to disturb the unity of this family.

In his disobedience, Adam rejected God's care and determined to search for happiness in his own way, not God's. He failed to surrender himself entirely to his Father in heaven. Thus original sin proved to be man's first obstacle to salvation.

114. What are the effects of original sin?

Human nature so fallen, (1) stripped of the grace that clothed it, (2) injured in its own natural powers, and (3) subjected to the dominion of death, is transmitted to all people. Thus the sin of humankind is very great, has caused sorrow and ruin, and weighs down on every one.

VATICAN COUNCIL II . . .

▲ In the course of history, the use of temporal things has been marred by serious vices. Affected by original sin, men have frequently fallen into many errors concerning the true God, the nature of man, and the principles of the moral law.

This has led to the corruption of morals and human institutions and not rarely to contempt for the human person himself. *(Apostolate of the Laity, 7)*

What divine revelation makes known to us agrees with experience. Examining his heart, man finds that he has inclinations toward evil too, and is engulfed by manifold ills which cannot come from his good Creator. Often refusing to acknowledge God as his beginning, man has disrupted also his proper relationship to his own ultimate goal as well as his whole relationship toward himself and others and all created things. *(Church in the Modern World, 13)*

EXPLANATION . . .

● (1) Adam's sin cut him off from God. He was stripped of the grace God had given him.

(2) His human nature was injured in its natural powers.

(3) When Adam sinned, sickness and the certainty of death entered his life. Adam's descendants suffered in the same ways: they were not able to experience living union with God; they failed in their respect for each other; their bodies were afflicted with the evils which accompany sickness and death.

Sin began when man first refused to be dependent upon God. The effect of this first sin was death and being separated from God. Therefore we are born into this world separated from our loving Father and subject to death. This situation is called "original sin."

The main sign of sin in the world is rejecting God. Sin brought death and especially the death of Jesus Christ who came to give life. Other signs of our sinful condition are war, poverty, hunger, hatred of people, violence, and other injustices.

All of us except Jesus are subject to original sin. In God, the Son can never be separated from the Father. Also, by a special grace Mary was born free of original sin. This grace is called the "immaculate conception."

115. What is personal sin?

Personal sin is that committed by the individual. By it a person, acting knowingly and deliberately, violates the moral law.

VATICAN COUNCIL II . . .

▲ Pulled by manifold attractions man is constantly forced to choose among them and renounce some. Indeed, as a weak and sinful being, he often does what he would not, and fails to do what he would (cf. Rom 7:14ff). *(Church in the Modern World, 10)*

EXPLANATION . . .

● **Sin is saying "no" to God. We sin when we refuse God's love and turn down his invitation to give of ourselves to God and others. We sin through personal acts of selfishness that cause harm to others or ourselves. But we often sin by not doing something—by refusing to move out of self toward God or to others. We can express sin in our thought, word, deed, or omission. The action must be a conscious and deliberate violation of the moral law.**

116. What are the effects of personal sin?

By committing personal sin, the sinner (1) fails in love of God; (2) turns away from, or even back from, his lifetime goal of doing God's will; (3) may even, by serious offense (mortal sin), break his relationship with the Father.

VATICAN COUNCIL II . . .

▲ Christians throughout history have always regarded sin not only as a transgression of divine law but also—though not always in a direct and evident way—as contempt for or disregard of the friendship between God and man (cf. Isa 1:2-3), just as they have regarded it as a real and unfathomable offense against God and indeed an ungrateful rejection of the love of God shown us through Jesus Christ, who called his disciples friends and not servants (cf. Jn 15:14-15). *(Apostolic Constitution on Indulgences, Paul VI, Jan. 1, 1967, 2)*

The very existence and the gravity of the punishment [of sin] enable us to understand the foolishness and malice of sin and its harmful consequences. *(Ibid., 3)*

EXPLANATION . . .

● **(1) Mortal sin is a rejection of God which destroys the life shared between God and the sinner. We can lose God's life regained for us by our Redeemer Jesus Christ. A serious violation of the law of God is called a mortal sin, a deadly sin, because it destroys God's life, grace, in** the human soul. A less serious sin (venial sin) is a lesser refusal by which one fails to do what God asks. It is a small violation of the law of God and does not deprive the soul of God's life, but it is a weakening of love for God and a damage to self and others. Venial sins open the way to serious sins.

(2) Sin is refusing to let God have his way in our life. We turn away from God because we want to live without regard for his will. We choose whatever we think will make us happy even though it does not fit into God's plan for our eternal happiness. We fail to trust God completely when we sin. Serious sin makes us unhappy and sometimes even slaves to sin. Jesus said, "Everyone who commits sin is a slave of sin" (Jn 8:34).

(3) The effect of mortal sin is separation from God and damage to ourselves and others. If we do not wish to change and continue to refuse to do what God wants us to do, the separation from God lasts. The Church calls this permanent separation from God "hell."

117. What is necessary to make a sin serious?

The Christian must have (1) clear knowledge of right and wrong, (2) so as to be able to choose with an informed conscience to love God and avoid offending him, and (3) the matter must be grave.

VATICAN COUNCIL II . . . *(Church in the Modern World, 17)*

▲ Man's dignity demands that he act according to a knowing and free choice that is personally motivated and prompted from within, not under blind internal impulse nor by mere external pressure. Man achieves such dignity when, emancipating himself from all captivity to passion, he pursues his goal in a spontaneous choice of what is good, and procures for himself, through effective and skillful action, apt helps to that end.

EXPLANATION . . .

● (1) Those who commit sin must realize what they are doing and that it is a serious offense against God.

(2) There must be full consent of the will. A person acting under any circumstance which deprives them of free will would not be guilty of mortal sin.

(3) The offense in itself must be serious, that is, something that has been forbidden or commanded by God under pain of losing his friendship.

The Good Shepherd finds the sheep which has strayed. He brings the sinner back to his fold.

118. What should the sinner be aware of when seeking forgiveness from God?

The sinner should remember (1) the sufferings and the death on the cross which Christ endured to destroy the effects of sin, (2) the power of grace which is greater than that of sin, and (3) the superabundant love of God which restores the penitents and draws them toward salvation.

VATICAN COUNCIL II . . .

▲ No one is freed from sin by himself and by his own power, no one is raised above himself, no one is completely rid of his sickness or his solitude or his servitude. On the contrary, all stand in need of Christ, their model, their mentor, their liberator, their Savior, their source of life. *(Missionary Activity of the Church, 8)*

EXPLANATION . . .

● **(1) Jesus Christ in his perfect love for us died on the cross to make up for our personal sins and to regain for us the life of grace and to make up for the sin of Adam. Sin is an offense against God. Only God can forgive our sins. God chose his Son to be the one to suffer and to die for our sins. Jesus is called our Savior because he saved us from sin. He is called our Redeemer because he paid the price for us; he bought us back.**

(2) In the sacrament of Penance Christ meets sinners, forgives their sins, and gives them again the peace that belongs to God's children. He also gives them added power of grace to overcome sin in the future. He gives them the strength to be faithful to God's law of love: to love God with all their heart, and their neighbor as themselves for the love of God. Jesus gives sinners the help they need to forgive their brothers and sisters even as Christ has forgiven them, to root grudges out of their life and to gain the ability to work in harmony with others in God's family.

(3) Christ wants his people to be one even as he and his Father are one. He told the first members of the Church that they had to love one another even as he loved them. Sin weakens this unity by causing disharmony and division. As the Good Shepherd, Christ knows his sheep. When one strays, he goes out in search of it. Finding it, he places it on his shoulders and returns rejoicing to the fold. This shows the joy which Christ feels when a sinner has a change of heart.

Especially in the sacrament of Penance Christ and the Church come to us with pardon and peace. Having sought us out, Jesus forgives our sins and restores us to the happiness of God's family. The priest, in Christ's name and in the name of all who are incorporated in Christ, welcomes us back to the full friendship and joy of the Church.

But Christ and the Holy Spirit expect us to be sorry for our sins and to have a change of heart. When we encounter Christ in this sacrament, we pledge to reverse our sinful ways. We promise to make genuine moral improvements in our lives. A continual conversion to Christ and his Church is required of us. We must continue to fight our sinful desires and refrain from whatever causes us to hurt God's family.

DISCUSSION QUESTIONS

1. What is sin? (112)
2. How did man abuse his liberty? (113)
3. What are the effects of original sin? (114)
4. What is personal sin? (115)
5. What are the effects of personal sin? (116)
6. What is mortal sin? (116)
7. What is venial sin? (116)
8. What is necessary to make a sin serious? (117)
9. What should give us hope in seeking forgiveness of our sins? (118)

Part Six – MORAL LIFE

Chapter 17

THE MORAL LIFE OF CHRISTIANS

119. What did Christ direct his apostles to teach?

Christ directed his apostles to teach the observance of everything that he had commanded them when he said, "Teach them to observe all that I have commanded you" (Mt 28:20).

VATICAN COUNCIL II . . .

▲ In his gracious goodness, God has seen to it that what he had revealed for the salvation of all nations would abide perpetually in its full integrity and be handed on to all generations. Therefore Christ the Lord, in whom the full revelation of the supreme God is brought to completion (cf. 2 Cor 1:20; 3:13; 4:6), commissioned the apostles to preach to all men that Gospel which is the source of all saving truth and moral teaching, and to impart to them heavenly gifts. *(Divine Revelation,* 7)

What was handed on by the apostles includes everything which contributes toward the holiness of life and increase in faith of the People of God; and so the Church, in her teaching, life and worship, perpetuates and hands on to all generations all that she herself is, all that she believes. *(Divine Revelation,* 8)

EXPLANATION . . .

● **Before Jesus departed from this earth, he gave special instructions to his apostles. He told his apostles to go forth and preach the gospel of the New Covenant to every nation, for he intended his kingdom, the Church, for all people. They gathered those who believed into communities, uniting them to Christ and one another through God's holy word and the Mass.**

120. What must we do if we are to respond generously to God's love?

To respond to God's love we must (1) believe the things which are to be believed, and (2) do or avoid those things which are to be done or avoided.

VATICAN COUNCIL II . . .

▲ "The obedience of faith" (Rom 13:26; cf. 1:5; 2 Cor 10:5-6) "is to be given to God who reveals, an obedience by which man commits his whole self freely to God, offering the full submission of intellect and will to God who reveals" (Vatican I), and freely assenting to the truth revealed by him. To make this act of faith, the grace of God and the interior help of the Holy Spirit must proceed and assist, moving the heart and turning it to God, opening the eyes of the mind and giving "joy and ease to everyone in assenting to the truth and believing it" (Vatican I). To bring about an ever deeper understanding of revelation the same Holy Spirit constantly brings faith to completion by his gifts. *(Divine Revelation, 5)*

Only by the light of faith and by meditation on the word of God can one always and everywhere recognize God in whom "we live, and move, and have our being" (Acts 17:28), seek his will in every event, see Christ in everyone whether he be a relative or a stranger, and make correct judgments about the true meaning and value of temporal things both in themselves and in their relation to man's final goal. *(Apostolate of the Laity, 4)*

EXPLANATION . . .

● **(1) The Church continues teaching what Jesus taught and studies the changing conditions of human life in the light of the gospel so as to help people to know what God asks of them. The teaching of the Church includes all the truths of faith which Jesus taught.**

(2) The teaching of the Church also includes all those things which are to be done or avoided in order that the followers of Jesus might live

the Christian life according to his will. It is our duty as Christians to respond to God's love by faith and action. If we truly love God we shall endeavor to do his holy will.

121. What is Christian morality?

Christian morality is a positive response to God, by growing in the new life given through Jesus Christ. It defines a way of living worthy of a human being and an adopted child of God.

VATICAN COUNCIL II . . .

▲ The Gospel of Christ constantly renews the life and culture of fallen man; it combats and removes the errors and evils resulting from the permanent allurement of sin. It never ceases to purify and elevate the morality of peoples. *(Church in the Modern World, 58)*

EXPLANATION . . .

● **The Church expresses her teaching by stating ideals, by making judgments about the morality of certain actions, and by making laws concerning human behavior. It is the will of God that we become sharers in Christ's risen life and children in his holy family. We are to live a life worthy of members of a community of worshipers and believers, destined for heaven.**

122. How is Christian morality supported?

Christian morality is supported and guided by the grace and gifts of the Holy Spirit.

THE BIBLE . . .

✠ *Such hope will not be doomed to disappointment, because the love of God has been poured into our hearts through the Holy Spirit that has been given to us.* (Rom 5:5)

VATICAN COUNCIL II . . .

▲ Now, the gifts of the Spirit are diverse: while he calls some to give clear witness to the desire for a heavenly home and to keep that desire green among the human family, he summons others to dedicate themselves to the earthly service of men and to make ready the material of the celestial realm by this ministry of theirs. Yet he frees all of them so that by putting aside love of self and bringing all earthly resources into the service of human life they can devote themselves to that future when humanity itself will become an offering accepted by God (cf. Rom 15:16). *(Church in the Modern World, 38)*

EXPLANATION . . .

● **So that we may live well as God's children, the Holy Spirit helps us in many ways. He persuades us to hold each other in high esteem. He gives us a common bond of friendship so that we may become a community of love, united in Christ because we share his life of grace. He causes us to have the desire and power to do things pleasing to our heavenly Father. The Spirit makes clear what Jesus taught us in the gospel, and he gives us help to fight Satan and remain true to Jesus and the Catholic Church to the end.**

These activities of the Spirit are sometimes called actual graces. Without these helps it is impossible to do anything toward our own salvation or the salvation of others.

123. What is conscience?

Conscience is a personal judgment that something is right or wrong because of the will and law of God. Conscience is not feeling nor self-will although these may affect the degree of culpability (guilt).

VATICAN COUNCIL II . . .

▲ In the depths of his conscience, man detects a law which he does not impose upon himself, but which holds him to obedience. Always summoning him to love good and avoid evil, the voice of conscience when necessary speaks to his heart: do this, shun that. For man has in his heart a law written by God; to obey it is the very dignity of man; according to it he will be judged (cf. Rom 2:5-16).

Conscience is the most secret core and sanctuary of a man. There he is alone with God, whose voice echoes in his depths. In a wonderful manner conscience reveals that law which is fulfilled by love of God and neighbor (cf. Mt 22:37-40; Gal 5:14). *(Church in the Modern World, 16)*

EXPLANATION . . .

● **Conscience is an awareness of what God is asking us to do at a given time. It helps us to know when we act sinfully. Our conscience tells us**

whether an action is right or wrong, a mortal or a venial sin. Our conscience is our mind judging on moral matters. Therefore, it must be instructed. We must learn from Christ, teaching through his Church.

124. Must each person follow his conscience?

Christian freedom needs to be guided in questions of day-to-day living. Each person must have a right conscience and follow it.

VATICAN COUNCIL II . . .

▲ In fidelity to conscience, Christians are joined with the rest of men in the search for truth, and for the genuine solution to the numerous problems which arise in the life of individuals from social relationships. Hence the more right conscience holds sway, the more persons and groups turn aside from blind choice and strive to be guided by the objective norms of morality. Conscience frequently errs from invincible ignorance without losing its dignity. The same cannot be said for a man who cares but little for truth and goodness, or for a conscience which by degrees grows practically sightless as a result of habitual sin. *(Church in the Modern World, 16)*

EXPLANATION . . .

● **The moral life of Christians is guided by the grace and gifts of the Holy Spirit. We do not always know whether our conscience is right. But we can train our conscience over a period of time by listening to the Word of God in the gospels and in the Church and by being attentive to the inspiration of the Holy Spirit within us. Our conscience can be so developed that it will learn to know the call of God in every situation and help us to respond faithfully to him.**

125. What is the duty of the teaching authority of the Church?

It is the duty of the teaching authority of God's Church, or Magisterium, to give guidance for applying the enduring norms and values of Christian morality to specific situations of everyday life.

VATICAN COUNCIL II . . .

▲ The Church is, by the will of Christ, the teacher of the truth. It is her duty to give utterance to, and authoritatively to teach that truth which is Christ himself, and also to declare and confirm by her authority those principles of the moral order which have their origins in human nature itself. *(Religious Freedom, 14)*

EXPLANATION . . .

● **Christian freedom needs to be ruled and directed in the specific circumstances of human life. Accordingly, the individual conscience of the faithful must be obeyed at all times, though it requires appropriate formation under the guidance and teaching of the universal magisterium whose duty it is to explain the whole moral law authoritatively, in order that it may rightly and correctly express the objective moral order.**

During the Second Vatican Council it was the Holy Spirit who guided the Fathers in their deliberations and final decisions.

126. What is the duty of the conscience of the Catholic Christian?

The conscience of the Catholic Christian must pay respectful and obedient attention to the teaching authority of God's Church.

VATICAN COUNCIL II . . .

▲ Although the individual bishops do not enjoy the prerogative of infallibility, they nevertheless proclaim Christ's doctrine infallibly whenever, even though dispersed through the world, but still maintaining the bond of communion among themselves and with the successor of Peter, and authentically teaching matters of faith and morals, they are in agreement on one position as definitively to be held. This is even more clearly verified when, gathered together in an ecumenical council, they are teachers and judges of faith and morals for the universal Church, whose definitions must be adhered to with the submission of faith. *(The Church, 25)*

EXPLANATION . . .

● **The authority of the Church is the right, power, and duty to govern the members of the Church. All authority comes from God for the well-being of those who are subject to authority. Our Lord entrusted his authority to the Church he founded. "All authority in heaven and on earth has been given to me. Go, therefore, and make disciples of all nations, baptizing them in the name of the Father, and of the Son, and of the Holy Spirit, and teaching them to observe all that I have commanded you" (Mt 28:18-20). Since the Church speaks to us in the name of God we must be respectfully obedient to her teaching.**

127. What is the teaching of the Church on obedience due to bishops?

In matters of faith and morals, the bishops speak in the name of Christ and the faithful are to accept their teaching and adhere to it with a religious assent of soul. The religious submission of will and of mind must be shown in a special way to the authentic teaching authority of the Roman Pontiff, even when he is not speaking *ex cathedra*.

VATICAN COUNCIL II . . .

▲ Bishops, teaching in communion with the Roman Pontiff, are to be respected by all as witnesses to divine and Catholic truth. In matters of faith and morals, the bishops speak in the name of Christ and the faithful are to accept their teaching and adhere to it with a religious assent. This religious submission of mind and will must be shown in a special way to the authentic Magisterium of the Roman Pontiff, even when he is not speaking *ex cathedra*; that is, it must be shown in such a way that his supreme Magisterium is acknowledged with reverence and the judgments made by him are sincerely adhered to, according to his manifest mind and will. *(The Church, 25)*

EXPLANATION . . .

● We serve God and his Church by fulfilling our obligations to honor, love, respect, and obey the Pope as the successor of St. Peter, our bishops, who are our shepherds, and our priests ordained for our spiritual service.

The integrity of the truth is ensured by the special assistance of the Holy Spirit whom Christ has given to his Church. Revelation is the whole complex of events and words through which God has manifested himself to us. As the Church lives by her faith she comes to a fuller and deeper understanding of it. The message must also be adapted to the changing historical needs of God's People. In this process there is great danger of misinterpretation and error. That is why the apostles were constantly concerned about keeping the message intact and preserving it from all deviations.

In view of the dangers inherent in the historical development of the faith, the Church needs special divine assistance if she is to preserve the truth intact and know for certain what she has to believe. Christ promised this assistance of the Holy Spirit to the apostles and through them to the Church. He said, "The Advocate, the Holy Spirit, whom the Father will send in my name, will teach you everything and remind you of all that I have said to you" (Jn 14:26).

The Church can speak with such authority because she knows that, thanks to the assistance of the Spirit promised by Christ, she cannot err when she believes or teaches a doctrine as belonging to the deposit of the faith, that is, "ex cathedra." This freedom from error is called "infallibility."

The Pope and bishops might be called the organs of that infallibility with which Christ has endowed his Church. When they teach infallibly, they represent the whole Church—not, however, as delegated by the faithful but by virtue of the authority received from Christ. Hence the faithful are to accept their teaching and adhere to it with a religious assent of soul.

128. What is the duty of the Christian concerning moral values which are absolute?

The Christian must know that there are moral values which are absolute and never to be disregarded or violated by anyone in any situation. Fidelity to them may require heroism of the sort we see in the lives of the saints.

VATICAN COUNCIL II . . .

▲ All must hold to the primacy of the objective moral order, that is, this order by itself surpasses and fittingly coordinates all other spheres of human affairs—the arts not excepted—even though they be endowed with notable dignity. For man, who is endowed by God with the gift of reason and summoned to pursue a lofty destiny, is alone affected by the moral order in his entire being. *(Media of Social Communication, 5)*

EXPLANATION . . .

● The conscience itself of Christians must be taught that there are norms which are absolute, that is, which bind in every case and on all people. That is why the saints gave witness to Christ through the practice of heroic virtues. Martyrs suffered even torture and death rather than deny Christ. St. John declared, "Dearly beloved, if our hearts do not condemn us, we can approach God with confidence and receive from him whatever we ask, because we obey his commandments and do whatever is pleasing to him" (1 Jn 3:21-22).

129. What does obedience to the Holy Spirit include?

Obedience to the Holy Spirit includes a faithful observance of the commandments of God, the laws of the Church, and just civil laws.

VATICAN COUNCIL II . . .

▲ Since this mission goes on and in the course of history unfolds the mission of Christ himself, who was sent to preach the gospel to the poor, the Church, prompted by the Holy Spirit, must walk in the same path on which Christ walked: a path of poverty and obedience, of service and self-sacrifice even to death, from which death he came forth a victor by his resurrection. *(Mission Activity of the Church, 5)*

EXPLANATION . . .

- Like the Father and Jesus, the Spirit is a Divine Person. He is the living flame of the infinite love between the Father and the Son. The Father and Son have sent the Spirit to bind us to themselves and to each other in sincere Christian love. Without the assistance of the Holy Spirit, we can do nothing toward our salvation. The Spirit gives us the power to make a lasting commitment to Christ, and also the help needed to keep that commitment.

  We should let the Spirit have his way with us. He will bend our wills and touch our hearts if we will let him. We ought to pray each day for the strength to say yes to what the Spirit wants to accomplish in us. Obedience to him includes a faithful observance of the commandments of God, the laws of the Church, and just civil laws.

130. What is the duty of a Christian if civil laws are not just?

Christian witness is especially powerful when it defends the values of God rather than those of the world.

Christians are bound to defend the values of God rather than of the world.

THE BIBLE . . .

✠ *"We must obey God rather than men!"* (Acts 5:29)

VATICAN COUNCIL II . . .

▲ Political authority, both in the community as such and in the representative bodies of the state, must always be exercised within the limits of the moral order and directed toward the common good with a dynamic concept of that good—according to the juridical order legitimately established or due to be established. When authority is so exercised, citizens are bound in conscience to obey. *(Church in the Modern World, 74)*

EXPLANATION . . .

● **Remembering that our Lord called us "the salt of the earth," "the light of the world," good Christians should take an interest in and participate in civic affairs. Only in this way can they expect to carry the principles of Christ into civic affairs. Christian witness must defend the values of God rather than those of the world. Peter and the apostles replied to the high priest as they stood before the Sanhedrin, "We must obey God rather than men!" (Acts 5:29).**

DISCUSSION QUESTIONS

1. What instructions did Jesus give his apostles? (119)
2. How should we respond to God's love? (120)
3. How does the Church express her teaching of morality? (121)
4. How does the Holy Spirit help us to live as God's children? (122)
5. What is conscience and what is its function? (123)
6. What is the duty of the Magisterium of the Church? (125)
7. Why must the conscience of the Catholic Christian obey the teaching authority of the Church? (126)
8. What are our obligations toward the Pope and bishops? (127)
9. What is infallibility? (127)
10. What is our duty concerning absolute moral values? (128)
11. What does obedience to the Holy Spirit include? (129)
12. What is our duty concerning unjust civil laws? (130)

Learn from ME for I am meek and humble of Heart

Chapter 18

THE PERFECTION OF CHRISTIAN LOVE

131. What is the special characteristic of Christian moral teaching?

The special characteristic of Christian moral teaching is its total relationship to the love of God, or charity.

VATICAN COUNCIL II . . .

▲ The greatest commandment in the law is to love God with one's whole heart and one's neighbor as oneself (cf. Mt 22:37-40). Christ made this commandment of love of neighbor his own. For he wanted to equate himself with his brethren as the object of this love when he said, "As long as you did it for one of these, the least of my brethren, you did it for me" (Mt 25:40). *(Apostolate of the Laity, 8)*

EXPLANATION . . .

● **The moral teaching of Jesus is summed up in the two commandments he gave his Church: "You shall love the Lord your God with all your heart, and with all your soul, and with all your mind, and with all your strength. . . . You shall love your neighbor as yourself" (Mk 12:30-31). Other words and examples of Jesus tell of how these commandments are to be practiced.**

132. Why is love of God the soul of morality?

Love of God is the soul of morality because (1) God is love. (2) In God's plan that love reaches out in Jesus Christ to unite all people in mutual love. (3) All commandments and norms for this moral teaching are summed up in faith working through charity.

THE BIBLE . . .

✠ *Owe nothing to anyone except the debt of love you owe one another. If you love your neighbor, you will have fulfilled the Law. The commandments, "You shall not commit adultery, You shall not kill, You shall not steal, You shall not covet," and every other commandment are all summed up in this one saying, "You shall love your neighbor as yourself." Love cannot result in any harm to the neighbor; therefore love is the fulfillment of the Law. (Rom 13:8-10)*

In Christ Jesus neither circumcision nor lack of circumcision is worth anything. All that matters is faith expressing itself through love. (Gal 5:6)

VATICAN COUNCIL II . . .

▲ "God is love, and he who abides in love, abides in God, and God in him" (1 Jn 4:16). God pours out his love into our hearts through the Holy Spirit, who has been given to us (cf. Rom 5:5); thus the first and most necessary gift is love, by which we love God above all things and our neighbor because of God. *(The Church, 42)*

EXPLANATION . . .

● (1) God loves us. He always has loved us and always will love us. He has loved us from the moment he thought of our creation. He will love us for all eternity. St. John tells us of the depth of God's love for each individual. "For, God so loved the world that he gave his only Son, so that everyone who believes in him may not perish but may attain eternal life" (Jn 3:16).

Because God loves every human being with an undying, deep love St. John goes so far as to call God "love." "Dearly beloved, let us love one another because love is from God. Everyone who loves is born of God and knows God. Whoever does not love does not know God, because God is love" (1 Jn 4:7-8).

God watches over us every moment of our existence. Every beat of our heart depends on him. God gave us all the good things in life that we have, our life, our health, our family, our friends, our possessions. God made us his children in Baptism and promised to grant us eternal life with him in heaven, if we are faithful to him.

He gives us the privilege of sharing his divine life through grace. He continues to grant us the blessings of the Catholic Church, especially through the sacraments and God's truth. Through his immense love for us he forgives our sins if we repent.

In speaking of the Father's love Jesus said, "Everyone who asks will receive, and those who seek will find, and to those who knock the door will be opened. Is there a father among you who would hand his son a snake when he asks for a fish, or hand him a scorpion when he asks for an egg? If you, then, despite your evil nature, know how to give good gifts to your children, how much more will the heavenly Father give the Holy Spirit to those who ask him!" (Lk 11:10-13).

The heavenly Father gives us God the Holy Spirit to live within us and guide us to keep in touch with the Father in prayer, to help us understand his words, and to make our life and love like that of Jesus. Before his departure for his death, Jesus said, "But when the Spirit of Truth comes, he will guide you into all the truth. . . . The Father himself loves you because you have loved me and have come to believe that I came from God" (Jn 16:13, 27).

Whenever we think of God's great love for us we ought to desire to love God in return. Our one aim in life should be to be united with God through love that expresses itself in faithful service. Our life must be a joyous life with God.

(2) Jesus Christ in his perfect love for us died on the Cross to make up for our personal sins and to regain for us the life of grace and eternal life with God. Christ is our mediator with God. God's love reaches us through Jesus Christ, the God-Man. Christ and his Father sent the Holy Spirit into the hearts of the apostles. The Spirit—the love of God in the Trinity—was God's supreme gift to the Church. The great work of the Spirit was to unite us into a community of love. He still incorporates us in Christ by bringing us many gifts.

His chief gift is his personal presence in those who believe and follow Christ. By means of his personal presence and the gift of sanctifying grace, the Spirit makes us pleasing to God and holy. Through sanctifying grace he makes us children in the family of God and unites us in faith and charity to Christ and to each other. As a community of believers, we become heirs of God's kingdom. This is God's plan for us, a plan that has its source in God's love.

(3) All commandments and norms of Christian morality are summed up in faith working through charity. St. Paul says, "In Christ Jesus neither circumcision nor lack of circumcision is worth anything. All that matters is faith expressing itself through love" (Gal 5:6). Charity is everything.

All of Christianity is love. His kingdom is love. We are created to love, grow through love, and finally find ourselves by loving. St. Paul said, "If in speaking I use human tongues and angelic as well, but do not have love, I am nothing more than a noisy gong or a clanging cymbal" (1 Cor 13:1).

133. What does responding freely and perfectly to God's Will mean?

Responding freely and perfectly to God and God's Will means (1) keeping the commandments and living in his love; (2) accepting and practicing the "new commandment" of charity.

VATICAN COUNCIL II . . .

▲ Indeed, in order that love, as good seed, may grow and bring forth fruit in the soul, all of the faithful must willingly hear the Word of God and accept his will, and must complete what God has begun by their own actions with the help of God's grace. These actions consist in the use of the sacraments and in a special way the Eucharist, frequent participation in the sacred action of the Liturgy, application of oneself to prayer, self-abnegation, lively fraternal service and the constant exercise of all the virtues. *(The Church, 42)*

EXPLANATION . . .

● (1) Jesus said, "As the Father has loved me, so have I loved you. Remain in my love" (Jn 15:9).

(2) One can tell the true Christian by the love he shows for others. Jesus said that this is how his followers can be identified. "I give you a new commandment: love one another. Just as I have loved you, so you should also love one another. This is how everyone will know that you are my disciples: if you love one another" (Jn 13:34-35).

Jesus washes the feet of his apostles and gives them his "new commandment" of love.

134. What is one's greatest responsibility and dignity?

One's greatest responsibility and their source of greatest dignity is, sustained by faith, to live a life of love of God and of others.

VATICAN COUNCIL II . . .

▲ Charity, as the bond of perfection and the fullness of the law (cf. Col 3:14; Rom 13:10), rules over all the means of attaining holiness and gives life to these same means. It is charity which guides us to our final end. It is the love of God and the love of one's neighbor which points out the true disciples of Christ. *(The Church, 42)*

Such a life [of union with Christ] requires a continual exercise of faith, hope and charity. *(Apostolate of the Laity, 4)*

EXPLANATION . . .

● The action of the Spirit of Christ is made clear when the peculiar characteristic of Christian moral teaching—which is love—is brought to light. All precepts and counsels of this moral teaching are summarized in faith working through love, and this is, as it were, its soul.

Jesus taught about God's way of life, that is, that God's life is love. God lives by forever giving himself. To belong to the kingdom means that we must live by love, too. Like Jesus, we must be willing to live for others.

St. John wrote: "God's love was revealed to us in this way: God sent his only Son into the world so that we might have life through him. This is what love is: not that we have loved God, but that he loved us and sent his Son as expiation for our sins. Beloved, since God loved us so much, we should love one another. . . . God abides in anyone who acknowledges that Jesus is the Son of God, and that person abides in God. We have come to know and to believe in the love that God has for us. God is love, and whoever abides in love abides in God, and God in him" (1 Jn 4:9-16).

We, therefore, are called to embrace, in faith, a life of charity toward God and others; in this lies our greatest responsibility and exalted moral dignity.

135. In what does one's holiness consist?

One's holiness, whatever their vocation or state of life may be, is the perfection of love of God.

VATICAN COUNCIL II . . .

▲ In the various classes and differing duties of life, one and the same holiness is cultivated by all who are moved by the Spirit of God, and who obey the voice of the Father and worship God the Father in spirit and in truth. These people follow the poor Christ, the humble and cross-bearing Christ in order to be worthy of being sharers in his glory. Every person must walk unhesitatingly according to his own personal gifts and duties in the path of living faith, which arouses hope and works through charity. *(The Church, 41)*

EXPLANATION . . .

● The life of Jesus shows us in a human way that God's life is a life of love. Father, Son, and Holy Spirit are forever giving themselves to each other. God asks us to be holy. To be holy means being like God. He wants us to be as much like him as possible. This means sharing more and more of our life with him so that he can complete the good work he began in us through his grace in Baptism when we first received his divine life and became his children.

Jesus reminded us of our obligation to be holy. "Strive to be perfect, just as your heavenly Father is perfect" (Mt 5:48). Our holiness is the perfection of love of God.

136. What is the importance of a religious vocation?

Accepting a religious vocation by men and women who show in this special and needed way their love of God and true service to humankind is important for humanity and for the Church.

VATICAN COUNCIL II . . .

▲ The holiness of the Church is fostered in a special way by the observance of the counsels proposed in the Gospel by our Lord to his disciples. An eminent position among these is held by virginity or the celibate state (cf. 1 Cor 7:32-34). *(The Church, 42)*

EXPLANATION . . .

• The religious state is expected to be the perfect following of Christ. It was instituted by our Lord, who in the gospel established it by counseling the practice of voluntary poverty, chastity, and obedience. Besides the profession of the three ordinary vows of religion, the observance of a rule of common life is an essential of the religious life.

Perfect love of God is the aim and ideal of the religious state. The religious state is a permanent condition of life, officially recognized as such by the Church, wherein a person binds himself or herself to strive after perfection.

God has called us to union with himself by holiness of life and the accomplishment of his work in the world. We can answer this call by the one theological virtue of charity—to love God and neighbor. Our apostolate is an expression of our love of God and consecration to him. Love is the energizing force of our witness in the world.

The perfection of Christian life essentially consists in love: first and foremost in the love of God, then in the love of neighbor. The whole life of a religious is to be one continuous act of love in the service of God and the Church. The apostolate of religious is to participate in the work of the Church. Hence their religious vocation is important for humanity and for the Church.

DISCUSSION QUESTIONS

1. What is the special characteristic of Christian morality? (131)
2. How does God show his love for us? (132)
3. How did Jesus show his love for us? (132)
4. How does the Holy Spirit show his love for us? (132)
5. Why is all Christianity summed up in love? (132)
6. How do we respond to God's will? (133)
7. Why is living a life of faith through love one's greatest responsibility? (134)
8. Why does one's holiness consist in the love of God? (135)
9. What is the religious state? (136)
10. Why is the religious vocation important? (136)

Chapter 19

DUTIES FLOWING FROM LOVE OF GOD AND OTHERS

137. Where are the duties flowing from love of God and others to be found?

The duties and obligations flowing from love of God and others are to be found within the overall framework of (1) the Ten Commandments of God, (2) the laws of the Church, (3) the Sermon on the Mount, especially the Beatitudes, (4) the spiritual and corporal works of mercy, (5) and the theological and moral virtues.

VATICAN COUNCIL II . . .

▲ Let man be convinced that obedience is the hallmark of the servant of Christ, who redeemed the human race by his obedience. *(Mission Activity of the Church*, 24)

EXPLANATION . . .

● **(1) The covenant or agreement between God and his people included the Ten Commandments as an essential part of the message of salvation to Moses. Like the first People of God we Christians accept the commandments as a part of our agreement with him. As loving sons and daughters we see the commandments as our response to God's love for us. By keeping the commandments we surrender ourselves in obedience to God and unite ourselves with him.**

All the Ten Commandments can be contained in two commandments of love. The first three commandments show us how we must love God; the last seven commandments show us how to love others for the love of God. The Ten Commandments of God are of special importance in teaching the specifics of morality. The Old Testament, the New Testament, and the long use of the Church testify to this.

(2) From time to time the Church has listed certain specific duties of Catholics. Some duties expected of Catholic Christians today are the laws of the Church, traditionally called precepts of the Church.

(3) The ***Beatitudes*** express some of the high standards of Christ's kingdom and the reward promised for living according to them. In the Sermon on the Mount Christ tells us how to attain happiness in this life. The reward promised in each of these Beatitudes is primarily heaven. But if we live according to the plan of Christ we shall have a foretaste of the happiness of heaven in this life.

Christ tells us that we will be happy by doing for his sake the very things which we think will make us unhappy. He tells us that we must not set our hearts on money; that we must forgive our enemies and love them; that we must avoid all sin; that we must be willing to suffer for his sake. Christ has not only told us how to live; he has shown us by his example. What is more, he gives us all the help to follow his example.

(4) Some of the most important *works of mercy* are to help convert the sinner, advise the doubtful, instruct the ignorant, comfort the sorrowful, bear wrongs patiently, pray for the living and the dead, feed the hungry, clothe the poor, support the homeless, visit the sick, and bury the dead.

(5) We would not be able to love God or one another as children of God without a special gift from God, the gift of charity. It is one of the great powers which God gives us with the gift of the divine life. God also gives us the power to believe in him and the power to hope in him. These are the virtues of faith, hope, and charity, called ***theological virtues*** because they refer to God.

The moral virtues are: "*prudence* [that] disposes the practical reason to discern, in every circumstance, our true good and to choose the right means for achieving it" (CCC 1835); "*justice*...consists in the constant and firm will to give their due to God and neighbor (CCC 1807); *temperance* that inclines us to govern our appetites according to what is pleasing to God; *fortitude* that inclines us to do what God desires even when it is difficult.

138. What is the obligation of the Christian toward God?

Toward God Christians have a lifelong obligation of love and service. (1) The Will of God must be put first in the scale of our personal values, and must be kept there throughout life; (2) we must have toward God the attitude of a child to an all-good, all-loving Father, and must never think or live as if independent of God; (3) we must gladly give to God genuine worship and true prayer, both liturgical and private; (4) we must not put anyone or anything in place of God (which is idolatry, superstition, witchcraft, occultism); (5) we must not blaspheme God nor perjure ourselves; (6) we must show respect for persons, places and things related specially to God; (7) atheism, heresy, and schism are to be rejected in the light of one's duties to God.

VATICAN COUNCIL II . . .

▲ The root reason for human dignity lies in man's call to communion with God. From the very circumstances of his origin man is already invited to converse with God. For man would not exist were he not created by God's love and constantly preserved by it; and he cannot live fully according to truth unless he freely acknowledges that love and devotes himself to his Creator. *(Church in the Modern World, 9)*

EXPLANATION . . .

● **(1) Our Lord's first concern was to give honor to his Father in heaven. Doing his Father's will, he said, was food for him. We who are rooted in Christ and share his divine life are to share also in his devotion to the Father. Like our eldest brother Christ, we should approach the Father with reverence and obedience. Our first aim in life should be to do his holy will in all things.**

(2) Adoration or worship is the high honor we owe to God because God is all-perfect and we depend entirely on him. We adore God because God in his high perfection has willed to create us, to keep us in existence, to watch over us as a father watches over his children, to forgive our sins and even to make us like himself in divine grace. Realizing God's infinite perfection and his love for us, we acknowledge our total dependence on him. Our attitude toward him should be one of a devoted child to an all-loving Father.

(3) The virtue of religion—the first of all moral virtues—enables us to render homage to God because submission is due to him. This virtue inclines us to acknowledge by acts of worship the rights of God as the Beginning and the Last End of all things. We fulfill a duty of justice which the law of nature itself requires.

The offering of sacrifice is the supreme visible and social act of adoration. Sacrifice is an outward sign which expresses the intimate sentiments of one's heart when we render worship to God. When we perform acts of piety and recite vocal prayers, the words and gestures are intended to express the thought and intentions of the soul.

We worship God by fulfilling the duties of our state in life, by public adoration of God at Mass, by learning what God teaches, by prayer and sacrifice, by believing in God, hoping in him, and loving him with all our heart, and by practicing acts of love toward those whom God created—our neighbors.

But adoration must not be outward alone; it must be from the heart. This is true worship, as Jesus told the Samaritan woman: "The hour is coming, indeed it is already here, when the true worshipers will worship the Father in Spirit and truth. Indeed it is worshipers like these that the Father seeks" (Jn 4:23).

(4) The *First Commandment* is: "I, the Lord, am your God. You shall not have other gods besides me." It binds us to adoration. We honor God by praising him, by serving him, and by offering sacrifice to him. The First Commandment also warns us against any action that would lead us away from the true adoration of the living God; neglecting to learn the truths God has taught, or refusing to believe these truths once we understand them; leaving God's Church when we know it is the true Church; giving in to superstitious practices by which we show belief that certain persons or things have powers that only God has.

(5) The *Second Commandment* is: "You shall not take the name of the Lord, your God, in vain." This commandment directs us to have respect for God's name and everything connected with that name. Peter, filled with the Holy Spirit, spoke to the leaders of the people of Israel, "This [Jesus] is 'the stone rejected by you, the builders, that has become the cornerstone.' There is no salvation in anyone else, nor is there any other name under heaven given to men by which we can be saved" (Acts 4:11-12).

We honor God's name by invoking God with reverence in our prayers. The Church praises the name of God in her liturgical prayers, especially at Mass. We honor God when we call upon God in an oath to witness the truth of our statement, or when we make a vow to follow God more closely as religious do.

To use the name of God irreverently is to sin against this commandment. To use God's name with insolence, hate, or abuse is a serious sin. We should have nothing to do with blasphemy, perjury, or any other irreverent treatment of God's name.

(6) When we speak with reverence of the Holy Father, bishops, priests, religious sisters, and brothers dedicated to God, we honor God. It is sinful to speak irreverently about those dedicated to God. Holy things dedicated to God, such as the Bible, the altar, rosaries, should be treated with respect.

(7) Atheism, heresy, and schism are to be rejected as a failure to fulfill our duties toward God. The greatest way the faithful can help the atheistic world in coming to God is by the witness of a life which agrees with the message of Christ's love and of a living and mature faith that is manifested by works of justice and charity.

The *Third Commandment* is: "Remember to keep holy the sabbath day." We are obliged to offer Mass each Sunday (or Saturday evening) and holy day of obligation. Christ expects us to unite our hearts with his as he and the Church adore the Father. We praise the Father for his great glory, thank him for his abundant goodness, and ask for his continued help. We ask pardon for our sins.

The Mass is the highest form of worship. Sunday is a weekly reminder of Christ's Easter victory and of the joy which God's People share with Christ. By resting from our usual work, we find it easier to join with other Christians in making Sunday a day of celebration and thanks for the triumph of Jesus Christ.

139. What is the obligation of the Christian toward his neighbor?

Like Christ, Christians will show love (1) by concern for the rights of their neighbors—freedom, housing, food, health, right to work; (2) by showing to all others the justice and charity of Christ— to reach out in the spirit of the Beatitudes to help all others, to build up a better society in the local community and justice and peace throughout the world. (3) Their judgment and speech concerning others are to be ruled by the charity due all sons and daughters of God. (4) They will respect and obey all lawful authority in the home, in civil society, and in the Church.

VATICAN COUNCIL II . . .

▲ The greatest commandment in the law is to love God with one's whole heart and one's neighbor as oneself (cf. Mt 22:37-40). Christ made this commandment of love of neighbor his own and enriched it with a new meaning. For he wanted to equate himself with his brethren as the object of this love when he said, "As long as you did it for one of these, the least of my brethren, you did it for me" (Mt 25:40). *(Apostolate of the Laity, 8)*

EXPLANATION . . .

● (1) The second great commandment of God is like the first because it springs from the same principle and motive. Immediately beside the great and fundamental law of the kingdom of God, "You shall love the Lord your God with all your heart," there is the command: "And your neighbor as yourself" (Lk 10:27). The norm for the love of God is the totality of the very depths and powers of the soul—"with all your heart, with all your soul, with all your strength, and with all your mind."

The norm for the love of neighbor is self-love—"as yourself." But our Lord raised that to the sphere of the divine when he commanded us to love our neighbor as he loved us. The Redeemer's love for us is without limit. St. Paul tells us: "Thus, God proved his love for us in that while we were still sinners Christ died for us" (Rom 5:8).

The commandment of love of neighbor founded in the Old Testament is carried over into the new dispensation, where it is renewed. It takes on a new, special relationship to Christ, the God-Man, for he declared that this commandment of fraternal love is his favorite commandment. It is his own commandment. "This is my commandment: love one another as I have loved you" (Jn 15:12). This love is the sign by which his disciples will be clearly recognized.

Today we are challenged to live our life in such a way that we will bear witness to God by serving the needs of others. As Christians we can serve our neighbor by personally taking care of their spiritual, physical, and social needs. We can serve others personally through the ministries of medicine, nursing, teaching, social work, and many activities that help others in one way or another. Perhaps we can in some way be of service in society in the fields of business, education, law, government, public health.

Since not every Christian can be a servant professionally, each should minister according to the gifts and talents he has received from God. St. Paul says, "There are different varieties of gifts, but the same Spirit. There are different kinds of service, but the same Lord. There are different forms of activity, but the same God who produces all of them in everyone. To each of us, the manifestation of the Spirit is given for the common good" (1 Cor 12:4-7).

(2) We must bring our Christian faith—its beautiful truths and wonderful ideals—into a way of life based on the spirit of the gospel. If we really believe in Jesus Christ we know that we must reshape our life to the gospel and the spirit of the Beatitudes. This is the Christian life.

The Church urges us to serve God by serving others after the example of Jesus Christ. After he had washed the feet of his disciples, Jesus said to them: "Do you understand what I have done for you? You call me 'Teacher' and 'Lord,' and rightly so, for that is what I am. So if I, your Lord and Teacher, have washed your feet you also should wash one another's feet. I have given you an example. What I have done for you, you should also do" (Jn 13:12-15).

The Church calls upon Christians to live for others as Jesus lived and died for all. Such a life calls for sacrifice and earnest effort, but it promises to make our Christian faith alive and real. The Church wishes us to have room in our hearts for all people so that we might labor with them to build up human society.

By friendship with others the People of God can become a sign and instrument of union with God and of the unity of all humankind. A life of service to others is the best way of letting people know that God is present in the world and that he loves all of us. God serves our needs and in this way makes known to us his fatherly love and concern.

The Bishops of the United States further explain concern for our others in these words: "A loving concern for others should not be narrow or isolated; it should be universal, unlimited. 'By means of missionary activity the Church unceasingly gathers and directs its forces toward its own growth. The members of the Church are impelled to carry on such missionary activity by reason of the love with which they love God, by which they desire to share with all men in the spiritual goods of both this life and the life to come' ***(Mission Activity of the Church, 7).***"

(3) God commands us to think kindly. Jesus said, "Do not judge, so that you in turn may not be judged. For you will be judged in the same way that you judge others, and the measure that you use for others will be used to measure you. Why do you take note of the splinter in your brother's eye but do not notice the wooden plank in your own eye?" (Mt 7:1-3).

Kindness is a very positive virtue. Its essence is the strength of a person's self-control and the conquest of their egoism. Its object is the giving of self to others. This interior disposition inclines a person to think kindly, to wish well and to do good.

The basis of every type of love is kind thinking. Kindness excludes malicious and suspicious thoughts—thoughts which ascribe evil intentions and vicious purposes to others, thoughts which put an evil interpretation on the gestures, actions, words and even silence of others.

Our speech concerning others must also be ruled by charity. The sin of uncharitable talk is a vicious destroyer of internal unity within any family. It violates truth, justice and love. Our Lord's new law of love demands that we avoid not only bodily injury to our neighbors but also angry and uncharitable words and feelings against them, for even these internal sins offend God.

(4) The ***Fourth Commandment*** of God is: "Honor your father and your mother." Authority is the right, power, and duty to govern the members of a family, the members of the Church or the citizens of a country. All authority comes from God. The authority of parents is from God. St. Paul says, "Children, obey your parents in the Lord, for it is only right that you should do so. 'Honor your father and your mother.' This is the first commandment that is connected with a promise: 'that it may go well with you and that you may have a long life on earth' " (Eph 6:1-3).

Even the authority of the government comes from God. St. Paul says, "Let everyone submit himself to the governing authorities, for all authority is derived from God, and whatever authorities exist have been instituted by God" (Rom 13:1).

Authority comes from God for the well-being of those who are subject to authority, not for the honor or gain of those exercising the right and duty of governing. Christians possessing authority should consider themselves the servants of those they govern.

Jesus said, "Whoever wishes to be great among you must be your servant and whoever wishes to be first among you must be your slave. In the same way the Son of Man did not come to be served but rather to serve and to give his life as a ransom for many" (Mt 20:26-27).

Jesus was obedient to Mary and Joseph. He respected civil and temple authorities as well. He paid taxes and obeyed the regulations which were set up for the good of the society in which he lived. In these matters Christ was really showing respect for his Father in heaven, for it is from him that all authority stems.

We who are members of the Mystical Body of Jesus are to imitate the reverence which he showed for those in authority. We are commanded to give our parents consideration and affection. As children we owe them obedience.

Like our brother Christ, we must also obey legitimate civil authorities. All just laws, whether or not they please us, are to be accepted as expressions of God's will. In a special way the laws of the Catholic Church represent God's will. The Risen Christ speaks to us through the Church. We should look upon Church laws as commands from God himself.

Christ exercised his authority over others with charity. The way in which he gave orders to his apostles and sent them forth was always respectful and kindly. He knew that the Father had entrusted them to him and that it was his responsibility to lead them safely back to the Father. We, whom the Father has called to share the life of Jesus Christ, must use authority in a responsible, kindly way as Christ himself did. Parents should understand that their children have been entrusted to them by our Father in heaven. They should instruct their children about Christ and his Church, and should teach them to love their neighbor.

Parents who fail to exercise right authority over their children, children who fail to obey and honor their parents, citizens who offend the common good by violating laws, are all in some way offending Christ.

The Samaritan dresses the wounds of the injured man. Jesus urges us to imitate this example of compassion.

140. What are some of the sins against neighbor?

(1) In the area of justice: it is sinful to be selfishly apathetic toward others in their needs, to violate the rights of others—to steal, deliberately damage another's good name or property, cheat, not to pay one's debts, and to show anger, hatred, racism and discrimination.

(2) In the area of God's gift of life: the Christian cannot be anti-life and must avoid sins of murder, abortion, euthanasia, genocide, indiscriminate acts of war, and immoral methods of family limitation.

(3) In the area of speech: sins of lying, detraction and calumny are forbidden.

(4) In the area of sexuality: the Christian is to be modest in behavior and dress; there can be no premarital sex, fornication, adultery, or other acts of impurity or scandal to others; one must remain chaste, repelling lustful desires and temptations, self-abuse, pornography and indecent entertainment of every description.

VATICAN COUNCIL II . . .

▲ Coming down to practical and particularly urgent consequences, this Council lays stress on reverence for man; everyone must consider his every neighbor without exception as another self, taking into account first of all his life and the means necessary to living it with dignity (cf. Jas 2:15-16), so as not to imitate the rich man who had no concern for the poor man Lazarus (cf. Lk 16:18-31).

In our times a special obligation binds us to make ourselves the neighbor of every person without exception, and of actively helping him when he comes across our path, whether he be an old person abandoned by all, a foreign laborer unjustly looked down upon, a refugee, a child born of an unlawful union and wrongly suffering for a sin he did not commit, or a hungry person who disturbs our conscience by recalling the voice of the Lord, "As long as you did it for one of these the least of my brethren, you did it for me" (Mt 25:40). *(Church in the Modern World, 27)*

EXPLANATION . . .

● (1) The *Seventh Commandment* of God is: "You shall not steal." The *Tenth Commandment* is: "You shall not covet anything that belongs to your neighbor." All the goods of this world came from a good God. He has put at our disposal more than enough of this world's goods. Material goods that God gives us are not for ourselves alone. He gave them for us and for our family, but also that we may help others, especially those in need.

By the Seventh and Tenth Commandments God forbids taking something that belongs to another against his reasonable wish. Stealing, depriving another of their money or property by deceiving them, fraud, deliberately damaging the property of another, not paying just debts, not making a reasonable effort to find the owner of an article we have found, depriving a laborer of a just wage, wasting the time, money, or property of an employer, depriving our family of needed money by gambling, drinking, or foolish spending are all violations of these two commandments. If the damage is not serious, the sin is venial.

The Bishops of the United States explain the serious obligation of social justice in these words: "Social justice is a constitutive element of the Christian message. Christians have a serious obligation, therefore, to give to other persons their basic human rights. Individually, and collectively with other members of the ecclesial community, Christians must act to change social institutions and structures which are oppressive and deny human beings their basic rights.

"Sins of omission such as standing by while institutions and structures deny freedom and dignity to their members, without participating in some way, politically or socially, to bring about their liberation, are forbidden.

"Listed are oppressive situations calling for social action: whatever violates the integrity of the human person, such as: terror, torture, mutilation, slavery, or unjust coercion; whatever insults human dignity, such as: subhuman living conditions, arbitrary imprisonment or deportation, inadequate health services, and neglect of the aging; exploitation of the worker; every type of discrimination, whether social, economic, or cultural, whether based on sex or religion; invasion of privacy, unequal educational opportunities, inordinate concentration of wealth, consumerism, excessive exploitation of natural resources, sexism, massive expenditures for military purposes, and discriminatory taxation."

(2) The *Fifth Commandment* of God is: "You shall not kill." This commandment directs us to care for our body, mind, and soul and to care for the body and soul of our neighbor. Our own life and our own body are the means God gives us to serve him, to serve ourselves, and to serve our neighbor. We must take care of our body, its life and health. We must practice Christian self-discipline in the use of food, alcohol, and tobacco.

Christ came to give life, not to take it away. His followers, accordingly, are to oppose whatever tends to destroy or abuse human life: murder, suicide, abortion, mercy-killing, bodily mutilation, excessive use of drugs, drunkenness, fighting, anger.

(3) The *Eighth Commandment* of God is: "You shall not bear false witness against your neighbor." A good name consists in the esteem with which a person is held by others and the mutual confidence result-

ing from it. Mutual confidence based on mutual respect is the foundation of all family life. Without them, doubt, mistrust, suspicion make their appearance to disrupt a family, community or society.

Every unjustified violation of a good name is a sin both when the uncharitable talk is based on truth, which is detraction, and when it is based on a lie, which is calumny. Calumny is the greater sin because not only justice and love, but also truth is violated.

Revealing a person's hidden faults, gossiping about a person's known faults, exaggerating their faults, telling tales about them are ways of damaging a person's reputation. It is never permitted to tell a lie, because every lie is an abuse of a sacred power given to us by God. Lies start quarrels, discord, even separate friends.

(4) The *Sixth Commandment* of God is: "You shall not commit adultery." The *Ninth Commandment* is: "You shall not covet your neighbor's wife."

The virtue of Christian chastity is the virtue by which Christians regulate the use of their sexual powers according to the law of God. A Christian consecrates soul and body to Jesus Christ in Baptism. One who violates chastity violates dedication to Christ. Sexual passion that is implanted in us by God as a sacred power, is something holy. It is something good in itself and important in God's plan of creation and providence. The misuse of it is evil.

The full use of sexual passion is a right and privilege of those who are validly married. Therefore, adultery, fornication, masturbation, and the fully deliberate desire of committing these acts are seriously wrong. Though it is impossible to rule out all evil thoughts and desires from our minds, we can, at least, refuse to welcome them. Unwelcomed desires, no matter how wrong they seem, cannot defile our heart.

141. What are the duties of the follower of Christ toward self?

The Christian must (1) be another Christ in the world, a living example of Christian goodness; (2) be humble and patient in the face of one's imperfections, as well as those of others; (3) show a Christlike simplicity toward material things and the affluence of our society; (4) be pure in words and action even in the midst of corruption.

VATICAN COUNCIL II . . .

▲ All the faithful of Christ are invited to strive for the holiness and perfection of their own proper state. Indeed they have an obligation to so strive. Let all then take care that they guide aright their own deepest sentiments of soul. Let neither the use of the things of this world nor attachment to riches, which is against the spirit of evangelical poverty, hinder them in their quest for perfect love. *(The Church*, 42)

EXPLANATION . . .

● **(1) No one has ever spent himself for others like Christ when he dwelt among us. Love for his Father was the mainspring of all he ever did. Jesus Christ is the source of genuine personal influence. In their life in the world Christians should endeavor to personify the love of Christ in such a warm and attractive way that others will be induced to copy it. They communicate to others an impartial and selfless love which is as strong and as true as the love of Christ. Their external conduct should be marked by a dignity worthy of a Christian. By their example they can spread the faith that is in them, especially through the charitable assistance of their neighbor.**

(2) Self-denial is imitation of Jesus. Having come down from heaven with the purpose of showing us the way to eternal life, Jesus followed no other way than that of the Cross. He suffered for us that we might walk in his steps. He said, "Anyone who wishes to follow me must deny himself, take up his cross, and follow me" (Mt 16:24).

The true way to holiness is to love God and our neighbor for God's sake, and to sacrifice ourselves in order to fulfill better this great Commandment and the counsels related to it. We sacrifice ourselves because we love, because we want to love still more and because God loves a cheerful giver. Our patience in the face of our own shortcomings and those of others pleases God more than our zeal; our sufferings borne for love of God produce more fruit than our activity; our failures accepted with renewed confidence in God lead more souls to him than our successes. All that matters is that God may be glorified and that souls may be saved, especially our own.

(3) Renunciation of earthly possessions is one of the first sacrifices Christ asks of those whom he calls to share his mission. A Christian will love a spirit of simplicity and dependence upon God as Christ did; he will see in poverty of spirit a key to genuine freedom, and will see in it a way to become Christlike. Christ declared, "Blessed are the poor in spirit, for theirs is the kingdom of God" (Mt 5:3).

In a world that seeks earthly riches and material things feverishly, there is urgent need for those who, by the example of their spirit of simplicity and detachment, bear witness to the teaching of Christ that things spiritual, supernatural and divine have the highest value. The witness of this Christlike simplicity in Christians devoted to the glory of God and the salvation of souls is an inspiration to Christians themselves who easily neglect this high ideal through their anxious care to provide for the material needs of their families.

(4) In these days, when sensual love and the pleasures of the flesh are emphasized as necessary for the full enjoyment of life, the example of chastity is particularly impressive. To this world, where the body and sensuality count for so much, the true Christian by a life of decency in word and action proves that purity is possible, fruitful, and ensures a greater freedom to serve the needs of others.

142. What are some of the capital sins the Christian must avoid?

To be guarded against are the capital sins (1) of pride, with its many manifestations; (2) of sloth—spiritual, intellectual and physical; (3) of envy of others' success and of their financial and material possessions; (4) of intemperance—lack of self-control, abuse of one's bodily health by indulgence in food, alcohol, drugs.

VATICAN COUNCIL II . . .

▲ This gospel announces and proclaims the freedom of the sons of God, and repudiates all the bondage which ultimately results from sin (cf. Rom 8:14-17); it has a sacred reverence for the dignity of conscience and its freedom of choice, constantly advises that all human talents be employed in God's service and men's, and, finally, commends all to the charity of all (cf. Mt 22:39). *(Church in the Modern World, 41)*

EXPLANATION . . .

● Temptation is an inducement to sin. Deliberate sin, whether mortal or venial, is preceded by an inducement to sin, which is called temptation. The sources of temptation are three: the world about us, the devil, and our own inclinations to sin. These inclinations are: pride, covetousness, lust, anger, gluttony, envy, and sloth. If we pray, God will always give us strength to overcome temptation. In order to avoid sin we must also avoid any person, place, or thing which in all probability will lead us into sin. We should pray in particular for the grace to guard against the principal sources of sin, especially pride, sloth, envy, and intemperance.

143. What will the thought of the duties flowing from the love of God and people help the Christian to do?

The thought of the duties and obligations flowing from the love of God and people will help the Christian to (1) form a right conscience, (2) choose always what is right, (3) avoid sin and the occasions of sin, and (4) live in this world according to the Spirit of Christ in love of God.

VATICAN COUNCIL II . . .

▲ All Christ's faithful, whatever be the conditions, duties and circumstances of their lives—and indeed through all these—will daily increase in holiness, if they receive all things with faith from the hand of their heavenly Father and if they cooperate with the divine will. In this temporal service, they will manifest to all the love with which God loved the world. *(The Church, 41)*

EXPLANATION . . .

● (1) In order to sanctify our actions, we must see to it that they are inspired by supernatural love. Love must rule and guide us in all our actions that our whole life may be directed to God. Love comes to us from God. It is the splendid prerogative of the children of adoption. Following the advice of St. Paul, we should be "rooted and grounded in love" (Eph 3:17). "Everything that you do should be done in love" (1 Cor 16:14).

St. John wrote these words to the early Christians: "I rejoiced greatly when some of the brethren arrived and related how faithful you are to the truth" (3 John 3). John means that we should regulate all our conduct in accordance with the views and intentions of God and in conformity with our state of life.

Our conscience tells us whether an action is right or wrong, a mortal or a venial sin. Our conscience is our mind judging on moral matters. Therefore, it must be instructed. We must learn from Christ, who teaches us through his Church. Only with the guidance of the Holy Spirit can we form a right conscience.

(2) We need the light of strength of actual grace to choose always what is right and to do it. Hence we should frequently pray to the Holy Spirit to guide and help us.

(3) We need the help of the Holy Spirit especially to avoid sin and the occasions of sin. Since the world about us, the devil, and our own inclinations to sin are so powerful in the face of our human weakness, we must put our confidence in the even greater power of God's grace.

(4) The great Commandment of love requires of us that we act toward God as his children and that we act toward others as brothers and sisters, children of the same Father, members of the Mystical Body of Christ. Our duties toward God and toward our neighbor are set forth especially in the Ten Commandments. If we love God we will keep the first three commandments; they tell us our duties toward God. If we love

ourselves and our neighbor we will keep the other seven commandments; they tell us our duties toward ourselves and our neighbors.

The Ten Commandments flow from our very nature as human beings. Because we were created by God and depend on him completely we must, as intelligent responsible beings, acknowledge that dependence. We must praise God, love him, believe him, and show reverence for his name. Because each human being has certain rights which they receive from God, we must respect those rights.

In studying these commandments we are studying the laws which tell us how we, as human beings, must act toward God and toward others. But, more than that, we as children of God are studying the laws which help us fulfill the great law of Love. We will then live in this world according to the Spirit of Christ in love of God.

DISCUSSION QUESTIONS

1. Where are the duties flowing from love of God and neighbor to be found? (137)
2. Why should our first aim in life be the will of God? (138)
3. What are our duties toward God in the First Commandment? (138)
4. What are our duties toward God in the Second Commandment? (138)
5. What are our duties toward God in the Third Commandment? (138)
6. In what does the second great commandment consist? (139)
7. How do we show our concern for the rights of our neighbor? (139)
8. How do we show to all the justice and charity of Christ? (139)
9. Why must we think kindly of others? (139)
10. In what does the Fourth Commandment consist? (139)
11. In what do the Seventh and Tenth Commandments consist? (140)
12. In what does the Fifth Commandment consist? (140)
13. In what does the Eighth Commandment consist? (140)
14. In what do the Sixth and Ninth Commandments consist? (140)
15. How can we be a living example of Christian goodness? (141)
16. How do we express humility and patience toward others? (141)
17. How do we show Christlike simplicity? (141)
18. How do we give an example of chastity? (141)
19. What is temptation? What are its sources? (142)
20. How can we sanctify our actions? (143)
21. How do we form a right conscience? (143)
22. How can we overcome temptation? (143)
23. What does the great Commandment of Love require of us? (143)

Part Seven – THE CHURCH

Chapter 20

THE CHURCH, THE PEOPLE OF GOD

144. What is the Church?

The Church is the new People of God, prepared for in the Old Testament and given life, growth, and direction by Christ in the Holy Spirit.

VATICAN COUNCIL II . . .

▲ Israel according to the flesh, which wandered as an exile in the desert, was already called the Church of God (Neh 13:1; cf. Num 20:4; Deut 23:1ff). So likewise the new Israel which while living in this present age goes in search of a future and abiding city (cf. Heb 13:14) is called the Church of Christ (cf. Mt 16:18). For he has bought it for himself with his blood (cf. Acts 20:28), has filled it with his Spirit and provided it with those means which benefit it as a visible and social union. *(The Church, 9)*

The Church has been seen as "a people made one with the unity of the Father, the Son and the Holy Spirit" (St. Cyprian). *(The Church, 4)*

EXPLANATION . . .

● God made Israel a sacred community, dearer to him than all other nations. They were to be the bearers of God's blessings to the world. Through them he planned to reunite a torn and divided people. So that

they would not lose heart during their trials, he reminded them that he was caring for them like a loving Father. These were the first People of God. Even though they sinned, God remained faithful to them. He brought them out of Egypt and fed them in the desert. He said that he would always care for them because they were his special possession. He asked them to accept his love and to be his children.

After Israel had wandered in the desert for forty years, God led them, despite their sins, into the land originally promised to Abraham. Although Israel as a whole failed in their devotion to God, a few remained faithful. They were the remnants of the once great Israel. They depended on God alone. Through them he would keep his promise to send the world a Savior who would gather all people into God's family.

Jesus, God's own Son, born of Mary, was a descendant of David. With these scattered fragments of Israel, he built a new kingdom intended for all peoples. He brought peace to his people and freed their souls from sin and from the sadness which sin brings. He is our Savior.

To proclaim the Good News of salvation to all people everywhere in all time Jesus formed into one body his followers, the community of believers, the People of God. He called this body his Church. This was to be the new People of God.

145. How did the Church have its origin?

The Church is the work of God's saving love in Christ. Founded by Christ, it had its origin in his death and resurrection.

VATICAN COUNCIL II . . .

▲ The mystery of the holy Church is manifest in its very foundation. The Lord Jesus set it on its course by preaching the Good News, that is, the coming of the kingdom of God, which, for centuries, had been promised in the Scriptures: "The time is fulfilled, and the kingdom of God is at hand" (Mk 1:15; cf. Mt 4:17). In the words, in the works, and in the presence of Christ, this kingdom was clearly open to the view of men. *(The Church, 5)*

It was from the side of Christ as he slept the sleep of death upon the cross that there came forth "the wondrous sacrament of the whole Church." *(Sacred Liturgy, 5)*

EXPLANATION . . .

- To proclaim the message of salvation, to extend his kingdom, to be present in the world for all people, to teach us, to shepherd us, and to pour out his grace upon us Jesus entrusted to his twelve apostles the power, right, and duty in his Church to teach, to guide and to sanctify all people. Before ascending into heaven Jesus said to his apostles, "All authority in heaven and on earth has been given to me. Go, therefore, and make disciples of all nations, baptizing them in the name of the Father, and of the Son, and of the Holy Spirit, and teaching them to observe all that I have commanded you. And behold, I am with you always, to the end of the world." (Mt 28:18-20).

Through his death and resurrection, Jesus has earned for us the privilege of belonging to God's holy family. To enter that family we need sanctifying grace, a sharing in the life of Christ. We first get sanctifying grace when we are baptized.

By the power of the resurrection, we are inserted into the Mystical Body of Christ. Incorporated in Christ, we are no longer under the dominion of sin; with him we are heirs of heaven; we, like him, shall rise from the dead. Thus the Church had its beginning in the death and resurrection of Jesus.

The Church officially began when the Holy Spirit entered into the followers of Jesus and initiated them into the life of God. This happened on the day of Pentecost, a Jewish holy day. After his resurrection Jesus showed himself to his closest friends and others of his followers. When they came to believe that he had really conquered death, he withdrew his visible presence and lives on hidden in his Father. On Pentecost he sent his Spirit and life upon his followers as he had promised. The followers of Jesus announced to everybody the Good News of what Jesus had done and invited their hearers to believe in him and live by his Spirit.

146. What are the gifts of God to the Church?

In the Catholic Church are found (1) the deposit of faith, (2) the sacraments, and (3) the ministries inherited from the apostles.

VATICAN COUNCIL II . . .

▲ Jesus Christ, then, willed that the apostles and their successors—the bishops with Peter's successors at their head—should preach the Gospel faithfully, administer the sacraments, and rule the Church in love. It is thus, under the action of the Holy Spirit, that Christ wills his people to increase, and he perfects his people's fellowship in unity: in their confessing the one faith, celebrating divine worship in common, and keeping the fraternal harmony of the family of God. *(Ecumenism*, 2)

EXPLANATION . . .

● **(1) To carry on Christ's teaching the apostles were given the power and duty to teach Christ's doctrine to the world. They were appointed by Christ to be our shepherds or spiritual rulers so that through them and their successors he would lead us to the kingdom of heaven. Jesus said, "Whoever listens to you, listens to me, and whoever rejects you rejects me. And whoever rejects me rejects the one who sent me" (Lk 10:16). "Amen, I say to you, whatever you bind on earth shall be bound in heaven, and whatever you loose on earth shall be loosed in heaven" (Mt 18:18).**

(2) Christ taught the apostles that his grace was to be given to God's people through them. Through the apostles he would forgive sins. "If you forgive anyone's sin, they are forgiven. If you retain anyone's sins, they are retained" (Jn 20:23).

Through the apostles Christ would give his body and blood to the world. "Then he took bread and after giving thanks he broke it and gave it to them, saying, 'This is my body which will be given for you. Do this in memory of me.' And he did the same with the cup after supper, saying, 'This cup is the new covenant in my blood, which will be poured out for you' " (Lk 22:19-20).

He said to his apostles, "Go, therefore, and make disciples of all nations, baptizing them in the name of the Father, and of the Son, and of the Holy Spirit" (Mt 28:19).

Through the apostles and their successors, to whom these powers were entrusted, the Church administers the sacraments for the salvation of God's people.

(3) With the powers given them by Christ the apostles were to be his witnesses in the world. He said to them before ascending into heaven, "You will receive power when the Holy Spirit comes upon you, and then you will be my witnesses not only in Jerusalem, but throughout Judea and Samaria, and indeed to the farthest ends of the earth" (Acts 1:8).

Jesus continued, through his apostles, to be king, priest, and teacher to his people. The apostles gathered believers into communities and united them to Christ and to each other. The Catholic Church inherited these ministries from the apostles.

147. What is the Church able to do through these gifts of God?

Through these gifts of God, the Church is able to act and grow as a community in Christ, serving humankind and giving us his saving word and activity.

VATICAN COUNCIL II . . .

▲ In the human nature united to himself the Son of God, by overcoming death through his own death and resurrection, redeemed man and remolded him into a new creation (cf. Gal 5:15; 2 Cor 5:17). By communicating his Spirit, Christ made his brothers, called together from all nations, mystically the components of his own Body. In that Body the life of Christ is poured into the believers who, through the sacraments, are united in a hidden and real way to Christ who suffered and was glorified. *(The Church,* 7)

EXPLANATION . . .

● **Peter was Christ's chief ambassador on earth. The whole Church was entrusted to his care. The apostles shared their responsibility with others, called bishops. Today Christ continues, through his bishops, to be king, priest, and teacher to his Church.**

Priests share in the powers of Christ through ordination to the sacred priesthood. The Catholic priesthood has been handed down in the Catholic Church in an unbroken line from Christ and the apostles till the present day.

148. How does the Church share in the prophetic office of Christ?

Assembled by God's Word, the Church accepts that Word and witnesses to it in every part of the globe.

VATICAN COUNCIL II . . .

▲ When Jesus, who had suffered the death of the cross for humankind, had risen, he appeared as the one constituted as Lord, Messiah, and eternal Priest (cf. Acts 2:36; Heb 5:6; 7:17-21), and he poured out on his disciples the Spirit promised by the Father (cf. Acts 2:33). From this source the Church, equipped with the gifts of her Founder and faithfully guarding his precepts of charity, humility and self-sacrifice, receives the mission to proclaim and to spread among all peoples the kingdom of Christ and of God and to be, on earth, the initial budding forth of that kingdom. *(The Church, 5)*

EXPLANATION . . .

● **Through ordination of bishops and priests the powers of Jesus Christ have been handed down in the Catholic Church for two thousand years. Bishops and priests are those in Christ's Mystical Body who have the authority to teach for Christ, to shepherd his flock, and to dispense his graces to the world.**

Christ lives and works through his bishops and priests in his Church. He said the work of his Church would go on even to the end of the world. "Go, therefore, and make disciples of all nations, . . . teaching them to observe all that I have commanded you. And behold, I am with you always, to the end of the world" (Mt 28:19-20).

149. Why is the Church missionary?

The Church is missionary by its very nature, and every member of the Church shares the command from Christ to carry the Good News to all.

VATICAN COUNCIL II . . .

▲ Divinely sent to the nations of the world to be unto them "a universal sacrament of salvation," the Church, driven by the inner necessity of her own catholicity, and obeying the mandate of her Founder (cf. Mk 16:16), strives ever to proclaim the gospel to all men. The apostles themselves, on whom the Church was founded, following in the footsteps of Christ, "preached the word of truth and begot churches" (St. Augustine). It is the duty of their successors to make this task endure "so that the word of God may run and be glorified" (2 Thes 3:1) and the kingdom of God be proclaimed and established throughout the world. *(Mission Activity of the Church, 1)*

EXPLANATION . . .

● The Church is in reality its members. The Christian community must act as a servant after the example of its Founder, Jesus Christ. It must serve the larger human community by sharing with it the riches of its faith and sharing in works that concern the welfare of the whole human family. Christian witness is giving testimony to the loving presence of God in the world. The Church gives Christian witness by its very existence as a community of faith and love, by the preaching of the gospel, and especially by service to others.

As the community of believers the Church must live the life of Jesus in his Spirit, and show his love by her life of fellowship and service to others. St. Luke says of the first Christians: "They devoted themselves to the teaching of the apostles and to the communal fellowship, to the breaking of bread and to prayers" (Acts 2:42).

150. Why is the Church a society with leaders?

By God's design, the Church is a society with leaders—with a hierarchy. As such, it is a people guided by its bishops, who are in union with the Pope.

THE BIBLE . . .

✠ *To him who loves us and has washed away our sins with his blood and made us to be a kingdom and priests to serve his God and Father—to him be glory and power forever and ever. Amen. (Rev 1:5-6)*

VATICAN COUNCIL II . . .

▲ This Sacred Council, following closely in the footsteps of the First Vatican Council, with that Council teaches and declares that Jesus Christ, the eternal Shepherd, established his holy Church, having sent forth the apostles as he himself had been sent by the Father (cf. Jn 20:21); and he willed that their successors, namely the bishops, should be shepherds in his Church even to the consummation of the world. And in order that the episcopate itself might be one and undivided, he placed Blessed Peter over the other apostles, and instituted in him a permanent and visible source and foundation of unity of faith and communion. *(The Church, 18)*

EXPLANATION . . .

● Christ conferred on the apostles and their successors the duty of teaching, sanctifying, and ruling in his name and power. But the laity, too, share in the priestly, prophetic, and royal office of Christ and therefore have their own role to play in the mission of the whole People of God in the Church and in the world.

The laity exercise a true apostolate by their activity on behalf of bringing the gospel and holiness to people, and of penetrating and perfecting the temporal sphere of things through the spirit of the gospel. Incorporated into Christ's Mystical Body through Baptism and Confirmation, they are assigned to the apostolate by the Lord himself. They are consecrated into a royal priesthood and a holy people in order that they may offer spiritual sacrifices through everything they do, and may witness to Christ throughout the world.

The activities which make up the Church's witness are these: preaching the Word of God and teaching its meaning; celebrating God's action in her liturgy; ministering to the spiritual and physical needs of the faithful. The Church celebrates God's gift of man principally in the Mass and sacraments.

151. Who is the Pope?

The Pope (1) is the Bishop of Rome, the Vicar of Christ, (2) he has succeeded to the office of Peter in his care and guidance of the whole flock of Christ, and (3) is the head of the college of bishops.

THE BIBLE . . .

✠ *When they had finished breakfast, Jesus said to Simon Peter, "Simon, son of John, do you love me more than these?" He replied, "Yes, Lord, you know that I love you." Jesus said to him, "Feed my lambs." Jesus said to him again, "Simon, son of John, do you love me?" He replied, "Yes, Lord, you know that I love you." Jesus said to him, "Tend my sheep." Jesus said to him a third time, "Simon, son of John, do you love me?" Peter was hurt that Jesus had asked him a third time, "Do you love me?" "Lord," he said to him, "you know everything. You know that I love you." Jesus said to him, "Feed my sheep." (Jn 21:15-17)*

VATICAN COUNCIL II . . .

▲ In this Church of Christ the Roman Pontiff, as the successor of Peter, to whom Christ entrusted the feeding of his sheep and lambs, enjoys supreme, full, immediate, and universal authority over the care of souls by divine institution. (*Office of Bishops*, 2)

EXPLANATION . . .

● (1) The Pope, the Bishop of Rome, is the successor of St. Peter, being supreme shepherd of the Church of Christ and having all the rights, powers, and duties of Peter.

(2) Jesus solemnly told Peter he was to be supreme shepherd, the head of the Church. "And I say to you: You are Peter, and on this rock I will build my Church, and the gates of the netherworld will not prevail against it. I will give you the keys of the kingdom of heaven. Whatever you bind on earth shall be bound in heaven, and whatever you loose on earth shall be loosed in heaven" (Mt 16:18-19).

Christ gave Peter, the supreme shepherd of souls, the holy task of giving the entire People of God his teaching and his grace. After his resurrection Jesus said to Simon Peter, "Simon, son of John, do you love me more than these?" He replied, "Yes, Lord, you know that I love you." Jesus said to him, "Feed my lambs" (Jn 21:15).

The Pope is the successor of St. Peter. He is the highest Christian teaching authority in the world; he is the supreme ruler or shepherd of the Catholic Church.

(3) While the Pope is the successor of St. Peter, the Catholic bishops are the successors of the other apostles. Christ established the apostles as a type of college or ruling body. As a college or body they were jointly responsible for the evangelization of the whole world. To the whole college Christ addressed his great missionary command, "Go, therefore, and make disciples of all nations, baptizing them . . ." (Mt 28:19).

Peter says Jesus is the Son of the living God, and Jesus makes him the head of his Church.

As a college, at the Council of Jerusalem, the apostles decided the question whether the Jewish customs should be imposed on non-Jewish converts: "It is the decision of the Holy Spirit and also our decision not to lay any further burden upon you beyond these essentials" (Acts 15:28).

Christ appointed Peter head of the apostolic body because he was to be the visible center of unity in the faith and life of the community. To him Jesus also said, the night before his passion and death: "Simon, Simon, behold, Satan has desired to sift all of you like wheat. But I have prayed that your own faith may not fail. And once you have turned back, you must strengthen your brethren" (Lk 22:31-32).

152. What does the community of faith owe the Pope and bishops?

The community of faith owes the Pope and bishops respect and obedience, for in exercising his office of father and pastor, a bishop should stand as one who serves.

VATICAN COUNCIL II . . .

▲ Bishops, teaching in communion with the Roman Pontiff, are to be respected by all as witnesses to divine and Catholic truth. In matters of faith and morals, the bishops speak in the name of Christ and the faithful are to accept their teaching and adhere to it with a religious assent. This religious submission of mind and will must be shown in a special way to the authentic magisterium of the Roman Pontiff, even if he is not speaking ex cathedra; that is, it must be shown in such a way that his supreme magisterium is acknowledged with reverence, the judgments made by him are sincerely adhered to, according to his manifest mind and will. *(The Church, 25)*

EXPLANATION . . .

● We serve God and his Church by fulfilling our obligations implied in the Fourth Commandment of God, to honor, love, respect, and obey the Pope as successor of St. Peter, our bishop who is our shepherd and our priests ordained for the loving service of the faithful.

All should obey their bishop as Jesus obeyed his Father; they should obey priests as if they were apostles. Bishops and priests, on the other hand, are expected to exercise their office of father and pastor, ever at hand to serve the flock of Christ.

153. What is the gift of infallibility in the Church?

The Roman Pontiff, the head of the college of bishops, enjoys infallibility in virtue of his office, when, as the supreme shepherd and teacher of all the faithful, he proclaims by a definitive act some doctrine of faith and morals.

VATICAN COUNCIL II . . .

▲ This infallibility with which the Divine Redeemer willed his Church to be endowed in defining a doctrine of faith and morals extends as far as the deposit of Revelation extends, which must be religiously guarded and faithfully expounded. And this is the infallibility which the Roman Pontiff, the head of the college of bishops, enjoys in virtue of his office, when, as the supreme shepherd and teacher of all the faithful, who confirms his brethren in their faith (cf. Lk 22:32), by a definitive act he proclaims a doctrine of faith and morals. *(The Church, 25)*

EXPLANATION . . .

● Infallibility is a gift of the Holy Spirit by which the Church's faith is protected from error. The Holy Spirit remains in the Catholic Church to enable her to continue the work of Christ in the world. He guides the bishops and priests of the Church in their holy work of Christ—teaching his doctrine, shepherding souls, and giving grace to the people through the sacraments.

When the Church teaches solemnly in the name of God, the teaching is infallible, that is, it cannot be mistaken in matters of faith or morals. When the Pope teaches solemnly in his official capacity as head of the Church, that is, "ex cathedra," or when the bishops assembled with the Pope in Council solemnly pronounce upon a matter of faith or morals, that doctrine is the infallible teaching of the Church and is a matter of divine faith.

Moreover, when the Pope and the morally unanimous body of bishops throughout the world teach that a certain doctrine has been revealed by God, this teaching is infallible even though it has not been solemnly defined. For it is still Christ teaching through his universal Church.

When the Pope speaks on a matter of faith or morals, but not "ex cathedra," his teaching is not of itself infallible. However, the Pope is not merely a private individual, nor is he merely a private theologian. He

is the official head of the Church on earth, the Vicar of Christ, and his teaching demands respect, obedience, and assent.

154. How does the teaching authority of the Church guide the faithful in truth?

Jesus willed that the bishops, the successors of the apostles, should be shepherds in his Church. He placed Peter over the other apostles, and instituted in him a permanent source and foundation of unity of faith and fellowship.

VATICAN COUNCIL II . . .

▲ The apostles, by preaching the gospel everywhere (cf. Mk 16:20), and it being accepted by their hearers under the influence of the Holy Spirit, gathered together the universal Church, which the Lord established on the apostles and built upon Blessed Peter, their chief, Christ himself being the supreme cornerstone (cf Rev 21:14; Mt 16:18; Eph 2:20). *(The Church, 19)*

In the Church there is a diversity of ministry but a oneness of mission. Christ conferred on the apostles and their successors the duty of teaching, sanctifying, and ruling in his name and power. *(Apostolate of the Laity, 2)*

EXPLANATION . . .

● The Pope is a visible sign of Jesus and the symbol of unity for the Church. Together with the bishops, and as their head, he teaches and governs the universal Church.

The bishops are visible signs of Jesus in each locality and the symbol of unity for the Church there. Each diocesan bishop is responsible for teaching and governing of the Church in that locality. Nationwide, all the bishops, together with the Pope, are the official witnesses to the faith of the whole Church and are responsible for her life throughout the world.

To be a Catholic means fundamentally to believe that Jesus Christ, the Son of God, established a Church to continue and to carry on his work of redemption. But the average Catholic cannot sound the depths of philosophical and theological arguments. He finds his security and peace in the teaching authority of the Church, to which Christ promised immunity from error through the help of the Holy Spirit, in teaching people what they must believe and what they must do to attain salvation.

155. What is the role of the Holy Spirit in the Church?

(1) The Holy Spirit preserves the Church as the body of Christ and his bride, so that—despite the sins of its members—it will never fail in faithfulness to him and will meet him in holiness at the end of the world. (2) The Holy Spirit also helps the Church constantly to purify and renew itself and its members.

VATICAN COUNCIL II . . .

▲ The Spirit dwells in the Church and in the hearts of the faithful as in a temple (cf. 1 Cor 3:16; 6:19). In them he prays on their behalf and bears witness to the fact that they are adopted sons (cf. Gal 4:6; Rom 8:15-16, 26). The Church, which the Spirit guides in the way of all truth (cf. Jn 16:13) and which he unified in communion and in works of ministry, he both equips and directs with hierarchical and charismatic gifts and adorns with his fruits (cf. Eph 4:11-12; 1 Cor 12:4; Gal 5:22). By the power of the Gospel he makes the Church keep the freshness of youth. Uninterruptedly he renews it and leads it to perfect union with her Spouse. The Spirit and the Bride both say to Jesus, the Lord, "Come!" (cf. Rev 11:17). Thus the Church has been seen as "a people made one with the unity of the Father, the Son and the Holy Spirit" (St. Cyprian, St. Augustine). *(The Church, 4)*

EXPLANATION . . .

● (1) Every Christian receives the Holy Spirit in the sacrament of Baptism and in the sacrament of Confirmation. The Holy Spirit with the Father and the Son actually lives in the Christian. Jesus said, "Whoever loves me will keep my word, and my Father will love him, and we will come to him and make our abode with him" (Jn 14:23).

Through the Holy Spirit a Christian shares in the life of grace, God's life in his soul. St. Paul reminds the Christian that he is holy because the Holy Spirit dwells in him. "Do you not realize that you are God's temple, and that the Spirit of God dwells in you? If anyone destroys God's temple, God will destroy that person. For the temple of God is holy, and you are that temple" (1 Cor 3:16-17).

The Holy Spirit enlightens our minds to accept and believe the teaching of Jesus and gives us the strength to live according to it. An openness to God and a willing response to the guidance of his Holy Spirit is necessary for holiness. St. Paul says, "Do not quench the Spirit" (1 Thes 5:19).

Holiness is expected from the whole Church. Giving himself to all, God makes it possible for all people to give themselves completely to him and to others. All are called to holiness according to the gifts and talents each possesses.

Saints are those whom the Church has declared to be true models of holiness. There are many other people about whom the Church has said nothing and whose holiness is known only to God and a very few others. These are saints also.

The Holy Spirit brings about a union between Christ and his members. This union is one of the great mysteries of our faith. St. Paul described this union as the body of Christ. Christ himself is head of that body, while those who belong to him are its members. They are united closely with the head and with each other by a strong interior bond, which is the Holy Spirit. We call this body the Mystical Body of Christ. The Church is also called the Bride of Christ.

(2) So that we may live well as God's children, the Holy Spirit helps us in many ways. His activities are sometimes called actual graces. Without these helps it is impossible to do anything toward our salvation or the salvation of others. With the help of the grace of the Holy Spirit the Church is constantly purified and renewed spiritually.

156. How can the Church be modernized?

To help its members, the Spirit-guided Church can modernize in those areas that permit change.

VATICAN COUNCIL II . . .

▲ Every renewal of the Church is essentially grounded in an increase of fidelity to her own calling. Undoubtedly this is the basis of the movement toward unity. Christ summons the Church to continual reformation as she sojourns here on earth. The Church is always in need of this, insofar as she is an institution of men here on earth. *(Ecumenism, 6)*

EXPLANATION . . .

● The aims of Christian renewal, as outlined in the declarations of Vatican Council II which opened October 11, 1962, are: (1) To impart an ever-increasing vigor to the Christian life of the faithful; (2) To adapt to the needs of the times those aspects of the Church which are subject to change; (3) To strengthen whatever can promote union among all who believe in Christ; (4) To foster whatever can help to call the whole of humankind into the household of the Church.

There are many areas in the Church which permit change, such as liturgy, marriage laws, religious practices. Adjustments are necessary to any genuine renewal of the Church, but these must be made in accordance with the spirit and decisions of Vatican Council II. However, the faithful are to be solidly and fully instructed in the teaching and authentic tradition of the Catholic Church.

But the most important change is to take place in the individual Catholic. This is the area where Christian renewal begins. Only after one has begun to improve their own spiritual life will each one acquire the necessary zeal and power to promote the Christian renewal in others.

DISCUSSION QUESTIONS

1. Why is the Church the new People of God? (144)
2. Why does the Church have its origin in the death and resurrection of Christ? (145)
3. What is the deposit of faith in the Church? (146)
4. How did Christ give the apostles the power to forgive sins? To consecrate at Holy Mass? To teach? (146)
5. What ministries did the Church inherit from the apostles? (146)
6. How does the Church serve humankind? (147)
7. How does the Church share in the prophetic office of Christ? (148)
8. How does the Church express her missionary character? (149)
9. What duties did Christ confer on the apostles and their successors? (150)
10. How do the laity exercise a true apostolate? (150)
11. What are the activities that make up the Church's witness? (150)
12. Why is the Pope the Vicar of Christ? (151)
13. Why is the Pope the head of the bishops? (151)
14. Why do we owe respect and obedience to the Pope and bishops? (152)
15. What is the gift of infallibility? (153)
16. How are the faithful guided in truth? (154)
17. How does the Holy Spirit help the Church? (155)
18. What are the aims of Christian renewal? (156)

Chapter 21

THE CHURCH AS A COMMUNITY

157. Why is the Church a community?

(1) The Church is a community sharing together the life of Christ, a people assembled by God. (2) Within this assembly there is a basic equality of all persons. (3) There are different responsibilities for each in the Church.

VATICAN COUNCIL II . . .

▲ They are fully incorporated in the society of the Church who, possessing the Spirit of Christ, accept her entire system and all the means of salvation given to her, and are united with her as part of her visible bodily structure and through her with Christ, who rules her through the Supreme Pontiff and the bishops. *(The Church, 14)*

EXPLANATION . . .

● **(1) The Church is the worldwide community of those whom God has called to give witness to his Son Jesus and to the new life he has brought to them. This assembly is called "the People of God" and "the body of Christ."**

The description of the Church as the People of God and the body of Christ helps all of us to see ourselves as one with a group to whose destiny we are tied, and whose welfare we share. This is the reality of

Baptism; we are joined to Christ, to the whole Christ, Christ and his people, the Church.

If we are thus joined in Christ, he is truly one of us in a very real and intimate sense. For if the Church is seen as a successor to Israel, then Jesus, the Messiah and Head of the new People of God is seen as rooted in humanity. The infant Jesus is the Son of Mary, as well as Son of God. He is of the people of Israel, of the tribe of Judah, of the house of David.

It is through his humanity that each of us is united to Christ as our Savior. The Divinity of Christ must not be slighted; but it must not cancel out his true humanity. Each time we use the phrase the "People of God" we see Christ, greater than Moses, who shares a truly human nature with Moses and like him leads the People of God from slavery to freedom, from death to life. Christ is Our Passover. We look to the daughter of Zion, Mary, whose Son is Jesus. This brings home the fact that he is one of us, truly Emmanuel, our God with us.

(2) In describing the Church as the People of God emphasis is placed on the fact that the Church is composed of people. It includes the Pope, bishops, priests, and all the laity. That is why the Council said: "The Church is a people made one with the unity of the Father, the Son and the Holy Spirit." In this assembly of people there is a basic equality of all persons.

(3) Just as God made Moses the leader of his people in the Old Testament, so Christ gave to his apostles and their successors the right to teach and to command in his name. These powers are given for the service and welfare of the People of God. Hence there are different responsibilities in the Church. The People of God are important because they are made to the image and likeness of God, and because they are joined to Christ, the only-begotten Son.

158. Is there a difference between the ministerial priesthood and the priesthood of the people?

The Church is also a priestly people. But the ministerial priesthood is essentially different from "the priesthood of the people." Yet all are united and equal as the one People of God.

VATICAN COUNCIL II . . .

▲ Christ the Lord, High Priest taken from among men (cf. Heb 5:1-5), made the new people "a kingdom and priests to God the Father" (Rev 1:6; cf. 5:9-10). The baptized, by regeneration and the anointing of the Holy Spirit, are consecrated as a spiritual house and a holy priesthood, in order that through all those works which are those of the Christian man they may offer spiritual sacrifices and proclaim the power of him who has called them out of darkness into his marvelous light (cf. 1 Pet 2:4-10).

Therefore all the disciples of Christ, persevering in prayer and praising God (cf. Acts 2:42-47), should present themselves as a living sacrifice, holy and pleasing to God (cf. Rom 12:1). Everywhere on earth they must bear witness to Christ and give an answer to those who seek an account of that hope of eternal life which is in them (cf. 1 Pet 3:15).

Though they differ from one another in essence and not only in degree, the common priesthood of the faithful and the ministerial or hierarchical priesthood are nonetheless interrelated: each of them in its own special way is a participation in the one priesthood of Christ. *(The Church, 10)*

Christ gave to his apostles and their successors the right to teach and command the People of God in his name.

EXPLANATION . . .

● Jesus Christ is a compassionate priest of God sent to us. Our high priest is one of us, a mediator between us and the Father. Christ wanted his sacred priesthood to be shared by others because his work and his authority, his teaching, his sacrifice, and his grace were for all people of all time. He appointed the apostles to be his priests to carry on his work in the world.

By the imposition of the hands of the bishop a man is made a priest, becoming a representative of Christ and having the priestly powers of Christ, just as the apostles by ordaining priests and bishops passed on their priestly powers to others so that the work of Christ the priest would be continued in the world.

The first work of a priest is to offer sacrifice to God for the sins of the people. Priests offer Christ in sacrifice at Mass. They teach in the name of Christ, baptize, forgive sins, give Christ's body and blood in Holy Communion, anoint the sick, bless persons and things with the blessing of Christ, are official witnesses for Christ and his Church at the marriages of Catholics. This is the ministerial priesthood.

By Baptism the faithful are made one body with Christ and members of the People of God. Sharing, in their own way, in the priestly, prophetic, and kingly functions of Christ, they have a part of their own in carrying out the mission of the whole Christian people in the Church and in the world. St. Peter says, "But you are 'a chosen race, a royal priesthood, a holy nation, a people claimed by God as his own possession,' so that you may proclaim the praise of him who called you out of darkness into his marvelous light" (1 Pet 2:9).

What distinguishes the laity is their "secular character." Although those in holy orders can at times be engaged in secular activities and professions, they are by reason of their vocation especially and professedly ordained to the sacred ministry. Living in the world, they are called by God to work for the sanctification of the world like a leaven, from within, by carrying out their proper tasks according to the spirit of the gospel. They are consecrated into a royal priesthood and a holy people in order that they may offer spiritual sacrifices through everything they do and may witness to Christ in the world.

Within the basic equality of all the members there is a diversity of functions. The distinction which the Lord made between sacred ministers and the rest of the people of God involves union, since pastors and the other faithful are bound together by their mutual need. Priests should minister to the needs of one another and of the other faithful. The faithful, in turn, should cooperate enthusiastically with their priests. All—clergy, religious, and laity— are brothers and sisters in the Mystical Body of Christ.

159. What is the vocation to holiness in the Church?

In the Church every individual has a call from God, a vocation to holiness.

THE BIBLE . . .

✠ *There is one body and one Spirit, as well as one hope to which you have been called by your vocation, one Lord, one faith, one baptism, one God and Father of all, who is over all and through all and in all. (Eph 4:4-6)*

VATICAN COUNCIL II . . .

▲ Thus it is evident to everyone that all the faithful of Christ, of whatever rank or status, are called to the fullness of the Christian life and to the perfection of charity. *(The Church, 40)*

EXPLANATION . . .

● When God created man, he bestowed upon him the gifts of supernatural life, of divine sonship. He was alive with the very life of God. But man sinned, and by sin he lost the gift of divine life. Left to himself, man was incapable of winning back the divine life. But God in his infinite mercy conceived the wonderful plan of the redemption. He sent his only-begotten Son into the world to save humankind.

Christ became Man. He took our sinfulness upon himself and stood in the place of all people before his Father. He accepted death and on Calvary paid the penalty for all people's sins. Since he was God's Son, the bonds of death could not hold him. He rose again to life. With him all humankind passed from death to life, returned to the Father's sonship, and enjoyed the intimacy of his love.

With Christ we have already died to sin and risen to newness of life. He will pour into our souls that very life of divine sonship that filled him in his own resurrection. This he did through the sacrament of the Church he founded. In the Church Christ wills to continue his own life in us for the glory of the Father. This Christ-life within us is the holiness to which God has called every individual in the Church.

This Christ-life means that we open our minds to him by faith so that we have the same outlook that he had. We open our hearts to him that he may live in us his own life of love and self-surrender to the Father. We pattern our conduct on his so that in all things we become like him, our Model. St. Paul said, "It is no longer I who live, but it is Christ who lives in me" (Gal 2:20).

160. Why does every individual in the Church deserve respect?

(1) In the Church every individual deserves respect, since all join in the one cause of Christ. The Pope and the bishops coordinate this work, in every rite, diocese, parish, and mission. (2) In each, no matter how small or poor or isolated, "Christ is present, and by his power the one, holy, Catholic and Apostolic Church is gathered together."

VATICAN COUNCIL II . . .

▲ Indeed, the spirit of unity should be promoted in order that fraternal charity may be resplendent in the whole apostolate of the Church, common goals may be attained, and destructive rivalries avoided. For this there is need for mutual esteem among all the forms of the apostolate in the Church and, with due respect for the particular character of each organization, proper coordination. (*Apostolate of the Laity*, 23)

This Church of Christ is truly present in all legitimate local congregations of the faithful which, united with their pastor, are themselves called church in the New Testament. (*The Church*, 26)

EXPLANATION . . .

● (1) Commitment to Christ is the key to the total transformation of one's character which is expected of his followers by Jesus Christ. The principal cause of hypocrisy in the lives of Christians, or resistance to basic Christian principles, is that too many people who profess to be

Christians have not made a total commitment of their entire being to Christ. They become victims of a double allegiance: "To serve both God and mammon."

The complete commitment to Christ that makes one a full Christian is an enduring act of one's free will, aided by the grace of God. Total commitment includes the whole of one's nature, spiritual and physical, intellectual and emotional, and the only faculty that can commit one's whole nature to anything is the will. This internal commitment of the mind and heart and will manifests itself by a life lived in conformity with the principles which Christ taught.

Dedication to Christ means obeying the commandments, fulfilling the duties of our state of life, accepting the sufferings God permits in our life, striving to perform our actions for the love of God, working to spread the reign of Christ. Every individual in the Church who thus joins in the one cause of Christ by total commitment to him deserves our deepest respect.

(2) Christ came to earth to incorporate all humankind into himself, to make all people one with him, members of the Body of which he is the head. This incorporation into the death and resurrection of Christ is brought about through Baptism.

In addition to Baptism, Christ has given us the Holy Eucharist as a means of union with him. Through the grace of these sacraments, Christ is present in us, and by his power the Catholic Church is gathered together in every parish, no matter how small.

DISCUSSION QUESTIONS

1. How do we share together the life of Christ in the Church? (157)
2. In what sense is the Church a community? (157)
3. Why is the ministerial priesthood different from "the priesthood of the people"? (158)
4. Why does every individual in the Church have a call to holiness? (159)
5. Why does every individual in the Church deserve respect? (160)

Chapter 22

THE QUEST FOR UNITY

161. Why is Christian unity in faith and love God's will?

Christ willed that all who believe in him be one, so that the world might know that he was sent by the Father.

THE BIBLE . . .

✠ *"I pray not only on behalf of these, but also for those who through their word will come to believe in me. May they all be one. As you, Father, are in me and I in you, may they also be in us so that the world may believe that you have sent me." (Jn 17:20-21)*

VATICAN COUNCIL II . . .

▲ Today, in many parts of the world, under the inspiring grace of the Holy Spirit, many efforts are being made in prayer, word, and action to attain that fullness of unity which Jesus Christ desires. This Sacred Council exhorts all the Catholic faithful to recognize the signs of the times and to take an active and intelligent part in the work of ecumenism. *(Ecumenism, 4)*

EXPLANATION . . .

● **There is but one Church. Jesus brought the same Good News to all and called them to the same new life. His Church is the union of those who follow his call.**

The night before he died Jesus prayed for Christian unity. "I pray . . . also for those who through their word will come to believe in me. May they all be one. As you, Father, are in me and I in you, may they also be in us so that the world may believe that you have sent me" (Jn 17:20-21).

St. Paul speaks of this unity when he pleaded with the early Christians to preserve it. "As a prisoner for the Lord, I implore you to behave in a manner worthy of the calling you have received, with all humility, gentleness, and patience, bearing with one another in a spirit of love. Make every possible effort to preserve the unity of the Spirit through the bond of peace. There is one body and one Spirit, as well as one hope to which you have been called by your vocation, one Lord, one faith, one baptism, one God and Father of all, who is over all and through all and in all" (Eph 4:1-5).

The Roman Catholic Church is the worldwide community of the followers of Jesus that is united around the Pope.

162. What is the duty of Catholics with regard to Christian unity?

(1) Prayer and work for Christian unity are essential to Catholic life. (2) Catholics should be deeply, personally concerned over the present, sad divisions of Christians. (3) Catholics should take the first steps in ecumenical dialogue. (4) They should try to make the Church more faithful to Christ and to its heritage from the apostles.

VATICAN COUNCIL II . . .

▲ In certain special circumstances, such as the prescribed prayer "for unity," and during ecumenical gatherings, it is allowable and indeed desirable that Catholics should join in prayer with their separated brethren. Such prayers in common are certainly an effective means of obtaining the grace of unity, and they are a true expression of the ties which still bind Catholics to their separated brethren. "For where two or three are gathered together in my name; there am I in the midst of them" (Mt 18:20). *(Ecumenism, 8)*

EXPLANATION . . .

● (1) The Church is one because there is only one Jesus and he communicates the same life of God to all who believe in him. At this basic level all Christians are truly united and the Church is one. If we truly love Christ, we shall do all in our power, by prayer and work, that Christ's will and prayer for unity may be realized: "That all may be one."

(2) But the Church is not one because historical differences and bitterness have driven the followers of Jesus apart so that much of their Christian life is not shared with one another. Besides, people's understanding of Jesus and the meaning of his life and teaching differs and sometimes these differences prevent Christians from coming together.

There are many churches because in the long history of Christianity there have been serious differences among our Lord's followers over the meaning of his Gospel and the way of living his life. As a result divisions and separate groups have appeared. These groups are principally the Roman Catholic Church, the Eastern Orthodox Church, the Anglican Church, and the various Protestant Churches. This sad condition should deeply concern a zealous Catholic.

(3) Ecumenism is the acceptance of the basic unity of the Church and the effort to make this unity present and visible in the whole life of the Church. Concerned Catholics should take the first steps in ecumenical dialogue.

(4) The ability of the Church to fulfill its Christ-given mission in our time is closely bound up with the development of a dynamic spirit of stewardship in our Catholic people. This spirit includes not merely the support of the Church and the dedication of time and effort to Church projects, but the faithful carrying out of the gospel of Christ in one's own life and a dedicated commitment to extend Christ's message to others.

It is our privilege to be not merely servants of God, but partners; not merely hirelings, but his children. This realization gives to Christian stewardship its sense of hope and gratitude, its light and joy, its consciousness of God's boundless resources. We are heirs with Christ. We share in his unfathomable riches and we should lovingly dispense them to others.

163. What do Catholics recognize in their quest for Christian unity?

Catholics recognize (1) the unique fullness of the Catholic Church which they believe to be the ordinary means of salvation, and which they desire to share with others. But they also recognize (2) that Catholics can be enriched by the authentic insights into the gospel as witnessed by other religious traditions.

At the Last Supper Jesus prayed to his Father for those who believe in him, "that all may be one as you, Father, are in me, and I in you."

VATICAN COUNCIL II . . .

▲ This Church, constituted and organized in the world as a society, subsists in the Catholic Church, which is governed by the successor of Peter and by the bishops in communion with him, although many elements of sanctification and of truth are found outside of her visible structure. These elements, as gifts belonging to the Church of Christ, are forces impelling toward Catholic unity. *(The Church, 8)*

EXPLANATION . . .

● (1) Catholics believe that Jesus Christ entrusted his work of redemption to his Church. He said to his first disciples, "As the Father has sent me, so I send you" (Jn 20:21). "Whoever listens to you listens to me, and whoever rejects you rejects me. And whoever rejects me rejects the one who sent me" (Lk 10:16). Not to the individual, but to the Church was the promise made by Christ: "I will ask the Father, and he will give you another Advocate to be with you forever" (Jn 14:16).

On Pentecost the Holy Spirit descended upon the apostles in the form of fiery tongues and welded them into the strong foundation upon which Christ's Church was to be built. They who had been ignorant, weak and timid now went bravely forth to confront the world and to win it for their Master.

Catholics believe that only through the Church can we know for sure what God wills us to believe and to do in order to attain salvation. Without the Church, religion becomes merely a matter of opinion and conjecture, with no one having any assurances as to what is true and false.

Catholics believe that only through the Church can we find security and certainty about the meaning and destiny of our human lives. For the Christian Catholic life is not meaningless. We are not at the mercy of a blind, unreasonable fate. We know that we are walking in the sunlight of truth, under the loving care of our Father in heaven and with the guidance of the Church, our spiritual mother upon earth. Catholics recognize the unique fullness of the Catholic Church, which they believe to be the ordinary means of salvation.

The Church is Christ, living and working in the members of his Mystical Body. As we have love and loyalty for Christ, so must we also have love and loyalty for his Church. We must love God's Church; we must listen to her teaching; we must be faithful to the laws which, as the mother of all souls, she finds necessary for our guidance along the way of salvation. All of us who have received the immense treasure of the faith must guard it and pass it on to the generations who will come after us.

(2) But Catholics also recognize that they can be enriched by valuable insights into the gospel as witnessed by other religious congregations and traditions. This recognition should aid them in their quest for Christian unity.

164. What other unity should concern the Catholic?

A still wider unity must be a concern of Catholic life and education: the unity of all people under God.

VATICAN COUNCIL II . . .

▲ The present-day conditions of the world add greater urgency to this work of the Church so that all men, joined more closely today by various social, technical and cultural ties, might also attain fuller unity in Christ. *(The Church, 1)*

EXPLANATION . . .

● The Catholic layperson's vocation is to be Christ's witness in the world of social, economic, and political activity. In the world we must contribute to the growth of the kingdom of God; one must be another Christ passing among us.

In the small circle of one's home and in the wide arena of public affairs, the Catholic layperson has been called to help steer the world heavenward. We must work in the making of laws and in the shaping of social doctrines and practice. We must be engaged day by day in developing our country's prosperity and in bettering the lot of the poor.

It is the Catholic layperson's vocation to join their work with the work of Christ by seeking to change the kingdom of the world into the kingdom of God. The layperson's vocation is to consecrate the world for Christ. If the world is made a better place to live in, and if the many millions of those who now do not know Christ become members of his kingdom, it will be because intelligent and zealous lay people have sincerely and successfully tried to fulfill the vocation which is theirs. In this way they help to bring about the unity of all people under God.

165. How is this concern for wider unity shown?

Religious education must show Christlike respect for all people of good will, beginning with our elders in faith, the Jewish people, and reaching out to those others who with us believe in God.

EXPLANATION . . .

● As Christ sends his apostles to teach and to be witnesses to him in the world, so, too, he would have the Catholic laity participate in this mission. The duty of proclaiming the gospel and making its influence felt in people's lives belongs not only to bishops and priests, but also to the laity. Every Catholic man and woman is called by God to be an apostle, that is, a messenger of Christ to the world.

The soul of the apostolate is love. We must first show Christlike respect for all people of good will, reaching out especially to those who with us believe in God.

166. Why must we respect every human being?

(1) We must show sensitive appreciation of the dignity and unique value of every human being because God has given to us intrinsic dignity, freedom and eternal importance. (2) The Church rejects as un-Christian any unjust discrimination or injustice because of race, national origin, ethnic origin, color, sex, class, or religion.

THE BIBLE . . .

✠ *If someone says, "I love God," but at the same time hates his brother, he is a liar. For whoever does not love the brother whom he has seen cannot love God whom he has not seen. (I Jn 4:20)*

VATICAN COUNCIL II . . .

▲ God, who has fatherly concern for everyone, has willed that all men should constitute one family and treat one another in a spirit of brotherhood. *(Church in the Modern World, 24)*

The Church reproves, as foreign to the mind of Christ, any discrimination against men or harassment of them because of their race, color, condition of life, or religion. On the contrary, following in the footsteps of the holy Apostles Peter and Paul, this Sacred Synod ardently implores the Christian faithful to "maintain good fellowship among the nations" (1 Pet 2:12), and, if possible, to live for their part in peace with all men (cf. Rom 12:18), so that they may truly be sons of the Father who is in heaven (cf. Mt 5:45). *(Non-Christian Religions, 5)*

In all of Christ's disciples the Spirit arouses the desire to be peacefully united, in the manner determined by Christ, as one flock under one shepherd, and he prompts them to pursue this end. *(The Church, 15)*

EXPLANATION . . .

• (1) Creatures reflect God in the sense that each mirrors in its own limited way the boundless reality and beauty of God. Men and women, because they have a spiritual soul, have dominion over the other earthly creatures and are a more perfect image of God than anything else on this earth.

Men and women are from God, therefore they are for God. They were placed on this earth to know and love God and be happy with him forever in the next world. They were made for God and will live forever with God in heaven if they will love him now. Because of these reasons each one has a unique dignity and value as a human being; each is free and will live forever. This makes every person deserving of respect.

(2) When Jesus was asked the question, "Who is my neighbor?" he replied by telling the story of the Good Samaritan, which teaches us that our neighbor is every person, not only those who belong to our race, our country, our religion. Even those who hate us and injure us must be included in our love. Therefore the Church rejects every kind of discrimination and injustice which would harm any human being.

DISCUSSION QUESTIONS

1. Why did Christ will that all who believe in him be one? (161)
2. In what sense is the Church one? (162)
3. In what sense is the Church not one? (162)
4. What is ecumenism? (162)
5. Why do we believe that only through the Church can we know for sure what God wills us to believe and do? (163)
6. How can Catholics be enriched by other religious traditions? (163)
7. What is the Catholic layperson's vocation in the world? (164)
8. What must religious education show with respect to unity? (165)
9. Why must we respect every human being? (166)

Chapter 23

THE CHURCH AS THE INSTITUTION FOR SALVATION

167. Why is the Church an institution for salvation?

Established by Christ as (1) a fellowship of life, charity and truth, the Church is a community of the People of God with Christ as leader and head. (2) It is a structured institution to which Christ has given the mission of bringing the message of salvation to all people.

THE BIBLE . . .

✠ *"All authority in heaven and on earth has been given to me. Go, therefore, and make disciples of all nations, baptizing them in the name of the Father, and of the Son, and of the Holy Spirit, teaching them to observe all that I have commanded you. And behold, I am with you always, to the end of the world."* (Mt 28:18-20)

VATICAN COUNCIL II . . .

▲ That messianic people has Christ for its head, "who was delivered up for our sins, and rose again for our justification" (Rom 4:25), and now, having won a name which is above all names, reigns in glory in heaven.

The state of this people is that of the dignity and freedom of the sons of God, in whose hearts the Holy Spirit dwells as in his temple. Its law is the new commandment of love as Christ loved us (cf. Jn 13:34). Its end is the kingdom of God, which has been begun by God himself on earth, and which is to be further extended until it is brought to perfection by him at the end of time, when Christ, our life (cf. Col 3:4), will appear, and "creation itself will be delivered from its slavery to corruption into the freedom of the glory of the sons of God" (Rom 8:21).

So it is that this messianic people, although it does not actually include all men, and at times may look like a small flock, is nonetheless a lasting and sure seed of unity, hope, and salvation for the whole human race. Established by Christ as a communion of life, charity, and truth, it is also used by him as an instrument for the redemption of all, and is sent forth into the whole world as the light of the world and the salt of the earth (cf. Mt 5:13-16). *(The Church,* 9)

EXPLANATION . . .

● **(1) Through Jesus Christ we have been made members of the family of God, the People of God. We are joined to Christ and to one another in a union which is far closer than any union on earth. Our Lord compared it to the sublime union of the Blessed Trinity: "May they all be one. As you, Father, are in me and I in you, may they also be in us" (Jn 17:21).**

We are one with Christ and with one another in the union of the Mystical Body of Christ here on earth. So close is this union that whatever we do or fail to do to one another we do or fail to do to Christ himself. Jesus said, "Amen, I say to you, whatever you did for one of the least of these brethren of mine, you did it for me" (Mt 25:40). Therefore we must have special love for our fellow members in the Mystical Body of Christ because in loving the members of his Body we are loving Christ. In practice, we must treat all people as we would treat Christ himself. Christ died for all.

(2) The Church is also a structured institution. Hence there are two kinds of authority in the Church: the ordinary authority every society has to organize and direct its own affairs, and the special authority given by Jesus to his disciples to teach and act in his name. The Church exercises her ordinary authority by enacting laws to regulate her internal affairs, to promote the good of all, and to fulfill the purposes of the Church. The

Church exercises the special authority given by Jesus in her teaching, worship, and service done in the name of Jesus. His person and power are present to her when she acts under this authority.

The Pope and the bishops exercise authority for the Church. Others, clergy and laity, can share in the exercise of the Church's authority in different degrees.

The Church speaks the Good News of God's doings in the world. She does this through her teaching and preaching, through her life and worship, through her Bible and the writings of her prophets, and sometimes through the words of a single Christian expressing their hopes. The mission of the Church is to bring the message of salvation to all people.

God has called to be witnesses all those who believe that God has revealed and given himself to us in Jesus Christ. The Church gives this witness by proclaiming in the world by word and deed what God has done in Jesus Christ. The Church must live the life of Jesus in his Spirit, and show his love by her life of fellowship and service to others.

168. What is the Church's contact with the world?

The Church is not of this world, and can never conform itself to this world. But (1) it both speaks and listens to the world, (2) and strives to be seen by the world as faithful to the gospel. Engaged in the world, (3) it always has heaven in view, toward which the People of God are journeying.

VATICAN COUNCIL II . . .

▲ Christians, on pilgrimage toward the heavenly city, should seek and think of those things which are above (cf. Col 3:1-2). This duty in no way decreases, rather it increases, the importance of their obligation to work with all men in the building of a more human world. *(Church in the Modern World, 57)*

EXPLANATION . . .

● **(1) To his Church Christ gave the commission to spread the message of salvation to the ends of the earth. Among all the gifts which God has given to us, the gift of the good news of the Gospel is one of the greatest. Here God reveals his secret plan, hidden from the eyes of** ages past, to save humankind and to give each one a share in his divine life through Jesus Christ his Son. Therefore the Church both speaks and listens to the world, without being of the world and conformed to the world.

(2) Much of the effective work of bringing the gospel of Christ to the world must be done by Catholic lay people. Lay people are challenged to make holy the actual world in which they live. They are mediators, go-betweens for the Church and the world. They discover Christ as the way, the truth, and the life, and then bring him into the world. As citizens of both the Church and the world, they are meant to be the bridge that connects them. The priest stands between God and people; the layperson stands between the Church and the world.

(3) The Church ministers to people's spiritual needs by providing a community of faith, where people can find support and guidance in their quest for God. Within this community the Holy Spirit gives and strengthens the life of God through the sacraments, prayer, and works of service. The sacraments are special actions in the Church through which the life of God is communicated to his people.

The Church also ministers to the physical needs of people by giving material aid to those in distress and by working with other concerned people in helping to overcome the causes of suffering, and building up a better life for them. Though the Church is deeply involved in the world and its needs, it always has heaven in view, and continues to be a light to lead people to eternal life with God.

DISCUSSION QUESTIONS

1. Why is the Church a fellowship of life, charity, and truth? (167)
2. Why is the Church a structured institution? (167)
3. How does the Church make contact with the world? (168)
4. How does the Church minister to the spiritual needs of people? (168)
5. What is the position of the Catholic layperson in the world? (168)
6. How does the Church minister to the physical needs of people? (168)

Chapter 24

MARY, MOTHER OF GOD, MOTHER AND MODEL OF THE CHURCH

169. What is Mary's place in the Church?

The (1) "ever-virgin Mother of Jesus Christ our Lord and God," Mary is in the Church in a place highest after Christ, (2) and also is very close to us as our spiritual Mother.

VATICAN COUNCIL II . . .

▲ The Virgin Mary, who at the message of the angel received the Word of God in her heart and in her body and gave Life to the world, is acknowledged and honored as being truly the Mother of God and Mother of the Redeemer. *(The Church, 53)*

The maternity of Mary in the order of grace began with the consent which she gave in faith at the Annunciation and which she sustained without wavering beneath the cross, and lasts until the eternal fulfillment of all the elect. Taken up to heaven she did not lay aside this salvific duty, but by her constant intercession continues to bring us the gifts of eternal salvation. *(The Church, 62)*

EXPLANATION . . .

● (1) The origin and foundation of the spiritual motherhood of Mary is intimately associated with the Incarnation. The source of this motherhood is the generous consent which she gave to the angel of the Annunciation, who had come to ask her consent to God's wish that she should become the Mother of his Son. In the plan of God, the salvation of the world had been made dependent on Mary's decision at that moment. But she not only consented, she also willed with a clear understanding of the meaning of the mission which was being confided to her.

(2) At the Incarnation, Mary gave Jesus to us. On Calvary, Jesus gave us his Mother. Acting as the One Mediator, he fixed the new plan of redemption. As Master, he assigned to his Mother a place near to him, yet still of a secondary order subordinated to him; but this place, in relation to all humankind, is all-powerful, unique. Christ, the Head himself, has appointed her to be the Mother of the Whole Christ.

170. What are some of Mary's special gifts from God?

Some of the special gifts from God to the Virgin Mary are: (1) being Mother of God, (2) being preserved from all stain of original sin, (3) being assumed body and soul to heaven, and (4) having a special place in the history of salvation.

VATICAN COUNCIL II . . .

▲ The Immaculate Virgin, preserved free from all guilt of original sin, on the completion of her earthly sojourn, was taken up body and soul into heavenly glory, and exalted by the Lord as Queen of the universe, that she might be the more fully conformed to her Son, the Lord of lords (cf. Rev 19:16) and the conqueror of sin and death. *(The Church,* 59)

EXPLANATION . . .

● (1) The Blessed Virgin is the collaborator with the Divine Word and with the Holy Spirit in the mighty work of the Incarnation. She occupies the same essential role in the work of sanctification of souls. Her dignity as the Mother of God and our Mother, her function as mediatrix of all graces and her own perfect holiness obtain for her a place of great importance in the sublime work of imitating Christ.

(2) In view of the merits of her Divine Son, Mary alone enjoyed the privilege of being preserved from original sin. From the moment of her conception God willed that she should crush the head of the serpent,

having decided from all eternity to make her the Mother of the Incarnate Word. Mary was never, even for an instant, subject to the evil spirit. She was always in the state of sanctifying grace. On December 8, 1854, Pope Pius IX officially proclaimed this great dogma, making himself the mouthpiece of all Christian tradition.

(3) After a most blessed death Mary was triumphantly assumed into heaven with soul and body and was crowned Queen of Heaven by her own Son. The dogma of the Assumption—one of the most ancient and solemn of Mary's feasts—was defined at Rome, November 1, 1950, by Pope Pius XII.

(4) Having meditated on the Scriptures, Mary understood that she was being asked to become the Mother of the Savior of humankind and that this Son was being given to her for the redemption of the human race. She was to be the Mother of all people gathered together into a new People of God, reconciled with God through a New Alliance, saved in oneness with him who was to become her Son. She willed to become our Mother in becoming the Mother of Christ the Savior.

171. What is the wish of the Church concerning devotion to Mary?

The Church urges that special veneration be given to Mary, due to her as Mother of Christ, Mother of the Church, and our spiritual Mother. This veneration is to be taught by word and example.

THE BIBLE . . .

✠ *"My soul proclaims the greatness of the Lord and my spirit rejoices in God my Savior. For he has looked with favor on the lowliness of his servant; henceforth, all generations will call me blessed." (Lk 1:47-48)*

VATICAN COUNCIL II . . .

▲ Having now been assumed into heaven, with her maternal charity she cares for those brothers of her Son who are still on their earthly pilgrimage and remain involved in dangers and difficulties until they are led into the happy homeland. All should devoutly venerate her and commend their life and apostolate to her maternal care. *(Apostolate of the Laity, 4)*

Let the entire body of the faithful pour forth instant supplications to the Mother of God and Mother of men. Let them pray that she, who aided the beginnings of the Church by her prayers, may now, exalted as she is above all the angels and saints, intercede before her Son in the fellowship of all the saints. May she do so until all families of people, whether they are honored with the title of Christian or whether they still do not know the Savior, may be happily gathered together in peace and harmony into one People of God, for the glory of the Most Holy and Undivided Trinity. *(The Church*, 69)

EXPLANATION . . .

- The Church has always urged that special veneration be given to Mary. Pope St. John XXIII said: "Devotion to Mary is the best and surest road to a deeper understanding of the teaching of the Divine Master, and it helps us make our lives correspond in every way to the vocation by reason of which 'we should be called children of God; and such we are' (1 Jn 3:1). . . . For each one of you, may this act of devotion to Mary be a pledge by which you oblige yourself to strive each day to live a life that will be more truly Christian, and more filled with the spirit of Mary, with a more refined love for each other and with a more solid participation in Catholic activities" (Nov. 13, 1960).

Pope St. Paul VI solemnly brought the third session of Vatican Council II to a close, November 21, 1964, in the presence of the entire body of the Church's bishops with the words: "For the glory of the Virgin Mary and for our own consolation, we proclaim Mary the Mother of the Church, that is, of the whole People of God, of the faithful as well as of the pastors, and we wish that through this title the Mother of God should be still more honored and invoked by the entire Christian people."

The Bishops of the United States remind our citizens that our country is under the protection of the Blessed Virgin Mary. "Since 1859 the United States has enjoyed a special relationship with the Blessed Virgin Mary. In that year, at the request of the American Bishops, Pope Pius IX placed the country under the protection of the Immaculate Conception."

172. Why does the Church honor the other saints?

The Church likewise honors the other saints who are already with the Lord in heaven because (1) they inspire us by the heroic example of their lives (2) and intercede for us with God.

VATICAN COUNCIL II . . .

▲ When we look at the lives of those who have faithfully followed Christ, we are inspired with a new reason for seeking the City that is to come (Heb 13:14; 11:10), and at the same time we are shown a most safe path by which among the vicissitudes of this world, in keeping with the state of life and condition proper to each of us, we will be able to arrive at perfect union with Christ, that is, perfect holiness.

In the lives of those who, sharing in our humanity, are nevertheless more perfectly transformed into the image of Christ (cf. 2 Cor 3:18), God vividly manifests his presence and his face to men. He speaks to us in them, and gives us a sign of his kingdom, to which we are strongly drawn, having so great a cloud of witnesses over us (cf. Heb 12:1) and such a witness to the truth of the gospel.

Nor is it by the title of example only that we cherish the memory of those in heaven, but still more in order that the union of the whole Church may be strengthened in the Spirit by the practice of fraternal charity (cf. Eph 4:1-6). For just as Christian communion among wayfarers brings us closer to Christ, so our companionship with the saints joins us to Christ, from whom as from its Fountain and Head issues every grace and the very life of the People of God. *(The Church, 50)*

It is supremely fitting, therefore, that we love those friends and co-heirs of Jesus Christ, who are also our brothers and extraordinary benefactors, that we render due thanks to God for them and "suppliantly invoke them and have recourse to their prayers, their power and help in obtaining benefits from God through his Son, Jesus Christ, who is our Redeemer and Savior" (Council of Trent). For every genuine testimony of love shown by us to those in heaven, by its very nature, tends toward and terminates in Christ who is the "crown of all saints," and, through him, in God who is wonderful in his saints and is magnified in them. *(The Church, 50)*

EXPLANATION . . .

● **(1) Because of our union with Christ we are united with all those who share his life in the larger family of God, the Communion of Saints. We on earth, members of the Church Militant, still fighting the good fight as soldiers of Christ, still journeying on our way to our Father's** house, are helped by the prayers and encouragement of the victorious and blessed members of the family, the Church Triumphant in heaven. We honor the saints and endeavor to imitate the example of their virtuous lives.

(2) We manifest the love and unity which is ours in the Communion of Saints also by praying to the saints in heaven as our patrons and intercessors with God. Not only is their intercession with God very powerful because of the love they have shown him on earth, but we also share in their merits gained by their heroic life.

Mary and Joseph bring Jesus to the temple to offer him to the Lord. They intercede for us with Jesus Christ.

173. What is our duty toward the deceased?

We (1) show reverence to the bodies of those who have gone before us in death and (2) pray for deceased relatives, friends and all the faithful departed.

VATICAN COUNCIL II . . .

▲ Fully conscious of this communion of the whole Mystical Body of Jesus Christ, the pilgrim Church from the very first ages of the Christian religion has cultivated with great piety the memory of the dead, and "because it is a holy and wholesome thought to pray for the dead that they may be loosed from their sins" (2 Mac 12:46), also offers suffrages for them. *(The Church, 50)*

This Sacred Council accepts with great devotion this venerable faith of our ancestors regarding this vital fellowship with our brethren who are in heavenly glory or who having died are still being purified. *(The Church, 51)*

EXPLANATION . . .

● **(1) We show reverence to the bodies of the deceased because they were temples of the Holy Spirit and are destined to rise gloriously.**

(2) We, who are still able to increase the divine life within us, still able to win God's favors by our cooperation with the grace of Christ, can help the suffering members of God's family, those who are being purified in purgatory. Purgatory is the way in which our relationships with God and others are strengthened after death when we have neglected penance in our life. They, in turn, although unable to help themselves, can and do pray for us. Through the Communion of Saints we are one with those loved ones and friends who rest in Christ.

DISCUSSION QUESTIONS

1. Why is Mary in the Church in a place highest after Christ? (169)
2. Why is Mary our spiritual Mother? (169)
3. What is the meaning of the divine motherhood? The Immaculate Conception? The Assumption of Mary into heaven? (170)
4. Why does the Church urge special devotion to Mary? (171)
5. Why does the Church honor the saints? (172)
6. What are our duties toward the deceased? (173)

Part Eight – FINAL REUNION

Chapter 25

FINAL REUNION WITH GOD

174. Why do Christians look forward to their final reunion with God?

During this earthly life, Christians look forward to their final reunion with God. They long for the coming of "our Lord Jesus Christ, who will transform our lowly bodies so that they will be conformed to his glorified body" (Phil 3:21).

THE BIBLE . . .

> ✠ *When this perishable body puts on imperishability, and this mortal body puts on immortality, then will the words that are written be fulfilled: "Death has been swallowed up in victory. Where, O death, is your victory? Where, O death, is your sting?" The sting of death is sin, and the power of sin is the Law. But thanks be to God who gives us the victory through our Lord Jesus Christ. (1 Cor 15:54-57)*

VATICAN COUNCIL II . . .

> ▲ We do not know the time for the consummation of the earth and of humanity (cf. Acts 1:7) nor do we know how all things will be transformed. As deformed by sin, the shape of this world will pass away (cf. 1 Cor 7:31). But we are taught that God is preparing a new dwelling place and a new earth

where justice will abide (cf. 2 Cor 5:2; 2 Pet 3:13), and whose blessedness will answer and surpass all the longings for peace which spring up in the human heart (cf. 1 Cor 2:9; Rev 21:4-5).

Then, with death overcome, the sons of God will be raised up in Christ, and what was sown in weakness and corruption will be invested with incorruptibility (cf. 1 Cor 15:42, 53). Enduring with charity and its fruits (cf. 1 Cor 13:8; 3:14), all that creation (cf. Rom 8:19-21) which God made on man's account will be unchained from the bondage of vanity. *(Church in the Modern World, 39)*

EXPLANATION . . .

● **At the second coming, all the dead will be raised, not only those who died in union with Jesus. The Father will raise us up too because of Jesus. Because of him he loves all of us and will raise up all who turn to him in faith. St. Paul says, "For we believe that Jesus died and rose again, and so too do we believe that God will bring forth with Jesus those who have fallen asleep in him" (1 Thes 4:14).**

Jesus promised that someday he would raise up all those who had been entrusted to him. By rising from the dead, they will share in his resurrection in the fullest way.

The victorious return of Christ at the world's end is surely the reason behind the strong hope which is in us now. St. Paul says, "But our citizenship is in heaven, and from there we await our Savior, the Lord Jesus Christ" (Phil 3:20).

175. When will the final realities come about?

The final realities will come about only when Christ returns with power to bring history to its appointed end.

VATICAN COUNCIL II . . .

▲ When Christ shall appear and the glorious resurrection of the dead will take place, the glory of God will light up the heavenly City and the Lamb will be the lamp thereof (cf. Rev 21:24). *(The Church, 51)*

EXPLANATION . . .

● **Christ, even as he was condemned to death before the court in Jerusalem, proclaimed that he was king. He prophesied that he would**

return to earth one day, no longer in poverty and humiliation, but in triumph to judge the living and the dead. His enemies will be forever vanquished, and he will bring history to its appointed end.

176. What will happen when Christ returns with power?

When Christ returns with power as Judge of the living and the dead (1) he will hand over his people to the Father. (2) Then only will the Church reach perfection and enter into the fullness of God.

VATICAN COUNCIL II . . .

▲ The Church, to which we are all called in Christ Jesus, and in which we acquire sanctity through the grace of God, will attain its full perfection only in the glory of heaven, when there will come the time of the restoration of all things (Acts 3:21). At that time the human race as well as the entire world, which is intimately related to man and attains to its end through him, will be perfectly reestablished in Christ (cf. Eph 1:10; Col 1:20; 2 Pet 3:10-13). *(The Church, 48)*

EXPLANATION . . .

● The great event of the second coming in power and glory is, at the same time, the act of judgment, of the raising of the dead in their bodies and of the transformation of the world.

(1) When Christ has subjected all things to himself, he will deliver his dominion to the Father. "Then comes the end, when Christ hands over the kingdom to God the Father, after he has destroyed every sovereignty and authority and power" (1 Cor 15:24). United to man through Christ, the whole creation shares in his continual sacrifice and perfect worship of the Trinity in the Holy Spirit. St. Paul says, "When all things are subjected to him, then the Son himself will also be subjected to the one who made all things subject to him, so that God may be all in all" (1 Cor 15:28).

(2) Death is the beginning of resurrection; the particular judgment places the individual in his proper setting in the history of salvation, and this is confirmed in the general judgment. Heaven and hell need for their completion the coming of Christ, who, by raising up their bodies, restores both the blessed and the lost human condition they once had, giving them the bodies corresponding to their state. The soul demands its body, the new humanity requires to be fulfilled in the res-

urrection of the body. Thus in the renewal of all things, the new creation, as part of the universe, is eternally perfected. Then only will the Church reach perfection and enter into the fullness of God.

177. Until the Lord's arrival in majesty, what happens to his disciples?

Until the Lord's arrival in majesty, (1) some of his disciples are pilgrims on earth, (2) some have finished this life and are being purified, and (3) others are in glory, beholding clearly God himself three and one, as he is.

VATICAN COUNCIL II . . .

▲ When the Lord comes in his majesty, and all the angels with him (cf. Mt 25:31), death will be destroyed and all things made subject to him (1 Cor 15:26-27). Meanwhile some of his disciples are exiles on earth, some having died are purified, and others are in glory beholding "clearly God himself triune and one, as he is."

But all in various ways and degrees are in communion in the same charity of God and neighbor and all sing the same hymn of glory to our God. For all who are in Christ, having his Spirit, form one Church and cleave together in him (cf. Eph 4:16). Therefore the union of the wayfarers with the brethren who have gone to sleep in the peace of Christ is not in the least weakened or interrupted, but on the contrary, according to the perpetual faith of the Church, is strengthened by communication of spiritual goods. *(The Church, 49)*

EXPLANATION . . .

● **(1) Once we have received sanctifying grace in baptism, it then becomes a matter of the greatest importance that we preserve this supernatural gift to the very end. The more the soul is purified of self, the more responsive does it become to the action of God. The degree of sanctifying grace will determine the degree of our happiness in heaven.**

(2) Anyone who dies in the grace of God, but is not free from all sins and all punishment due for sins, cannot go to heaven at once. Those who still have to do penance for their sins go first to *purgatory* (a word which means "cleansing state").

After Jesus ascended into heaven, two angels said to the disciples, "This Jesus who has been taken up from you into heaven will come back in the same way as you have seen him going into heaven" (Acts 1:11).

Purification is a matter of purging the soul and preparing it for the full perfection of the supernatural life which it already possesses. The soul itself must complete what was wanting in its fidelity and honor to God on earth. The soul's final turning to God happens through suffering. The real element effecting this cleansing and fulfillment of the soul in purgatory is its living love of God, which it possessed on leaving this life.

The soul in purgatory is animated by an ardent desire for absolute holiness, and this is for the sake of pleasing God. Purgatory will continue to exist until the whole world is judged on the Last Day. After the judgment there will be nothing but heaven and hell.

(3) The *beatific vision* is an immediate vision of God. This person-to-person union with him is the happiness of heaven. The full flowering of supernatural life to which God in his infinite mercy raised us is the future eternal life.

In order that we may be capable of this direct vision of God, God will give us a supernatural power which we call the Light of Glory, which can be bestowed only on a soul that already is united with God by means of sanctifying grace.

The beatific vision is a union of the soul and God—God possessing the soul and the soul possessing God in a unity so complete as to be infinitely beyond the happiness of any human love. This happiness is eternal; it is the essential happiness of heaven for which we were created.

178. Why should we face death with courage and joy?

(1) The Lord's resurrection means that death has been conquered. So we have reason to live, and to face death, with courage and joy. (2) In the risen Christ we live, we die, and we shall live again. (3) We look ahead to a homecoming with God our loving Father.

VATICAN COUNCIL II . . .

▲ Although the mystery of death utterly begs the imagination, the Church has been taught by divine revelation and firmly teaches that man has been created by God for a blissful purpose beyond the reach of earthly misery. In addition, that bodily death from which man would have been immune had he not sinned will be vanquished, according to the Christian faith, when man who was ruined by his own doing is restored to wholeness by an almighty and merciful Savior. For God has called man and still calls him so that with his entire being he might be joined to him in an endless sharing of a divine life beyond all corruption. *(Church in the Modern World, 18)*

EXPLANATION . . .

● **(1) Death is the separation of body and soul from each other. Though the soul continues in being, it is disturbed by the dissolution of the body, for the soul loses the organ through which it acted. One day our life will be overtaken by age or sickness or accident and then by death. But Christians believe that their existence is not entirely cut off from the world by death. Death is the passage over the threshold of earthly life to other life beyond.**

Christ gave death a new significance, changing it into an event bringing salvation. He did this by becoming man and taking death on himself, representing all humankind, as Adam had done so disastrously. In his death Jesus gave himself as a perfect sacrifice to the heavenly Father. He expiated Adam's surrender to Satan, and in him the surrender of all humankind. From that time, one is delivered over to God through death.

By his death Christ gave death a new significance, changing it into an event bringing salvation.

(2) The resurrection of Christ is the most important testimony of Scripture to our resurrection in the body. Through Christ's merits God has set up his new order, according to which Christ should be the beginning of resurrection. St. Paul said, "Since death came into the world through a man, the resurrection of the dead has also come through a man. Just as in Adam all die, so all will be brought to life in Christ" (1 Cor 15:21-22). As the second Adam, who gives new life to all things, Christ achieves his final victory over the lord of death, who gained dominion over all humankind in the person of the first Adam.

(3) We believe that the just who have been made perfect through death and purgatory are now in heaven, though they have not yet risen in the body nor undergone the final judgment.

Heaven is the kingdom of God. It would be insufficient to consider heaven only as a state of reward from the standpoint of individual happiness; for it is primarily a spiritual realm manifesting God's glory. We are called to glorify God in heaven in a perfect manner. The essential element in this adoration and honor is love and self-surrender to him.

God is the highest good that we not only shall know and love, but also live, in a mysterious sharing of his life. This life is purest joy and everlasting rest, fullest attainment, quiet happiness. We look forward to this state of perfection, the greatest act of our whole life, surpassing any of this earth. So we should face death with courage and joy, looking ahead to a homecoming with God our loving Father.

179. Why should each of us think seriously of his responsibility about his eternal destiny?

Each person should consider seriously the awesome responsibility each has about one's eternal destiny because of the importance (1) of the individual judgment after death, (2) of the refining and purifying punishments of purgatory, (3) of the dreadful possibility of the eternal death of hell, and (4) of the last judgment. Yet we should consider these final realities in the light of Christian hope.

VATICAN COUNCIL II . . .

▲ Christ won this victory when he rose to life, for by his death he freed man from death (cf. 1 Cor 15:56-57). Hence to every thoughtful man a solidly established faith provides the answer to his anxiety about what the future holds for him. At the same time faith gives him the power to be united in Christ with his loved ones who have already been snatched away by death; faith arouses the hope that they have found true life with God. *(Church in the Modern World, 18)*

Since however we know not the day nor the hour, on our Lord's advice we must be constantly vigilant. Then, having finished the course of our earthly life (cf. Heb 9:27), we may merit to enter into the marriage feast with him and to be numbered among the blessed (cf. Mt 25:31-46). Thus we may not be ordered to go into exterior darkness where "there will be the weeping and the gnashing of teeth" (Mt 22:13; 25:30). *(The Church, 48)*

EXPLANATION . . .

● **(1) At the very instant the soul leaves the body it is judged by almighty God. This judgment is called the *particular judgment.* God illumines the soul so that the soul sees itself as God sees it— sees the state of grace or of unforgiven sin it is in, and what its sentence is to be in accordance with the infinite justice of God. But it is the Lord who judges, not we.**

The particular judgment is an act of God. It includes God's acceptance or rejection, according to the way one has determined their state by their way of life and final act of self-commitment. This action of God has what may be called a direction to the appropriate "place"—heaven, hell, or purgatory. This judgment is final and irrevocable. If we die without the least trace of sin upon our soul, the immediate sight of God in heaven will itself be our judgment.

(2) Few of us expect that our particular judgment will find us free from every trace of sin. That would mean being free not only from every trace of sin, mortal and venial sin, but also free from all undischarged temporal punishment—the debt of atonement we owe to God even after sin itself has been forgiven. This debt is paid in *purgatory.*

(3) Having deliberately cut itself off from God during life, the soul which has chosen self in preference to God, and which has died without turning back to God, has now no means by which it can establish contact with God. It has lost God forever, having died without that bond of union with God which we call sanctifying grace. It is hell. For such a soul, death, judgment and hell are simultaneous.

(4) The *general judgment* is called the last judgment, since it is not followed by another, and its sentence endures forever. It takes place on the last day, and, along with the resurrection of the body and the renewal of the world, is one element in the coming of the Lord with power.

The general judgment is something more than the promulgation of the sentence already passed on so many at the particular judgment, for it concerns also those who are still living on that day. The whole human race will be judged. Judgment will be passed too on the angels, both good and bad, indeed on the whole creation. Each individual person will once more be summoned to appear before the Lord as their judge.

In this judgment each person is given a view over their whole life and its significance. Each one sees it in the light of the Lord. The sentence which was passed upon us in our particular judgment will now be publicly confirmed. All our sins—and all our virtues too—will become known.

The thought of these final realities should fill us with Christian hope, but at the same time we should be aware of the responsibility we have of attaining eternal salvation.

180. When will each person fully reach his eternal destiny?

On the day of the last judgment each person will fully reach their eternal destiny.

VATICAN COUNCIL II . . .

▲ The promised restoration which we are awaiting has already begun in Christ, is carried forward in the mission of the Holy Spirit and through him continues in the Church. There we learn the meaning of our terrestrial life through our faith, while we perform with hope in the future the task committed to us in this world by the Father, and thus work out our salvation (cf. Phil 2:12). *(The Church, 48)*

EXPLANATION . . .

● **The primary happiness of heaven consists in this, that we shall possess the infinitely perfect God, and be possessed by him. We shall be personally and consciously united to God himself who is infinite Goodness and Truth and Beauty. God's love can fulfill every craving and desire of the human heart. We shall then experience a happiness which, once achieved, we can never lose. We shall fully reach this eternal destiny on the day of the last judgment.**

181. What will happen on the day of the last judgment?

(1) All of us will be revealed "before the judgment seat of Christ, so that each one may receive suitable recompense for his conduct in the body, whether good or bad" (2 Cor 5:10). (2) Then "the evildoers shall rise to be damned," and "those who have done good deeds will rise to life" (cf. Jn 5:29)—to a life eternally with God beyond what the heart can imagine, to receive the good things that God has prepared for those who love him.

THE BIBLE . . .

✠ *"Those who have done good deeds will rise to life, while those who have done evil will rise to judgment" (Jn 5:29).*

VATICAN COUNCIL II . . .

▲ Before we reign with Christ in glory, all of us will be made manifest "before the tribunal of Christ, so that each one may receive what he has won through the body, according to his works, whether good or evil" (2 Cor 5:10). At the end of the world "they who have done good shall come forth unto resurrection of life; but those who have done evil unto resurrection of judgment" (Jn 5:29; cf. Mt 25:46). *(The Church, 48)*

EXPLANATION . . .

● **(1) The office of judging all humankind at the end of the world is committed to our Lord Jesus Christ, not only as God but also as Son of Man or Messiah. Jesus himself taught us that he would be the judge of humankind. "Indeed, just as the Father raises the dead and gives them life, so does the Son give life to anyone he chooses. The Father judges** no one, for he has entrusted all judgment to the Son, so that all may honor the Son as they honor the Father" (Jn 5:21-23).

The divine reward of eternal life requires our faithfulness toward God. Liberated from sin and brought under servitude to God, Christians receive, as the fruit of their good works, the increase of personal sanctification and, in the end, eternal life which is the gift of God. St. Paul says, "However, now that you have been freed from sin and bound to the service of God, the benefit you receive is sanctification and the end is eternal life. For the wages of sin is death, but the gift freely given by God is eternal life in Christ Jesus our Lord" (Rom 6:22-23).

(2) God will reward everyone according to their works on the day of the general judgment, and will give an eternal life of happiness to those who persevere in good works to the end. He will punish unrepenting sinners. St. Paul says, "God will repay everyone in accordance with what his deeds deserve. To those who seek after glory and honor and immortality by persevering in good works, he will grant eternal life" (Rom 2:6-7).

In heaven we shall be absorbed in the possession of the infinitely perfect God, the greatest Love that exists, for which the keenest human love is but a pale shadow. We shall also see Christ, the God-Man, in his glorified manhood. We shall live in the community of the angels and saints.

Happiness in this life is never perfect, never complete. God, who is infinitely good, would not place in human hearts this desire for perfect happiness if there were no way in which the desire could be satisfied. Our union with God will be so complete that we cannot now even faintly imagine the joy of it. St. Paul wrote: "Eye has not seen, ear has not heard, nor has the human heart imagined what God has prepared for those who love him" (1 Cor 2:9).

We shall also know our loved ones in heaven who died in the grace of God, and shall rejoice at their presence. In heaven we shall find again all those relatives and friends.

At every moment on earth we must be prepared for death, but we need the time allotted to us by the will of God, whether it be long or short. We must live a Christian life deserving of a heavenly reward. Heaven and its happiness is worth this short life of sacrifice and pain.

The Bishops of the United States conclude their text on the *Basic Teachings for Catholic Religious Education* with these words: "The message of Jesus is meant to be applied to everyday life. Nowhere is this more evidently needed than in the perennial search for love and justice in society and personal relationships. [in this document,] Chapter Six, The Christian Life of Service, devotes itself to the ways in which Christ's message finds a concrete expression in modern society's quest for just, loving and humane living conditions."

DISCUSSION QUESTIONS

1. What is the resurrection of the body? (174)
2. When will the final realities come about? (175)
3. What will happen at the second coming of Christ? (176)
4. What is purgatory? (177)
5. What is the beatific vision? (177)
6. What is the meaning of death? (178)
7. How did Christ give a new significance to death? (178)
8. What is heaven? (178)
9. What is the particular judgment? (179)
10. What is the purpose of purgatory? (179)
11. What is the meaning of hell? (179)
12. What is the general judgment? (179)
13. How should the thought of final realities affect us? (179)
14. What is our eternal destiny? (180)
15. In what will the happiness of heaven consist? (181)

APPENDICES

APPENDIX A

THE TEN COMMANDMENTS OF GOD

1. I, the Lord, am your God. You shall not have other gods besides me.
2. You shall not take the name of the Lord, your God, in vain.
3. Remember to keep holy the sabbath day.
4. Honor your father and your mother.
5. You shall not kill.
6. You shall not commit adultery.
7. You shall not steal.
8. You shall not bear false witness against your neighbor.
9. You shall not covet your neighbor's wife.
10. You shall not covet anything that belongs to your neighbor.

THE BEATITUDES

1. Blessed are the poor in spirit, for theirs is the kingdom of God.
2. Blessed are those who mourn, for they will be comforted.
3. Blessed are the meek, for they will inherit the earth.
4. Blessed are those who hunger and thirst for justice, for they will have their fill.

5. Blessed are the merciful, for they will obtain mercy.
6. Blessed are the pure of heart, for they will see God.
7. Blessed are the peacemakers, for they will be called children of God.
8. Blessed are those who are persecuted in the cause of justice, for theirs is the kingdom of God. (Mt 5:3-10)

APPENDIX B

DUTIES OF CATHOLICS

1. To keep holy the day of the Lord's Resurrection: to worship God by participating in Mass every Sunday and Holy Day of Obligation:* to avoid those activities that would hinder renewal of soul and body, e.g., needless work and business activities, unnecessary shopping, etc.
2. To lead a sacramental life: to receive Holy Communion frequently and the Sacrament of Penance—minimally, to receive the Sacrament of Penance at least once a year (annual confession is obligatory only if serious sin is involved).*

   —minimally, to receive Holy Communion at least once a year, between the First Sunday of Lent and the Most Holy Trinity.*

Note:
(Duties traditionally mentioned as Precepts of the Church are marked with an asterisk)

The traditionally listed chief Precepts of the Church are the following six:

1. To assist at Mass on all Sundays and holy days of obligation.
2. To fast and abstain on the days appointed.
3. To confess our sins at least once a year.
4. To receive Holy Communion during the Easter time.
5. To contribute to the support of the Church.
6. To observe the laws of the Church concerning marriage.

3. To study Catholic teaching in preparation for the Sacrament of Confirmation, to be confirmed, and then to continue to study and advance the cause of Christ.
4. To observe the marriage laws of the Church:* to give religious training (by example and word) to one's children; to use parish schools and catechetical programs.
5. To strengthen and support the Church:* one's own parish community and parish priests; the worldwide Church and the Holy Father.
6. To do penance, including abstaining from meat and fasting from food on the appointed days.*
7. To join in the missionary spirit and apostolate of the Church.

APPENDIX C

ESSENTIAL PRAYERS

SIGN OF THE CROSS

In the name of the Father, and of the Son, and of the Holy Spirit. Amen.

THE LORD'S PRAYER

Our Father Who art in heaven, hallowed be Thy name; Thy kingdom come; Thy will be done on earth as it is in heaven. Give us this day our daily bread; and forgive us our trespasses as we forgive those who trespass against us; and lead us not into temptation, but deliver us from evil. Amen.

THE HAIL MARY

Hail Mary, full of grace! The Lord is with thee; blessed art thou among women, and blessed is the fruit of thy womb, Jesus. Holy Mary, Mother of God, pray for us sinners now and at the hour of our death. Amen.

DOXOLOGY

Glory be to the Father, and to the Son, and to the Holy Spirit. As it was in the beginning, is now, and will be forever. Amen.

THE APOSTLES' CREED

I believe in God, the Father almighty, Creator of heaven and earth, and in Jesus Christ, His only Son, our Lord, who was conceived by the Holy Spirit, born of the Virgin Mary, suffered under Pontius Pilate, was crucified, died and was buried. He descended into hell; the third day He rose again from the dead; He ascended into heaven, and is seated at the right hand of God the Father almighty; from there He will come to judge the living and the dead.

I believe in the Holy Spirit, the Holy Catholic Church, the communion of saints, the forgiveness of sins, the resurrection of the body, and life everlasting. Amen.

ACT OF CONTRITION

O my God, I am heartily sorry for having offended You, and I detest all my sins, because of Your just punishments, but most of all because they offend You, my God, who are all good and deserving of all my love. I firmly resolve, with the help of Your grace, to sin no more and to avoid the near occasions of sin.

ACT OF FAITH

O my God, I firmly believe all the truths that the holy Catholic Church believes and teaches; I believe these truths, O Lord, because You, the infallible Truth, have revealed them to her; in this faith I am resolved to live and die. Amen.

ACT OF HOPE

O my God, trusting in Your promises, and because You are faithful, powerful and merciful, I hope, through the merits of Jesus Christ, for the pardon of my sins, final perseverance, and the blessed glory of heaven. Amen.

ACT OF CHARITY

O my God, because You are infinite Goodness and worthy of infinite love, I love You with my whole heart above all things, and for love of You, I love my neighbor as myself. Amen.

HAIL, HOLY QUEEN

Hail, holy Queen, Mother of mercy; hail our life, our sweetness, and our hope. To you do we cry, poor banished children of Eve. To you do we send up our sighs, mourning and weeping in this vale of tears. Turn then, most gracious advocate, your eyes of mercy toward us. And after this our exile show unto us the blessed fruit of your womb, Jesus, O clement, O loving, O sweet Virgin Mary.

THE MYSTERIES OF THE ROSARY

The Joyful Mysteries

1. The Annunciation of the Archangel Gabriel to the Virgin Mary
2. The Visitation of the Virgin Mary to the Parents of St. John the Baptist
3. The Birth of Our Lord at Bethlehem
4. The Presentation of Our Lord in the Temple
5. The Finding of Our Lord in the Temple

The Luminous Mysteries

1. The Baptism of Jesus in the Jordan
2. Christ's Self-Manifestation at Cana
3. The Proclamation of the Kingdom of God
4. The Transfiguration of Our Lord
5. The Institution of the Eucharist

The Sorrowful Mysteries

1. The Agony of Our Lord in the Garden of Gethsemane
2. The Scourging of Our Lord at the Pillar
3. The Crowning of Our Lord with Thorns
4. The Carrying of the Cross by Our Lord to Calvary
5. The Crucifixion and Death of Our Lord

The Glorious Mysteries

1. The Resurrection of Our Lord from the Dead
2. The Ascension of Our Lord into Heaven
3. The Descent of the Holy Spirit upon the Disciples
4. The Assumption of Our Blessed Lady into Heaven
5. The Coronation of Our Blessed Lady as Queen of Heaven and Earth

TOPICAL INDEX

(Numbers refer to **Questions**)

A

Absolution, 65
Angels, 24
Anointing of the sick:
  effects, 77
  meaning, 75
  reception, 76, 78
Apostolate of laity, 61, 63, 164, 168

B

Baptism:
  effects, 59, 60, 62
Bible, 2
Bishops, 127, 152

C

Chastity, 141
Children, 97
Christ:
  Family, 94, 100
  Firstborn of brethren, 41
  Firstborn of creation, 20
  God, 34
  Holy Spirit, 42, 43, 45
  Judge, 176
  love for Father, 39
  love for us, 39, 132
  Man, 33, 34, 36
  Natures, 34
  obedience, 37
  Redeemer, 36, 38, 40
  Resurrection, 25, 145
  Sacraments, 53
  salvation, 48
  Savior, 21, 36
  teaching, 38, 41, 42
Church:
  authority, 126, 146, 150, 163
  community, 157, 167
  duties, 150
  Holy Spirit, 44, 45, 15
  infallibility, 127, 153
  institution, 167
  office of Christ, 60, 148, 150
  origin, 145
  People of God, 60, 144
  power, 146
  renewal, 156
  teaching of, 125, 156, 146, 154, 163
  Whole Christ, 31, 41, 172
  work of, 52, 125, 146, 148, 159, 168
  world, 168
Commandments:
  Christ's teaching, 119
  fifth to tenth, 140
  first to fourth, 139
  Great Commandment, 131
  morality, 121, 131
Communion, Holy:
  effects, 84, 85
  heavenly banquet, 85
  love of neighbor, 84,
  memorial, 84, 90
  reception, 86
  87, 88
Confirmation:
  duties, 63
  effects, 61, 62
  See: Holy Spirit
Conscience, 123, 126, 143
Contrition, 69
Creation:
  glory of God, 32
  meaning, 22, 26
  of man, 24
  revelation of God, 15, 22, 25

D

Death, 178, 179
Deceased, 173

E

Earth, new, 29
Ecumenism, 162
Eucharist:
  central act, 79
  Passover, 90
  reception, 86
  Reserved, 90
  (See: Mass; Communion)
  Union with Christ, 84

F

Faith:
  through charity, 134
  in Christ, 21
  in God, 16, 103
  Church, 126
Family, 98, 99, 100
Freedom, 107, 112, 111, 113, 117

G

God:
  all-good, holy, wise, merciful, 9
  love of God for us, 9, 105, 118, 120, 132
  our love for God, 12, 13, 14, 103, 143
Grace:
  actual, 103, 109, 122
  God's love, 41
  Holy Spirit, 102, 112, 129, 132
  indwelling, 104
  reception of, 51
  sacraments, 49, 51, 57, 157
  sanctifying, 103, 106

H

Heaven:
  beatific vision, 177, 178, 181

Eucharist, 85
new heavens, 29
Hell, 179
Holiness, 20, 41, 52, 66, 135, 156, 159
Hope in God, 10, 103, 118
Humility, 141

I

Incarnation:
meaning, 18,
purpose, 19
Infallibility (See: Church)

J

Jesus (See: Christ)
Judgment:
Last, 176, 179
Particular, 179

K

Kingdom of God, 41 (See: heaven)

L

Law, civil, 130
Love for God: 12, 13, 14, 103, 120, 132, 133, 137, 138, 134
Love for Christ, 16
Love of neighbor:
commandment, 139
duties, 139, 141, 160, 166
Eucharist, 84, 88
marriage, 97, 98
meaning, 12, 10, 132, 139

M

Mary, 18, 169, 170, 171
Mass,10 (See: Eucharist)
consecration, 81, 82
memorial, 80, 84
sacrifice, 83
Matrimony:
duties of married, 95, 98
family, 98, 99, 100
institution, 91
mixed marriage, 101
permanence, 96
purpose, 97
sacrament, 92, 93, 94

O

Obedience, 126, 128, 129, 133, 163
Orders:
duties, 74
effects, 73
meaning, 72, 158

P

Patience, 141
Penance:
effects, 65, 66, 71
forgiveness, 68, 118
meaning, 67
reception, 70, 71
sacrament, 64
People of God, 60, 144
Pope, 151, 127, 152
Prayer, 10, 103
Priests, 72, 73, 74, 158
Purgatory, 177, 179

R

Religion, 15
Religious, state, 136
Resurrection of Christ, 25, 145
Resurrection of body, 174, 175
Revelation of God, 2, 3, 6, 15
Revelation of Christ, 5, 6

S

Sacraments:
effects, 55
meaning, 49, 50, 53, 57
purpose, 54
reception, 51, 56, 57
work of the Spirit, 48
Saints, 172
Salvation, 1, 26, 27, 28, 30, 36, 37, 48
Sick, 75, 76, 77
Sin:
effects, 108, 113, 116
forgiveness, 65, 68, 69
freedom, 109
mortal, 116, 117
Penance, 64, 65, 66
personal, 112, 113, 115
original, 114
sacraments, 57
temptation, 109, 110
venial, 116
Spirit, Holy:
in Church, 45, 155
confirmation, 61
devotion to, 47
is faithful, 46, 122
love for us, 132
person, 42
work, 42, 44, 48, 102, 122

T

Teaching of Christ, 38
Temptation, 109, 142, 143
Trinity, 7, 132

U

Unbelievers, 16
Unity of Christians, 161, 162, 165, 166

V

Virtue, 141, 164 (See: holiness)
Vocation:
holiness, 159
religious life, 136

W

World, conditions, 17, 168

pray

praise

repent

ask

yield